Gender and International Migration in Europe

Gender and International Migration in Europe is a unique work which introduces a gender dimension into theories of contemporary migrations. As the European Union seeks to extend equal opportunities, increasingly restrictionist immigration policies and the persistence of racism deny autonomy and choice to migrant women. This work demonstrates how processes of globalization and change in state policies on employment and welfare have maintained a demand for diverse forms of gendered immigration.

The authors examine state and European Union policies of immigration control, family reunion, refugees and the management of immigrant and ethnic minority communities. Most importantly this work considers the opportunities created for political activity by migrant women and the extent to which they are able to influence and participate in mainstream policy-making.

This volume will be essential reading for anyone involved in or interested in modern European immigration policy.

Eleonore Kofman is Professor of Human Geography at Nottingham Trent University. **Annie Phizacklea** is Professor of Sociology at the University of Warwick. **Parvati Raghuram** is a Lecturer in the Department of International Studies, Nottingham Trent University. **Rosemary Sales** is Principal Lecturer in the School of Social Science at Middlesex University.

Gender, Racism, Ethnicity

Series Editors:
Kum-Kum Bhavnani, *University of California at Santa Barbara*
Avtar Brah, *University of London*
Gail Lewis, *The Open University*
Ann Phoenix, *The Open University*

Gender, Racism, Ethnicity is a series whose main concern is to promote rigorous feminist analysis of the intersections between gender, racism, ethnicity, class and sexuality within the contexts of imperialism, colonialism and neo-colonialism. Intended to contribute new perspectives to current debates and to introduce fresh analysis, it will provide valuable teaching texts for undergraduates, lecturers and researchers in anthropology, women's studies, cultural studies and sociology.

Other titles in the series:

White Women, Race Matters
Ruth Frankenberg

Fear of the Dark
Lola Young

Gendering Orientalism
Reina Lewis

Cartographies of Diaspora
Avtar Brah

'Other Kinds of Dreams'
Julia Sudbury

Against Purity
Irene Gedalof

Outsiders Inside: Whiteness, Place & Irish Women
Bronwen Walter

Gender and International Migration in Europe

Employment, welfare and politics

Eleonore Kofman, Annie Phizacklea, Parvati Raghuram and Rosemary Sales

London and New York

First published 2000
by Routledge
11 New Fetter Lane, London EC4P 4EE

Simultaneously published in the USA and Canada
by Routledge
29 West 35th Street, New York, NY 10001

Routledge is an imprint of the Taylor & Francis Group

© 2000 Eleonore Kofman, *Annie Phizacklea, Parvati Raghuram and Rosemary Sales*

Typeset in Baskerville by The Midlands Book Typesetting Company, Loughborough, Leicestershire
Printed and bound in Great Britain by TJ International Ltd, Padstow, Cornwall

British Library Cataloguing in Publication Data
A catalogue record for this book is available from the British Library

Library of Congress Cataloging in Publication Data
Gender and International migration in Europe : employment, welfare, and politics / Eleonore Kofman ... [et al.].
    p. cm. –– (Gender, racism, ethnicity)
    Includes bibliographical references and index.
    1. European Union countries––Emigration and immigration––Government policy. 2. Women immigrants––Government policy––European Union countries. 3. Women immigrants–– European Union countries. I. Kofman, Eleonore. II. Series.

JV7590 .G46 2000
325.4––dc21
                                                                00-042492

ISBN 0-415-16729-9 (hbk)
ISBN 0-415-16730-2 (pbk)

Contents

Tables

Chapter 1

Gender and international migration in Europe

Some theorists have proclaimed the current period as the 'age of migration' (Castles and Miller 1998). Temporary and permanent movements are globalizing, accelerating, diversifying and feminizing. The United Nations estimates that there are approximately 125 million migrants in the world today. The number of countries influenced by these migratory movements has also increased, with Europe emerging as an important player in migratory movements. Of the 15–16 million third country nationals living in Europe, about forty-five per cent are women.

The number of migrant women in Europe has been increasing rapidly, especially, in the last two decades. Men formed the majority of immigrants to Europe in the post-war period of reconstruction, in flows dominated by labour migration (Zlotnik 1995), although even during this period there were some groups among whom women predominated. In the past two decades women have migrated to join men now resident in Europe, and family reunification remains the major reason for entry of women into Europe. However, more women are also migrating independently, for economic reasons, as students and refugees. Women also form significant numbers of undocumented workers, as has been shown in legalization programmes in several European countries. Women, for instance, formed 28 per cent of migrants who were legalized in 1987 and 1988 in Italy.

The significance of women in migration to Europe lies not only in these increased numbers, but also through their contributions to economic and social life in receiving countries. Migrant women have always been active in the labour market, although their labour may be invisible where they work as unpaid members in family businesses (Morokvasic 1993) or as home-workers in casualized, poorly paid jobs in certain sectors such as clothes manufacturing (Phizacklea 1982). Increasingly, women have also found employment in certain skilled specialisms, such as nursing, teaching and computing. They may enter a country for training, for family re-unification, on work-permits, or as refugees and subsequently find employment in highly skilled jobs. However, for many migrant women, the move has also been accompanied by de-skilling. Racial and sexual discrimination in the labour market has led to unemployment, and to poor pay and conditions of work for those who have found employment. Some have set up businesses in their own right to combat some of this discrimination (Phizacklea and Ram 1996; Raghuram and Hardill 1998).

Migrant women also play an important role in welfare, both as providers and as recipients. The gendered nature of welfare provision, which prioritizes women's role as carers in society, is heightened during migration. They provide welfare through both their paid and unpaid labour. Many of the recent women migrants to Europe have moved to seek jobs in the casualized welfare sector, particularly domestic work and caring of dependent children, elderly and disabled, as state provision of welfare is not keeping pace with the requirements of ageing populations across Europe.

Migration into Europe has become an increasingly politically sensitive subject, with migrants often cast as dependent on welfare, or alternatively as creating unemployment for nationals by providing cheaper labour. Migration policies have come to occupy centre-stage in the agendas of some political parties. At the same time, a number of national and European level non-governmental organizations have formed around migration issues, campaigning for changes to laws governing both the entry and the rights of migrants. The politics of gender in migration has varied sharply between countries. In most countries women have been considered the vectors of integration and their familial role in raising the next generation has been highlighted. They are less often perceived to pose a threat to the employment of nationals, as female migrants are constructed as family-formers rather than labourers. On the other hand, the racialization of migrant women's experiences in policy debates has been especially marked in some countries, with the primary focus of policies for migrant women being social integration rather than professional integration (Council of Europe 1994).

In recent decades, there has been increasing community and

political activity among immigrant groups in European states. With notable exceptions, such as Great Britain and Sweden, immigrants had either limited or no rights of political association and representation until the 1980s. The transformation of immigrants into ethnic minorities has given them greater security and allowed them to engage in trade union and other forms of political activity. State strategies of incorporation have increasingly relied on immigrant association at local and national levels (Soysal 1994). Migrants, as possessors of disproportionately greater capital and skills than those who remain in their home country, have organized themselves to influence the politics of the home country. Some, such as the Kurds, have effectively organized at the Europe-wide level.

Despite this increasing presence of migrant women in Europe, and a recognition of feminization of migration (Castles and Miller 1998), mainstream literature on migration has continued to ignore their presence. Most studies appear to be gender-neutral while utilizing models of migration based on the experiences of men. Women, where their presence is acknowledged, are often treated as dependants, migrating under family reunion, and their contribution to the economies and societies of destination countries ignored (Simon and Bretell 1986). Over the past fifteen years, feminists have highlighted the heterogeneity of women's position within the migration stream, their presence in the labour market, their contribution to welfare and their increasing political activities. Yet, the migration of women continues to receive little attention in mainstream literature and migration theorists have not adequately taken on board the significance of gender in understanding migration today.

In this book, we aim to consolidate current work on migration of women in Europe and to highlight the significance of the female presence in European migration streams. We focus on gendered differences in migration trajectories and incorporate a gender dimension into theorizations of contemporary migrations. We argue that the importance of women lies not merely in their increased numbers, but in their specific position in the labour market and welfare systems of Europe and in the forms of political activity and organization, both in Europe and in their countries of origin.

European context

In the eighteenth and nineteenth centuries, Europe was a continent of emigration. Millions of Europeans moved to the New World and to the colonies that they established in all the other continents. The most significant permanent migration during this period was that to the settler societies, and towards the end of the century, to South Africa. Shorter-term movements to the colonies were also important. Colonial linkages influenced the stream of migration even among the ex-colonies. For example, Spanish and Portuguese migration to their Latin American colonies continued even after these countries gained their independence in the nineteenth century.

This pattern of emigration continued well into this century. Inter-war labour shortages in northern Europe encouraged labour migration from southern Europe. In 1931, there were more migrants in France than in migration-dominated settler societies such as the USA. Refugee movements also contributed to the migrant population. Refugees from Russia, Poland, and Germany, Jewish refugees from eastern Europe and those fleeing from the Spanish Civil War all moved both to western European and New World countries. On the whole, migration from Europe before World War II was male dominated with more men than women emigrating, although with some variations. Ireland, for instance, has had an overall female majority since the middle of the nineteenth century, and migration to the USA has been female dominated since the 1930s. Refugee movements were largely family migration and women formed a significant and visible part of the migration within Europe. Transitory movements of the elite from the colonies, primarily for education, but also for employment, occurred during these years. The numbers involved were relatively small, but in a number of cases their political impact in their home countries was large, especially as this elite often formed a significant caucus within independence movements in these countries.

In the post-war period, there have been different regimes of migration, with particular forms of entry dominating during certain periods (see Chapter 3). The period immediately after the World War II has been largely characterized by refugee movements. The war created millions of displaced persons in the late 1940s and 1950s. Germans expelled from erstwhile German-controlled areas moved primarily from east to west, Italians moved north, and the refugees expelled from the USSR moved primarily to France, UK, Switzerland and Sweden.

A number of colonies gained their independence during the first post-war decade, most significantly the big Asian countries, India in 1947 and Indonesia in 1948. Decolonization and the attendant dismantling of the colonial administrative services fuelled large-scale return migration of European colonizers. In fact, this return migration continued through the first decades after independence, as the presence of 'old colonials' in professional sectors such as education continued for some time.

For about twenty years from the mid 1950s, Europe went through a period of economic boom, which, along with the effects of the World War II, i.e. labour shortages and reconstruction, led to a great increase in labour migration. Early labour migration, including that from the colonies was male dominated although women without spouses also migrated. Women often used emigration as a way of negotiating difficult marital relations or overcoming gendered hierarchies within their home country (Morokvasic 1993). Most of the labour migration during this period focused on manufacturing and construction industries: industries that primarily employed men. However, female-dominated sectors of the labour market, usually in the caring professions, such as teaching, nursing and in domestic work, also experienced labour shortages. In Italy, female-led migration to meet demands for domestic work was common even in the 1970s.

Colonial linkages continued to fuel significant migratory moves throughout this period. As colonial empires collapsed and many countries received their independence, European nationals living in the colonies returned home. In the 1950s, most of the Dutch who lived in Indonesia decided to return to the Netherlands, accompanied by many Indonesian former civil servants and military personnel. The last big group immigrated in 1962, when former Dutch New-Guinea became a part of Indonesia. Similar moves also occurred within the British colonies. Throughout the 1960s, the UK received migrants from its colonies in Africa, particularly Kenya and Tanzania, but also refugee movements from its ex-colony Uganda in 1973. Most of these movements were family movements, with both men and women migrating.

The economic downturn in Europe following the oil crisis of 1973 altered the nature of migration into Europe. As economic growth slowed, guest-worker systems were shut down. The primary reason for migrants entering Europe now became family reunification and the proportion of women migrating into Europe increased. Towards the end of the decade, the expansion in the economies of the Mediterranean countries altered the migration profile of these countries from net exporters of labour to net importers of labour. Immigrants into southern Europe also included return migrants from northern Europe. For instance, Spanish migrants returned from Switzerland and Germany, and Yugoslavians from Germany.

Immigration from the colonies continued, although it took several forms. The Netherlands continued to receive migrants from its dependencies, principally Surinam, which gained its independence in 1975 from the Kingdom of the Netherlands. Surinamese concerns about the political and economic prospects in their country just prior to their independence in 1975, led to migration peaks in 1974, 1975 and 1980. The usual type of immigration was that of complete households, so that subsequent family reunification immigration was small in this group. Skilled migration also continued throughout this period, and once again the direction of migration followed established migration routes. Resettlement programmes for Chilean and Vietnamese refugees contributed significantly to refugee movements during this period.

The nature of international migration in Europe has undergone further changes in the past two decades. Geopolitical and economic changes have led to shifts in the definition and meaning of the 'international'. One major transformation has been the re-drawing of national boundaries, most notably the dissolution of some states such as the old Soviet Union, the Baltic states and Czechoslovakia, and the reunification of East and West Germany. Internal movements have become international migration for the post-Soviet nations, whereas the movement across what was one of the most highly policed borders, that between East and West Germany, has now become an internal movement. The re-drawing of boundaries has been accompanied by considerable ethnic conflict, leading to large flows of refugees. Eastern European countries, such as Hungary and Romania, have become transit points for countries of former USSR.

During the same period, boundaries between the fifteen states, which now form the European Union, have been opened up to the movement of capital, commodities and people, and this has influenced the way in which national boundaries are experienced by people. These changes will also affect the six other states that are preparing for admission and whose citizens will also acquire rights to free movement within the EU seven years after the country joins the Union. Internal border controls have eased for citizens of the member states and the implications of border crossings and migration have altered. Two per cent of EU workers, who are employed, work in a member state other than that in which they have citizenship. At the same time, controls over the movement of non-citizens have been strengthened and the term 'fortress Europe' has been used to reflect these shifts (Kofman and Sales 1992).

To summarize, despite the variations in numbers, the differential visibility and the politicization of certain migrant categories, during particular periods, a broad spectrum of migrant movements has occurred throughout the century. Even during the period that was dominated by labour migration, other forms of migration, such as family reunification and refugee movements, occurred.

Contemporary migration in Europe is also influenced by the major trends in recent migration: acceleration, diversification, feminization, and globalization (Castles and Miller 1998). The numbers of migrants throughout the world have increased. This is partly caused by the shifting nature of employment patterns, particularly an increase in the number of those working on short-term contracts and a consequent growth in short-term movements. Technological changes have led to greater mobility of both jobs as well as people. Another major source of migration is tourism. The numbers of tourists to Europe have increased and some of those entering on tourist visas have extended their stay through marriage, employment, or in order to study. More recently, the number of refugees and asylum-seekers has increased rapidly and they now form the largest group of migrants into Europe.

The nature of movements has also diversified in the 1990s. Migration is still influenced by labour shortages, although these shortages manifest as specific sectoral imbalances leading to niche markets for labour. The primary shift in labour demand through most of the industrialized world has been from industrial to service sector. These service sector jobs occur in gendered niches, where labour recruitment is influenced by the sexual division of labour. Women dominate some of these shortage sectors where local populations are unable to meet labour requirements such as domestic work, nursing and teaching. Thus, there has been an increase in women migrants in particular sectors of the labour market.

As the extent of connections between places have expanded and deepened, the directions of migration have become more differentiated and diverse. One major trend has been the increasing concentration of migrants in cities, particularly the financial capitals of the world: New York, London, and to a lesser extent Tokyo. These cities have become receivers of heterogeneous flows of population, disproportionately young, and, as in the case of London, with a number of national flows dominated by women (Kofman 1998).

Definitions and sources

So who is a migrant? There is no uniform criterion for defining a migrant, either across countries or across time. The two primary elements in defining the category have been the criteria of mobility, i.e. the period of entry and stay in a receiving country, and that of citizenship. In this section, we outline some of the differences in categorization arising out of the mobility criteria. The conditions for and rates of take up of citizenship across Europe are discussed in Chapter 4. While citizenship and migration policies are usually left to national legislation, the strengthening of the European Union has created a new category of citizenship with variable rights in EU member countries. For instance, full members of EU have rights of mobility and some political rights across EU, whereas citizens of countries that are not members of EU, but have signed up to the Schengen agreement, have rights of mobility and may be considered quasi-citizens of the new Europe. A significant category to emerge recently has been that of 'third country nationals', i.e. those who are citizens of non-EU countries, whose rights of mobility have not matched those of EU citizens.

Defining migrants is a contested process, involving processes of inclusion and exclusion. By defining migrants as non-nationals, they are categorized as not belonging, and this is used as a mechanism for restricting or denying rights to employment, welfare and political activity. Exclusion and inclusion are not only imposed, but also perceived. Hence, migrants who are accepted and even have citizenship in the host country may still perceive themselves as migrants, particularly in collective settings where shared ethnic grouping can become the definitive criteria for belonging, and differences between the groups and host populations become highlighted. Such perceptions are further sharpened by attitudes towards migration and migrant issues within the host population.

These process of exclusion are also ideological in that they conflate migrancy with racial 'otherness', so that the major criteria used to label migrants becomes that of the visible marker of 'race'.

But relatively 'invisible' communities, such as east Europeans in western Europe, may also be racialized, not through differences in colour but by public perceptions, particularly of their dependence on the welfare state. Racialization also operates as a legacy of colonialism, especially in countries such as the UK where the migrant populations are largely drawn from the ex-colonies of the host country. In France, the history of colonialism in Africa, particularly the Algerian problem, has been markedly different from that in the French Caribbean, and this difference is played out in attitudes towards migrants from these two regions. Here, 'race' as a marker is subservient to issues of religion. Islam becomes the primary axis of difference and the basis for denoting migrants.

Although there are no easy answers to the question of who is defined as migrant, academics have used the United Nations recommendations as a starting point. The United Nations recommends that a migrant is defined as a person who has moved to a country other than that of their usual residence and has been living in that country for more than one year. The country of destination effectively becomes their new country of usual residence (Eurostat 1994, 1997). However, varying definitions have been employed by different organizations in different countries and at different times and so migration data are always considered notoriously unreliable.

Each country has formulated its definitions in relation to the specificities of its own migration history, the demographic data collection systems that it has in place and the aims of its migration policy. Some of the criteria used within the European Union are an intention to stay (Belgium, Italy, Luxembourg and Spain), a minimum period of stay in the country (Portugal, Finland, Sweden, Denmark and Netherlands) and the nature of housing occupied (Germany). Countries vary in the minimum period of time that a resident is required to stay in a country before they are registered as immigrants, varying from just one month (Netherlands) to one year (Portugal, Sweden, Finland) (Eurostat 1995). These regulations vary between nationals and non-nationals. Criteria for defining emigration and immigration also differ. Furthermore, emigration data are not collected by some countries, most notably France, while Spain does not provide emigration data for emigration of non-nationals. Another major gap in the migration data occurs where nationals from certain countries are not categorized as immigrants, for example, the Irish in the UK and members of certain African countries in France; consequently the reliability of these statistical data are further undermined. The degree and nature of inclusion of asylum-seekers in immigration data also varies between countries. Diversity in national regulations in registration of refugees between date of physical entry and official recognition affect the comparability of data on refugees. Besides, the increasing number of undocumented migrants in Europe further limits the validity of migration statistics.

The nature of data collected by each country also alters through time. In Portugal, for instance, between 1941–1988, the source for emigration data collated by the Portuguese National Statistical Institute (INE) was the record of the emigrant passport. Since 1989, these passports have been abolished and the primary data collection source is now an Emigration Survey, the sample for which is obtained from the Employment Survey. Such data have the shortcomings inherent in their source. Comparability between any two data sets is therefore limited.

Even where countries utilize the same definition of migration, the data collection systems used may lead to wide variations in the nature of data collected. All secondary sources of data are influenced by the purposes for which they have been produced, in that they are skewed by the assumptions of those who produce the data. However, as migration has received more and more attention from the international community, the collection of information on migration has received priority. At an international level, both the European Union, in the shape of its Statistical Service (Eurostat), and the United Nations have established programmes for the harmonization of migration statistics. Such harmonization of data has been prioritized within Europe in order to achieve comparability of data.

Migrants vary in the distances they move, the reasons for movement, the nature of incorporation within the political system of the new country and in their degree of permanence. On these bases, we may distinguish those who move within Europe, from those who have moved from outside Europe, those who have travelled short distances from those who have travelled long distances. Migrants also differ in the extent and nature of their recognition and the attendant rights in the new country. Illegal migrants have very few rights, while the rights of legal migrants vary between countries and across different statuses. The rights to stay, the right to work, the right to move, the rights to welfare and the rights to partake in political activity, are all differently constructed and may not necessarily be coterminous.

Like other forms of categorization, the degree of permanence is difficult to use as a criterion as data for this is difficult to obtain. While it may be assumed that significant numbers will shift from temporary to permanent stay, there is increasing evidence that more and more migrants are transient, and may move, while return migration is also important among certain migrant streams. Reason for entry is the most widely used criterion in defining migrants. On the whole, migration legislation and policy utilise the reason for entry as the basis for granting other rights. However, as different categories of migrants have dominated in certain periods the relationship between rights, categories and their historical place must be scrutinized, rather than assumed (see Chapter 3).

Labour migration was for long considered the primary form of migration in Europe. Labour migrants are those who enter to seek work, and usually waged work. Although the migration discourse has until recently revolved largely around unskilled migrants, numbers of skilled people have also entered, especially on work permits. Family reunion migration pertains to those who enter as spouses or children of the primary migrant. When the children of migrant workers marry someone from the country of origin of the parent(s) this often leads to so-called family formation immigration. This type of immigration frequently occurred during the 1980s and had very specific impacts on men and women. Student migration has increased throughout this period, although there have been shifts in country of origin of student migrants. The rights to work in this category are limited and it is difficult to switch from a student visa to a work permit. Tourists who overstay or switch categories through marriage, by obtaining jobs and legalizing their stay are another important category of migrants. In recent years, the largest increase in migration to Europe has occurred under the category of asylum-seekers and refugees. Those who apply for asylum at the port of entry in Europe are termed asylum-seekers. Asylum-seekers have to obtain refugee status from the country that they entered, a long legal process.

Although data collected are based on criteria for entry, migrants often switch categories. One primary switching mechanism is marriage, but length of relationship, and period of stay together before and after migration are used as criteria to curtail switching. Thus, students may marry residents and gain rights to stay, but in the UK they have to remain with their spouse for at least one year after marriage. In most countries in Europe, where marriage between homosexuals is not recognized, this avenue will only be available to heterosexual couples.

Another question that arises is when do migrants stop being migrants? Do we include the children of migrants who have obtained citizenship but remain in visible minorities within the receiving state? The children of migrants, often called the 'second generation' form ethnic minorities in these states. Although these children may have access to citizenship, they often face forms of discrimination similar to that of migrants. In this book we have adopted the most inclusive definition of migrants and have incorporated some of the issues faced by 'ethnic minority' women, but the main focus is on migrants. However, ethnic minority itself carries with it many of the problems inherited from its migrant parents. It often denotes a cohesiveness, cultural and historical, collapsing for instance, the very divergent experiences of migrants, for example from rural Punjab to Nottingham in the UK with that of the double migrated east African Asians of Gujarati origin moving from Kenya to Leicester, UK. Furthermore, an ethnic community carries with it little of pejorative nature of being a minority. Hence, Americans in Germany may not be considered 'real' migrants, whereas Turks form a minority.

The official terminology used is related to the primary preoc-cupations of each nation state. For instance, in Britain, the dominance of the race relations paradigm has collapsed the issue of migration with that of 'race' (Miles 1989), whereas in France, the primary distinction remains that between immigrants (immigrés) and French nationals (Neveu 1994). French principles of universalism guarantee equal rights to all citizens so that citizen-ship becomes the primary criterion for difference whereas, in the UK, the historical legacy of the Commonwealth whose members all had access to British citizenship but whose conceptions of national identity are highly racialized. In Sweden, Belgium and the Netherlands the term minorities is used for all migrants, as they assumed that all migrants were likely to settle. On the other hand, Germany has assumed all migration to be temporary, referring to migrant-workers as *gastarbeiter* (guest workers).

The Migrants Forum, launched by the European Communities Commission to give voice to migrants has used both status and discrimination as criteria, although selectively, in defining its membership. It includes those who do not have voting rights in Europe, primarily third country nationals so that associations representing Italians in Germany are not included. However, Black organizations in the UK, whose members have UK and hence EU citizenship, are admitted to the Forum (Neveu 1994). Hence, migrant in this context is subtly predicated on the racial category non-White, and in opposition to the imaginary White Europe.

Thus, migrant is a contested term. The contents of the category alter across space and time, in different contexts, involve self-definition and exclusion, and a denial of access to rights

Definitional issues, sources and gender

These definitional issues often have specific impacts on women migrants. Data collected focuses on the head of the household, who is implicitly assumed to be male. Female-headed households are often neglected. Gender disaggregated migration data is now collected by all countries within Europe, but although they have been collected for some years, they often remain unpublished. Even where published data have been available it has not prompted much interest and has often not resulted in a gendered analysis of migration. One reason for this is that conceptualizations of migration were driven by the labour migration model where labour was assumed to be male, and women were thought to be economically inactive. Migrants were assumed to be single men in search of employment, although throughout the labour migration period, women both migrated and participated in the economy (see Chapter 3). However, among certain categories of migrants, such as skilled labour migrants and asylum-seekers, there is still little gender-disaggregated data available. Feminists have argued that the categories used to define migration are also not necessarily appropriate to the experience of female migrants. The limitations of the collection and categorization influence the forms of analysis that can be undertaken. Thus, what is required is gender-disaggregated data collection, gender-sensitive categorization and gendered analysis.

One way in which the limitations of quantitative data sources have been circumvented is through the use of interviews and oral histories of migrants. While quantitative data can be useful for assessing the numerical significance of women in migration streams, the nature of the migrant experience and the variations between different women migrants is better understood through the use of qualitative data. Qualitative data often provide a holistic view of women's experiences. These sources have been better able to reveal the different spatio-temporal dimensions of female migration, the multiplicity of causes for their moves and the often overlapping strategies used by women migrants. It provides a flavour of the heterogeneity of migration, the range of ages at which people migrate, the varying skills they bring with them, the different reasons for moving, and for staying or moving again, the social relations that facilitate migration and the regimes that influence migrant trajectories. They also highlight the significance of gender as a key variable in the experience of migration.

A number of other sources also provide detailed and graphic portrayals of the migration experience, even though such sources may not have been created explicitly in order to provide this information. The cinema, autobiography, photography, ethnographic pieces, to mention just a few, have increasingly been used as sources of information. Recently, a number of films have focused on aspects of migrant lives, emphasizing themes such as familial conflict across gender and generation, but also challenging stereotypical images of migrant groups. In France, for example, most of these films depict the lives of more 'settled' migrant communities such as those of north Africans by Malik Chibane in *Hexagone* (1994) and *La Douce France* (1995; Tarr 1999). Far fewer films have examined issues concerning the process of migration and the exploitation of undocumented migrants, an exception being the Belgian film *La Promesse* (1998). There has also been a growth of interest in literature written by migrants (King *et al.* 1995; Brinkler-Gabler and Smith 1997), which connects conditions in the homeland with the movement to the destination countries, and describes migratory experiences and relationships with the dominant society. It has usually been the largest and long-established migrant groups that have dominated cinematic and literary production, for example Asian and Caribbean in the UK, North African in France and Turkish in Germany.

Autobiographical accounts of women across different generations could be used to understand the changing class and gender experiences (Gabaccia 1995; Chamberlain 1994) used oral histories to demonstrate familial networks and the movements between the homeland and receiving countries. Commemorative historiography has also come of age, as for instance, with the literature and documentaries that have traced and explored the history of Caribbean migration to the UK since the late 1940s.

Feminist contributions to the analysis of European immigration

The first studies to incorporate women were written in the early 1970s by women of immigrant origin. Early feminist research on migration aimed to increase the visibility of women within migratory streams. In France, Morokvasic's work on Yugoslav women, which was the theme of her PhD thesis, pioneered discussions on the role of gender in migration, while Leonetti-Taboada, herself the daughter of Spanish Civil War refugees, worked on Iberian women. Since 1975, a number of conferences have focused on migrant women and International Labour Organization (ILO) provisions have been extended to migrant women. However, Morokvasic (1983, 1984) argued that despite a proliferation of studies, many have perpetuated the stereotype of women as wife and mother. What quickly became apparent was the diversity in women's experiences, and that women were migrating for employment, as parts of households or to join family members who had already migrated.

The first stocktaking occurred in the early 1980s in the shape of the UNESCO publication *Women on the Move* (1980), with chapters by Abadan-Unat and Morokvasic on Europe. Around the same time, Phizacklea offered a structuralist analysis of labour migration in *One Way Ticket* (1983a,b). Morokvasic (1984) also focused on labour migration but argued that access to employment does not necessarily emancipate women. Simon and Bretell (1986) subsequently produced an edited volume on migrant women where they also emphasized cultural elements influencing migration, family life and reproduction, and recognized a greater variety of migrant categories, including refugees. Taravella (1984) produced an early bibliography.

Since then studies of female migration have almost exclusively been based on case studies and biographical material. By the 1990s a large number of case studies had accumulated, some of which provided a more European-wide perspective (Campani 1993a,b; Morokvasic 1993; Wihtol de Wenden 1996). To some extent this occurred because of European integration and the impact of fortress Europe on migrant women (Kofman and Sales 1992; Lutz

1997). The European Commission and the Council of Europe supported and convened meetings such as the First European Conference in Athens in 1994: Migrant Women, Active Women. They produced European Committee on Migration country reports on *Migration, Cultural Diversity and Equality of Women and Men* (Gaspard 1994; Lutz 1994); *Confronting the Fortress* (European Women's Lobby 1995), adding to the literature on female migration in Europe.

Feminist literature has adopted divergent methods, sources and approaches to ways of knowing female migration and has varied with different disciplinary takes. Most works that have explored female migration to Europe have been undertaken by sociologists (Phizacklea 1983; Morokvasic 1983, 1984, 1997; Yuval-Davis and Anthias 1989; Brah 1996; Essed 1996; Koser and Lutz 1998). Initially this led to particular emphases in the literature, with a focus on the social construction of the labour market. More recent work has been heavily influenced by cultural analysis, with a focus on representations of migrants and on the meanings that they attach to their lived experiences, resulting in a relative neglect of new forms of migration and the changing structural factors and immigration legislation within which this migration occurs. The focus has shifted from the experiences of migrations to that of minorities, those with a more settled migrant status, and often children of migrants. However, the link to home is retained, as in the burgeoning literature on diaspora (Brah 1996; Anthias 1997).

Anthropologists, on the other hand, have largely explored migrant women's experiences and everyday lives in the context of their social networks. Because of the nature of anthropology, they have focused on issues of the 'homeland' and on culture and religion, particularly in the context of the 'tradition–modernity' debate. Historians have studied migrant trajectories across generations. Geographers have been slow to take an interest in gender and international migration, generally focusing more on internal migration and using large-scale data sets to a greater extent than many of the other disciplines mentioned above (Halfacree and Boyle 1999). However, recent years have seen an increase in interdisciplinary work on migration, drawing on multiple sources and methods in order to develop cross-disciplinary approaches to the study of migration (see above). Biographical studies and narratives are increasingly being incorporated into accounts of migration and are an example of shared methodologies.

The new fields of interest and the accumulation of studies, including those that are European-wide, have yet to make any substantial impact on theorizations of migration or European studies of migration. A selection of key texts confirms this silence and the assumption that the only migrant who counts is male (Collinson 1993; King 1993; Miles and Thranhardt 1995; Uçarer and Puchala 1997). It also reveals a continuing inability to incorporate into European research the recent meso level of analysis in migration research (Boyd 1989; Goss and Lindquist 1995; Lee 1996; Matthei Miller 1996; Bjeren 1997), which emphasizes the role of households and wider social networks in migration decisions. The genderless interpretation of migratory movements also takes no account of wider economic, social and cultural changes that have affected women and men, both migrant and indigenous. Feminist work has especially emphasized the significance of household strategies and power relations within it in deciding how and where to move, but this work has not been taken up in research on migration in Europe.

Many of these texts examine new forms of migration and processes of citizenship and exclusion. Wrench and Solomos (1993), though not incorporating female migration into a general framework, include chapters on migrant women (Lutz 1993; Brah 1993b). The one major exception is the volume on new migrations in Europe where one of the editors, Helma Lutz, is a leading researcher on female migrations in Europe. Morokvasic (1997) in rethinking the implications of mobility from eastern Europe for emigration and immigration has incorporated female and male protagonists. Ackers (1998) has explored for the first time the experiences of migrant women moving within Europe, adding a significant new perspective to the existing literature.

What has emerged has been a diversity of categories of migration, new and traditional: labour (legal and undocumented), family reunion and formation, marriage, prostitution, asylum seekers and refugees. The effects of immigration policy on the status and exclusion of women from the labour market and social rights is also generating attention (see Simon and Bretell 1986; Kofman and Sales 1997, 1998).

While there has been an increasing recognition of the rapidity and the significance of changes in migratory experiences in recent decades within Europe, and complex theorizations of these processes, there has been little attempt to acknowledge the explicitly gendered nature of these experiences in mainstream analysis (Kofman 1999). On the whole, gender has rarely been considered a significant analytical category within European literature on migration, which has remained gender blind. Migrants have been treated as asexual categories and feminists researching women have often focused on nationals rather than immigrant women.

Family reunion migration, despite its numerical significance in Europe, has tended in general to be neglected (Lahav 1996), reflecting the lack of interest in a migration of dependants whose labour market participation is supposedly of secondary consequence (Kofman 1999). Whilst allowing family reunion in principle, many states have made it more difficult to comply with the requirements of housing, income and no recourse to public support. The fastest growing category has been asylum seekers, which is dominated by men, though a sizeable female presence indicates the need to study this group. In addition, the absence of gender guidelines in the refugee determination process and the restrictive interpretation of the application of the Geneva Convention have negative consequences for female asylum seekers (Crawley 1997; special issue of Refuge 1997).

New societies of origin and destination as well as flows have become far more important, yet the ways in which such streams are gendered have so far received little attention. Migration into southern Europe has increased, often with high female flows in domestic labour from the Philippines, Cape Verde, South America and from eastern Europe (Albanians, Polish). Women in eastern Europe who have borne the brunt in the transition to market economy in the east and are often highly qualified, but forced to work in the domestic sector in Germany (Friese 1995), have moved west, sometimes adopting a rotational character to their migration (Morokvasic 1991a).

Crises of national identity and conflicting laws concerning personal status have pushed women to the fore in political debates around issues of the wearing of the headscarf, polygamy and excision. This has been especially charged in a country such as France where women have turned into the 'vectors of integration'. Wihtol de Wenden (1996) sees the social and cultural dimensions of female immigration posing acute dilemmas between principles of universality, equality of rights, encouragement of individualism, tolerance and respect for other cultures and religious pluralism and identities. Campani (1995) suggests that women are becoming increasingly active subjects in the process of migration. She comments that research on the networks, groups and sociability of migrant women is still rare, although in recent years in France the growth in local migrant women's groups has also led to more attention being paid to them (Quiminal 1997). Sudbury (1998) has examined migrant women's organizations in the UK, focusing largely on Black (African, Caribbean, Chinese, south Asian) women's organizations. She takes up the issue of emancipation as a strategy. She argues that such emancipation is not merely achieved through access to the world of work. It is necessary to understand the different migrant trajectories, the contexts of the choices made, the emancipatory motivation, the impact of migration on familial structures and the role and status of women. Women migrants have constructed different subject positions within key debates, organizing themselves to campaign on local issues, but it is unevenly acknowledged in academic research across Europe. Besides, although women have campaigned locally to achieve similar aims, there has been little attempt to bring them together or to use European political space to achieve their ends.

This book

In this chapter we have set the context for European migration this century. We have highlighted the significance of women migrants in Europe and existing feminist work in this field. In Chapter 2 we outline some of the key theoretical debates to which this book contributes. Chapter 3 details European migratory regimes and examines the position of women migrants in these flows. It aims to challenge conceptualization of male labour migration models to Europe and restore a more accurate historical picture of gendered immigration. Chapter 4 examines notions of citizenship and national variations in models of collective incorporation of migrants. It also explores the degree to which international conventions may provide additional rights and argues that citizenship continues to be a key objective for migrants and a primary modus for acquiring rights and combating social exclusion.

The next three chapters examine different aspects of migrant women in relation to employment, welfare and politics. In Chapter 5 we follow changes in the past few decades in a selected number of key states of migrant women's position in and contribution to the labour market. In Chapter 6 we examine different welfare regimes in Europe and the role of migrant women as providers, mediators and clients of welfare. In Chapter 7 we outline the range of political activities in which migrant women participate and the ways they attempt to negotiate and challenge power relationships at different levels ranging from the home and the private sphere, to the national level and the European sphere.

This book is not the product of a series of research projects designed specifically to elucidate key questions regarding migratory histories, employment, welfare, citizenship and politics. That would constitute a mammoth task. Hence, inevitably, the partial coverage of certain areas has been one of the major problems we have confronted in seeking to provide a fairly comprehensive picture of the situation prevailing in different European states. The book is also, to varying degrees, disproportionately dependent on British material. This arises for several reasons. Firstly the interest in gender and migration in the social sciences and the development of migrant women's groups has a longer history in the UK than in many other European countries. As we have seen, the major reviews of literature on women and international migration are found in English-language journals and books. Secondly, much of the available material in European states tends to be produced in the form of unpublished reports or small-scale publications. This makes it extremely difficult to access material uniformly throughout European states. In each state there may be particular preoccupations or an emphasis on certain groups, and often those who are considered problematic in terms of traditional customs by official organizations.

The authors have brought to bear their own expertise. Eleonore Kofman has undertaken research on the development of policies towards migrant women in France and is particularly interested in counteracting a truncated history of female migration in Europe. Rosemary Sales has been involved in projects concerning the settlement of refugees and the role of migrant women as advocates in the UK. Eleonore and Rosemary have worked together for almost a decade in researching issues of exclusion and citizenship facing migrant women in the European Union. Annie Phizacklea has a long-standing interest in specific sectors of employment involving migrant women across a number of European countries. Parvati Raghuram has been involved in researching migration issues in India, gender and ethnic minority enterprise in the UK, and is currently interested in issues of skilled migration to Europe.

Chapter 2

Gender and migration theory

While there has been a dramatic speeding up of contemporary processes of feminization of migration, our conceptualization of these developments has not moved as fast. Perhaps some of this glacial movement in theory is because of the long-standing stalemate between models based on classical economics and those that draw on a neo-Marxist political economy tradition. Both of these claimed to be gender-neutral, but were in fact based on a model of gender relations that assumed female dependence. As Truong has argued:

> At best these two paradigms can incorporate women as a norma-tive category in migration flows, and explain their migration in terms of individual rational decision based on wage differentials (neo-classical), or collective rational decisions of households and states based on the interest in remittances (neo-Marxian).
>
> (Truong 1996: 31)

Women migrate for a whole range of reasons such as poverty, displacement from the land, debt, and many other external constraints over which they have little control. These problems are shared with men, though their impact is always gendered. The deci-sion to migrate is influenced by wage differentials in sender areas and in receiving areas, but this is only one element in the decision to migrate. Some non-economic factors are especially important causes of emigration for women. Social constraints facing women (or their lack) also influence sex selectivity patterns in migration streams. Marital discord and physical violence, unhappy and broken marriages and the impossibility of divorce often influence women's decision to migrate. Migration also offers women and men the opportunity to transgress sex-role behaviour, but this is especially important for women, as the constraints on women's behaviour are usually greater than those on men. It often allows women to escape discrimination because of other aspects of their gendered lives, particularly those who have suffered because of age or their position within the family. These interrelate with perceived and/or real opportunities for women after migration and, thus, influence migration. Women may perceive migration as a means of resisting and escaping at least some aspects of the oppressive structures in which they live their lives. It may provide the opportunity to improve financially their own situation and that of their families; to avoid or leave unsatisfactory, perhaps violent, marriages; and perhaps to restore self-respect and justice through collective action and resistance in the course of migration (see Chapter 7). In this chapter we examine some of the ways in which the reasons for migration have been theorized, examining the major approaches to migration through a critical gendered lens. We attempt to link this literature with other key concerns in social sciences, which are interrelated with issues of migration but have been inadequately linked to migration theories.

Looking back and moving on

The primary focus of early theories of migration was to understand the reasons for migration. What are the factors influencing migration? Till the 1970s the most influential theories were those proffered by neo-classical theorists who viewed individual migration decisions as a result of push–pull factors. They located decision-making in individuals, rather than within wider social units, but also conceptualized the reasons for migration within a reductive economistic framework. Migration is the product of rational decisions made by individuals who sit down and weigh up the costs and benefits of a move, and migrate to the destination that maximizes the net economic returns on migration (see for instance Todaro 1969, 1976).

Despite Ravensteins's qualification of women as 'greater migrants than men', they were essentially left out of theoretical thinking. Where women's migration was analysed at all, the major trend was to conflate it with reasons usually cited for men. Effectively it adopted an 'add women and stir' approach. The experiences of women migrants were fitted into models created to understand, explain and predict male migration, thus assuming that women have the same reasons for migrating as men. Agency in these accounts was never viewed within the context of resisting oppressive and exploitative structures. They assumed that men and women would act in exactly the same way and have the same relationship to those structures.

From the mid- to late-1970s there was a wave of theorizing that drew heavily on Marxist political economy, dependency theory and world systems theory. Castles and Kosack (1973), Castells (1975), Nikolinakos (1975), Phizacklea and Miles (1980) and Meillassoux (1981) were all representative of this approach. At the heart of these historicized political economy accounts was a focus on the unequal distribution of economic and political power on a worldwide basis and the way in which migration is a mechanism for mobilizing cheap labour for capital. Castles and Kosack (1973), for instance, argued that labour migration was in fact a form of development aid given by the poor countries to the rich countries and that it is unrealistic to assume that individuals exercise free choice over migration given these global inequalities in economic and political power and the ways in which economically dominant states control migration to suit their labour supply needs. Racism was often viewed as an essential mechanism for the 'over exploitation of the so-called under-developed peoples' and for keeping the latter in a constant state of fear (Meillassoux 1981: 121).

Looking back, some of these accounts seem guilty of an oversocialized view of migrant workers as passive agents tossed around in the turbulent seas of international capitalism. There was a tendency to reduce human agency to the interests of the collective – the global working class. The role of agency is particularly vital for a gendered account of migration because it is so often assumed that women simply 'follow' men and that their role in migration is reactive rather than proactive. Some theorists were guilty of an obsession with economy and class to the exclusion of other divisions such as gender, although Castles and Kosack (1973) and Phizacklea and Miles (1980) did pay attention to the gender division of labour. Whatever their faults they provided an antidote to the anodyne explanations provided by neo-classical economics.

Early structuralist accounts continued to downplay the non-economic factors influencing emigration. This lacuna was particularly important in the context of understanding women's migration because the reasons often include marital discord and physical violence, the impossibility of divorce, and the prevalence of conservative social legislation and practices. Research carried out by Morokvasic in the mid-1970s was among the first to point out the extent to which migration represented not simply an enforced response to economic hardship by single, widowed or divorced women, but also a deliberate, calculated move on the part of individual gendered actors to escape from a society where patriarchy was an institutionalized and repressive force (Morokvasic 1983; see also Gray 1996 on Irish women). Given the low social esteem and worth accorded to girls in many societies, we should pay much closer attention to this as a motivating factor in women's migration. There is also evidence that women's ability to earn and send home remittances significantly increases their social worth in their home settings. Hence economic factors interact with and influence non-economic factors, and together affect the decision to migrate. Skrobanek *et al.* (1997) argue on the basis of research in Thailand that parents tacitly accept their daughter's involvement in sex work as long as she is sending money home.

> Parents may wield less power over their daughters' decisions and choices. This contrasts with the not-too-distant-past, when parents were the decision makers in all things. ... Now a family with several daughters is considered lucky.
>
> (Skrobanek *et al.* 1997: 74)

Structural accounts may have erred in the direction of capital-logic in the past but this is not to say that structure is unimportant. The explosion in the number of women from poor countries seeking to migrate in search of work is firmly linked to the feminization of poverty resulting from structural adjustment programmes and, particularly, their impact on women's work in both the waged and unwaged sectors of the economy. Such bodies as the International Monetary Fund insist that growing cash crops may create agricultural jobs for women, for example in the picking and preparation of fruit, vegetables and flowers, but these jobs are low paid and virtually always highly precarious. At the same time, this form of production deprives families of land for the growing of subsistence food and other cash-generating activities. State policy in many developing countries, particularly in Asia, has encouraged labour migration, often in competition with one another, as a way of relieving internal poverty and servicing foreign debt. Migrants may be legally required to remit a certain proportion of their earnings. But labour migration is ultimately demand driven and most demand for labour in the affluent and newly industrializing countries is now for women (Lim and Oishi 1996: 99).

The extent to which migration is institutionalized at both ends of the migration route is often overlooked. At the receiving end, women's experience of migration is mediated by immigration policies and rules that often, in very subtle ways, continue to treat women as confined to a male-regulated private sphere. In cases where women do enter as a spouse, their entry is conditional and reinforces dependency on their husbands (see Chapter 3). For women entering as independent workers the kinds of jobs available to them are often not officially considered 'work' because they are hidden within the home (domestic service) or otherwise considered to be part of the private domain (for example sex work). As we shall see in Chapter 5, while all women face the constraints of sex segregation in employment (even if for the highly qualified this may only be encountered when they hit the 'glass ceiling'), migrant women also face limits on their citizenship rights and an institutionalized racism that deems some low-level servicing jobs as 'what migrant women do'.

All these factors are part of broader structural contexts that constrain women's opportunities, but this does not mean that they cannot be challenged. It is important to recognize that notions of structural context and agency are heavily inter-related. Unless we do this, migrant women will continue to be viewed as passive victims, helpless in the face of the impersonal cycles of international capital and bowing to oppressive patriarchal structures. Patriarchal structures take many different economic, social and political forms throughout the world. Being a widow in certain cultures, for example, will bring with it a range of social and economic constraints from which migration may provide an escape route of a kind. But wherever a woman migrates to, she will enter a labour market that is highly segregated by sex and, unless she holds certain scarce and highly valued skills, she will find that employment choices are confined to a narrow band of servicing and caring work traditionally associated with women's role in the private sphere. Nevertheless, once agency is put firmly in the same frame as structural context, we can begin to analyse in a rather different way migrant women's economic contribution and their efforts to improve their own (and their family's) standard of living, their bid for self-respect and their contribution as collective agents in instigating political change through alliance and coalition building.

One way out of the impasse between structuralist and neo-classical approaches to migration has been to focus on the family or household as the key to understanding migration (for instance Stark 1984) and to study the decision to migrate as part of household strategies. Early literature on the household treated the homogenous household as the primary unit of analysis, retaining the myth that the household is a refuge from the selfishness of the outside world, in which the members behave altruistically towards one another. Its overriding ethos was to counteract the exclusive concentration on individual motivations for migration. It argued for a shift towards 'understanding how these small social units pool resources to organize a process as complex as international migration' (Portes 1997: 816). Goss and Lindquist (1995: 327) point out that the principal tendency within the migration literature was to reify the household and to conflate the interests of its members with those of the male household-head, ignoring the ways in which the household can be a primary site for the exploitation of labour and transfer of value. This conception of the household is

> unlikely to be applied uncritically to Western societies and is consistent with the ideological tendency in social sciences to romanticize peasant and community in the Third World. Somehow, members of Third World households, not burdened by the individualism of Western societies, resolve to co-operate willingly and completely, each according to their capacities, to collectively lift the burden of their poverty.
>
> (Goss and Lindquist 1995: 328)

This work embodied no analytical shift towards recognizing that households are deeply implicated in gendered ideologies and practices. Families were assumed to make their decisions as a group rather than on an individual basis, weighing up the costs and benefits to the family as a whole of the migration of its members. However, households are not the cosy rational decision-making units that neo-classical economics would lead us to believe. Migration decisions reflect the power relations within the household and are influenced by both individual as well as collective interests. A number of studies explored the ways in which gendered power influence migration.

Two excellent gendered accounts of migration can be found in the work of Grasmuck and Pessar (1991) and Hondagneu-Sotelo (1994), both of which take the household as central to their analysis and start from the premise that, 'The household, as we conceive it, has its own political economy, in which access to power and other valued resources is distributed along gender and generational lines' (Grasmuck and Pessar 1991: 202). Their empirical research presumably falls foul of Portes warning against 'making respondents' definitions of the situation the ultimate test for theoretical propositions, and points to the hollowness of the assumption that households make collective decisions. Hondagneu-Sotelo (1994: 95) concludes, 'Opening the household "black box" exposes a highly charged political arena where husbands and wives and parents and children may simultaneously express and pursue divergent interests and competing agendas.'

While we recognize the need to understand the complexity of household relations, and the existence of both mutual solidarity and conflict within them, there are good reasons why a number of scholars, almost exclusively women, have concentrated on single sex-focused research. The role of women in migration was almost completely ignored until the late 1970s (see Chapter 1). This research, along with some studies of the household and social networks (e.g. the work of Hondagneu-Sotelo 1994), has been aimed at giving women a voice. This voice had never been heard and is often at odds with the overriding assumption in much of the literature that women simply follow men in the migration process. This also challenged the notion that households are benign units in which power and resources are equally distributed. Feminist social science has questioned traditional epistemological assumptions, particularly in terms of what 'passes the test' of 'objective' empirical research (Stanley and Wise 1983; Harding 1987). As Mary Evans (1997: 122) argues 'feminism can claim to have developed one of the now great critical traditions within the Western academy, that of suggesting that the universalistic assumptions of knowledge in our society are false, and partial, because they are drawn from the experiences of only one sex.' By investigating the hitherto untold experience of women migrants, this work has contributed to the wider understanding of migratory processes.

There are other reasons why the household can never be a satisfactory unit of analysis in bridging the gap between micro-level understandings and the structural context within which migration takes place. First, households take many different forms, from the 'neat' nuclear family household to a vast extended form. Second, households are entrenched within and reflect a whole range of power structures, which are by no means static and uncontested. Gender has remained the only theoretical lens through which household migration has been analysed. In an article titled 'Immigration theory for a new century', Portes implicitly accepts this view by confining a discussion of gender and migration to a single page subtitled 'Households and gender'. However, he suggests the need for caution in relation to 'analyses that concentrate exclusively on the individual motivations of household members and the conflict of interests between them. This has often become the centre of gender-focused research' (Portes 1997: 816). Besides, as the example from Thailand discussed above illustrates, the balance of social and economic power may shift quite rapidly. Finally, households are only one part of a number of mid-level institutions that play a part in the migration process.

The limitations of the focus on households have led to an interest within migration research in the role of social networks and the other institutions that link individuals across time and space. The role of social networks in facilitating migration, employment and settlement came to pre-occupy many during the 1980s and into the 1990s (see Boyd 1989 for an overview), although they had always been treated as significant elements in the older theories of chain migration (Castles 1999). Boyd argues that a starting point for research on social networks is that 'structural factors provide the context within which migration individuals or groups make decisions. However, at this micro-level analysis, the decision to migrate is influenced by the existence of and participation in social networks, which connect people across space' (Boyd 1989: 645).

Social networks are important in sustaining migration flows (for example by providing information, accommodation and employment for incoming migrants) and provide an important link between the individual actor and the structural context that fashions migration flows. If we are to explain an individual's decision to migrate we must combine accounts of structural context (in which structure is seen as both constraining and enabling) with situational, micro-level understandings.

Social networks comprising households, friends and community ties are crucial for an understanding of settlement patterns, employment and links with the homeland. Once migration begins these networks come to function as causes of migration in themselves because they lower the costs and risks of migration and increase its expected returns (Massey *et al.* 1993). Networks constitute an important resource for migrants who use them to gain employment, housing and other resources in the migration setting. Much of what is being described here is the phenomenon of chain migration, or the passing of information from migration to home, particularly information on job vacancies that may encourage family members and friends to devise ways of migrating. Social networks are also central to Hondagneu-Sotelo's analysis of Mexican migration. She concludes that

> traditionally, gender relations in the networks have facilitated men's and constrained women's migration, but this is changing. While patriarchal practices and rules in families and social networks have persisted, through migration women and men reinterpret normative standards and creatively manipulate the rules of gender.
>
> (Hondagneu-Sotelo 1994: 96)

These social networks facilitate transnational links (Glick Schiller *et al.* 1992) in which migrants move regularly between and participate in more than one society. As Sutton (1992) notes in relation to Caribbean migration, there has been little reflection in this literature on gender aspects of the use of transnational networks. Women in particular have played nurturing roles (nurses, carers and domestic labour) and sustained households in societies of emigration and immigration.

The importance of social networks in facilitating migration is therefore well established, but they do not by themselves provide an adequate bridge between structure and agency because it fails to take into account the increasingly formalized nature of migration. In another innovative account Goss and Lindquist argue for a mid-level concept, which they call a 'migrant institution' that 'articulates' between various levels of analysis (Goss and Lindquist 1995: 317). This refers to an ensemble of social networks and intermediaries that represents a complex articulation of individuals, associations and organizations that extends the social action of and interaction between these agents and agencies across time and space (Goss and Lindquist 1995: 319). Applying Giddens's structuration thesis to migration from the Philippines, they argue that the key component of recent large-scale international migration, largely neglected in the literature, is the complex of international and national institutions that transcend the boundaries of states and locales, linking employers in the developed or rapidly developing economies with individuals in the furthest peripheries of the Third World (Goss and Lindquist 1995: 335). Recent evidence on women's migration underlines the increasing importance of such institutions that connect the most remote village in a complex but highly efficient manner with work in affluent countries. In Chapter 5 we shall discuss this in relation to sex work and domestic work.

Goss and Lindquist argue that individuals 'act strategically within the institution to further their interests, but the capacity for such action is differentially distributed according to knowledge or rules and access to resources, which in turn may be partially determined by their position within other social institutions' (Goss and Lindquist 1995: 345). Thus they see structures as both constraining and enabling.

Emigration has become institutionalized in south-east Asia and to some extent, the Indian sub-continent, from state institutions downwards. Without the huge ensemble of recruitment agents, overseas employment promoters, manpower suppliers and a host of other legal and illegal intermediaries, Asian labour migration since the mid-1970s would not have reached such a massive scale (Lim and Oishi 1996: 90). However, this growth has a number of gender-specific implications. It coincided with the increased demand for labour in specifically female dominated sectors such as domestic work and 'entertainment' (Truong 1996). Competition between Asian countries for the market share has contributed to the institutionalization of low wages in these female-dominated sectors (UN Secretariat 1995, quoted in Lim and Oishi 1996). It is likely that women are making more use than men of these recruitment agents, particularly those who will facilitate clandestine migration, because they have less access to information (Lim and Oishi 1996: 90). In exploring what they term 'institutional theory', Massey *et al.* (1993) maintain that the introduction of stringent immigration controls by affluent countries has created a lucrative economic niche for entrepreneurs and organizations who facilitate clandestine transnational population movements. Their activities include smuggling across borders, faking papers and arranging marriages. In turn, because these practices create a highly vulnerable underclass of migrants, new humanitarian organizations have been set up to provide a range of services such as legal advice, shelter and help with obtaining papers.

Massey *et al.* conclude that these processes lead to a number of hypotheses that are completely different from those that emanate from micro-level decision-making models. They argue that as organizations develop to support, sustain and promote international movement:

> the international flow of migrants becomes more and more institutionalized and independent of the factors that originally caused it. ... Governments have difficulty controlling migration flows once they have begun because the process of institutionalization is difficult to regulate.
>
> (Massey *et al.* 1993: 451)

This notion of 'migrant institution' represents a significant advance, in providing an account that can deal with the myriad of agencies and organizations now operating in the 'business' of migration and that have played a crucial role in the 'feminization' of labour migration at a global level since the mid-1970s. Goss and Lindquist's work demonstrates its relevance in the case of Filipino and other Asian migrations where the process of migration has been to a large extent 'institutionalized' at the level of the state. While not all migration processes are as formally institutionalized, different kinds of channels and professional organizations facilitate and regulate contemporary migration flows, including those of skilled migrants. A channel of migration refers to the ways in which migration is facilitated for individuals. It may range from the informality of relatives and friends to more official recruitment agencies and transnational corporations (Findlay and Li 1998; Gould 1988). Little research on gender differences in the use of channels has been done beyond the world of corporations that tend to give few overseas assignments to their female staff (Adler 1994). Similarly, there is much to be done on the role of professional bodies as regulatory institutions for purposes of accreditation in the state of destination (Iredale 1997).

Our discussion suggests the importance of the link between structure and individual agency in understanding the migratory process. We can distinguish analytically between three levels in order to characterize contemporary migration: (i) the migratory regime that includes the relations between the country of emigration and immigration, the conditions of entry and rights of residence, employment and so on, including the rights of family members; (ii) the migratory institution that includes formal state structures as well as mediators and facilitators, recruitment agencies and informal networks through which individuals and households negotiate migratory regimes; and (iii) individual migrants whose migration choices are conditioned by their own histories, social identities and resources as well as by the broader structural conditions. All three levels of analysis are highly gendered.

So far we have concentrated on some of the problems we encounter with existing migration theory and have tried to provide a more adequate gendered account. We now turn to the connection between migration flows and developments in feminist theory on race and ethnic studies.

Linking migration and ethnicity?

The theorization of migration has become increasingly divorced from that of ethnic relations and this separation has limited our understanding of both. A substantial literature that has developed on the causes of refugee flows and processes of resettlement has also tended to remain somewhat distinct from migration research.

The 'ethnic relations' literature has become preoccupied with diasporic communities (Cohen 1997), multiculturalism and hybrid identities (Werbner and Modood 1997) in settled communities. The interest in cartographies of diasporas is related to a more complex system of migration, often consisting of multiple moves by an individual and leading to the scattering of families across states and continents (Bhachu 1993; Brah 1996a), though not necessarily looking back to a fixed homeland as implied by the usual definition of a diaspora (Anthias 1997). In fact, recent literature on diaspora has increasingly argued that the experiences of those who have migrated once differs significantly from those who are multiple migrants. This literature has also tended to emphasize the cultural dimension of hybrid and transnational identities. Some have celebrated the potential of border zones whereas others (Bhabha 1994) maintain that hybrid subject positions occupying in-between spaces are best located to resist hegemonic practices. However, not all migrants find this border zone liberatory. For many, this space is one dominated by the 'terrorizing experience of border crossings' (Mitchell 1997). Besides, as Heitlinger (1999) argues, the degree to which highly cosmopolitan identities are easily acquired will depend on class position, education and facility with a world language and may be contrasted with the difficulties faced by the undocumented and the majority of asylum seekers. This class divide has troubled and kept apart academic work on migration from that on hybridities. These developments have meant that the links between migratory processes and the development of 'ethnic minority communities' have tended to be neglected. In the following chapters we attempt to develop some of these links, focusing on the ways in which immigration legislation and formal citizenship status impact on access to rights and therefore shapes the ways in which communities are formed and identities constructed. In particular, we examine the gendered hierarchy of citizenship rights in relation to employment, welfare and political action.

At the same time, although there has been an increasing recognition of the importance of female migration, the main trend within feminist theory has been an increasing preoccupation with questions of identity and the body. The very real material inequalities that women's different positionings at a global level represent have, at times, been relegated to second place behind issues of individual identity. In the following paragraphs we suggest ways in which some of these cultural understandings of gender and race can help inform our understanding of these material inequalities.

In the early 1980s, debates within feminism began to shift with an acknowledgement of the complex interactions between categories of class, 'race' and gender and the identities that they give rise to. An important marker for this shift was the intervention of Black and ethnic minority feminists in the USA and UK who began to question what they considered to be the false priorities of the women's movement, and the tendency of feminist theory to universalize White women's experiences in the affluent countries of the world. Key writers of this period were Angela Davis (1982) and bell hooks (1981) in the USA and Hazel Carby (1982) in the UK. The lively debate that followed has certainly not just been an academic one and is by no means over. It demonstrated, amongst other things, that the concept 'Black' as a way of categorizing all 'non-White' women's experiences is just as problematic as the all encompassing category of 'woman'. But this recognition of the huge range of 'differences' has spawned its own problems. As Mary Maynard has argued, if we accept that the bases of difference and diversity are endless, then we obscure the possibility of analysing the material inequalities between individuals that this diversity represents and, at the same time, fail to explore what experiences individuals might have in common (Maynard 1996: 20). Feminism risks falling into the same trap as multiculturalism, which Malik suggests 'represents not a means to an equal society, but an alternative to one, where equality has given way to the toleration of difference and indeed of inequality' (Malik 1996: 170).

Maynard's critique reflects a more general comment on the way in which many disciplines have moved away from a concern with the material to a preoccupation with the 'cultural'. While endorsing her concern, we would argue that it is important for us to look at the ways in which so-called 'cultural' issues, such as concerns with the body, sexuality and representation, might also be significant for a gendered account of migration. For instance, if we try to answer a seemingly 'material' question: 'why is domestic and sex work increasingly regarded as work that migrant women do?', we can provide a set of answers that rests largely within the material. That these are jobs that have traditionally been regarded as within the private sphere, are done by women, and to which little or no value has been attached. But this answer begs a whole range of other questions. Is it simply a question that migrant women can be paid less? Part of the answer is 'yes' but this is not sufficient. To provide a more adequate answer we have to look at how different racialized and gendered identities have been constructed over time and how those identities have been changing.

There is now a large literature that shows how, for instance, Black African women's identities were both racialized and sexualized in specific ways in the process of colonization and enslavement. Patricia Hill Collins argues that the portrayal of the 'Jezebel', or sexually aggressive Black woman under slavery, had a number of functions. On the one hand, their sexuality had to be controlled by forcing them to work alongside men, yet on the other hand they could also be expected to breed a new generation of slave labour power. The alternative image was the 'mammy', an asexual (always fat) woman who would wetnurse White children and 'slaveowners effectively tied the controlling images of Jezebel and Mammy to the economic exploitation inherent in the institution of slavery' (Collins 1990: 77). From the earliest travelogues of Africa to the contemporary film and music industry, Black women have been represented in highly sexualized ways. Other enslaved and colonized women were deemed 'exotic', but their eroticization was built on understandings of their being 'primitive', 'uncivilized', the 'other'. Pseudo-scientific arguments developed in the mid-nineteenth century claimed that one could divide the world's population into distinct and permanent 'racial' types and that these types represented a hierarchy of superiority and inferiority. 'Natives' were deemed capable of carrying out certain types of manual work for their colonizers, but nothing more. Writing in 1814 of Aboriginal people in Australia, the then governor argued 'it seems only to require the fostering Hand of Time, gentle Means and Conciliatory Manners, to bring these poor Unenlightened People into an important Degree of Civilisation' (quoted in Miles 1987: 189). But this racial hierachization was also sexualized, with White European women literally 'put on a pedestal' in contrast to the alleged physical and moral inferiority of the 'other' (Bhattacharya 1997).

Considerable evidence has subsequently been amassed to disprove these notions of racial type and hierarchy. The study of genetics for instance has shown that individuals of supposedly different 'races' may genetically be more alike than individuals of the alleged 'same race' (Goldberg 1994: 67). In spite of the evidence, this legacy is powerful in both material and cultural terms. Collins argues that contemporary pornographic images of African-American women nearly always represent bondage and slavery, the woman submissive to the power of White men (Collins 1990: 169). The sexualization of 'foreign' women and the embodiment of racism are crucial in answering the above question. The submissive but erotic 'other' can be treated differently: their cultural representation has real material effects.

This brings us back to several other threads that have yet to be successfully woven together in a more adequate gendered account of migration: the uneasy relationship between concepts of 'race', ethnicity and culture. These concepts are not merely the subject of heated academic debate, they are deeply embedded in policy and political action throughout the world. We cannot begin here to do justice to the scale of these issues, but we can at least address some of the academic traditions that they draw on and their implications for a gendered account of migration. So far we have used terms such as 'racial hierarchy', 'racialized' and 'racism' without defining them. All of these terms are drawn from a tradition that after the second world war witnessed a rapid development in the United States and Britain, but to a lesser extent in other parts of Europe. This difference has taken a much clearer form in the last decade: the use of the term 'race' has virtually disappeared in academic discourse in Europe, but not in the UK and USA.

Academics interested in the question of migration in Europe have on the whole been keen to move away from a form of analysis that has cast post-war migration as creating a situation where people of different 'races' were brought into relation with one another. Many felt that the continued use by social scientists of a discredited term such as 'race', because people act on perceptions of 'racial' difference, confers a kind of fixed analytical status on what is a social construction. The use of 'race' and analysis of racism differs markedly between European states. In Germany in the post-World War II years, it has been associated with the Holocaust so that discrimination against foreigners is reduced to the term 'hostility against foreigners' and there is little serious study of racism (Piper 1998). In France, although the discussion of immigration and racism only emerged recently, Guillaumin (1972, 1995) had already in the 1960s critiqued the notion that we could categorize populations into racial groups. For her 'race' is a product of racist ideology; she identified a specific constellation of historical factors that assigned a given nature to individuals and that was formed in the course of the nineteenth century at a time of rapid and radical political, social and economic change. By the end of the century, the theory of difference and inequalities, enshrined in the superiority and inferiority of groups, had passed into social and institutional practice.

A biologically determinist notion of 'race' need not necessarily be the basis for racist beliefs, but as Yuval-Davis (1997b: 49) has argued 'every racist construction has at least some dimension of a mythical embodiment of the "other" '. This embodiment is always sexualized, and often in contradictory ways. Of equal importance is what Barker (1981) has termed a 'pseudo-biological culturalism' that has nothing to do with notions of biological superiority or inferiority, but with notions of difference and the defence of separate cultures and identities as 'natural'. Stolcke (1995) argues that 'cultural fundamentalism' has in fact replaced the more traditional racist rhetoric of the political Right in Europe. Racialization reproduces social relations through a number of areas such as notions of sexuality, ideological discourses on nation and community, construction of socio-cultural norms and legal rules of immigration and nationality (Brah 1993a, this book Chapter 4).

Gender relations and sexuality are crucial in defining cultural boundaries and binary opposition between modernist European standards and 'unacceptable' traditional models, which are incapable of being incorporated within the nation. Religion has become the key signifier of incompatible differences. Islamic groups, regulated by patriarchal structures, are singled out as being too distinctive in their daily lives and social norms to be able to cohabit with groups whose practices are derived from Christian traditions (Pieterse 1991). This dichotomy is expressed in its most extreme variant by the Far Right in France, but it is by no means absent from the mainstream media and political discourse. The French National Front castigate the submissiveness of Islamic women imprisoned in the private sphere, on the one hand, and warn against the rampant sexuality of North African men preying on French women, on the other (Kofman 1997). This is an integral aspect of the defensive discourse of 'Europism' in which a pure Europe territory is symbolically cleansed of 'foreign and uncivilized elements' (Essed cited by Lutz 1997).

It is thus important to look at the ways in which racism works, why it is that certain groups are set apart from others through the attribution of certain negatively evaluated features, beliefs or actions, which are then used to justify their exclusion from equal access to certain resources including political rights. In an early attempt to answer that question, Rex argued (1970, 1973) that our search should begin with an analysis of colonialism and colonial societies where production based on unfree labour predominated and where the colonizers developed discourses alleging the innate inferiority of the colonized. He goes on to consider the legacy that these discourses have for the perception and treatment of migrant labour from colonies or ex-colonies. Curtis (1984) has shown how the Irish have been 'racialized' throughout the history of colonialism. At the height of 'scientific' racism the need to control the Irish was 'explained' in terms of supposedly smaller skulls than the Anglo-Saxon 'ideal'. Racial stereotypes of the Irish persist in Britain, although because Ireland is a member of the European Community, Irish people partake in the privileges of free movement with Europe. Miles (1989) has been one of the few British theorists to have rejected the exclusive use of a colonial model, typical of much of the British and American theorizing of the relationship between capitalism and racism, in explaining much of European racism in the nineteenth and twentieth centuries. As in many countries, racist ideology was early on directed against the Jews. The first Aliens Act in the UK was passed in 1905 to control the flow of Jewish immigrants from Eastern Europe.

Since the late 1980s, the relationship between immigration, racism and national identity has generated a number of comparative studies (Wrench and Solomos 1993; Wieviorka 1994). Such studies raise the problem of terminology. Race relations, an exclusively British term, cannot thus be easily exported (Neveu 1994). Wieviorka's analysis of the three dimensions contributing to the resurgence of racism and xenophobia has been highly influential in comparative studies. The first aspect is the social or the way in which a society is structured and stratified. Racism finds a fertile terrain in a society where social movements are breaking down and unemployment is increasing. A second series of conditions involves the State and the degree to which it ensures principles of equality and social redistribution and the functioning of its institutions, e.g. police, schools, immigration service, etc. He argues that a state that reduces welfare provision and enacts racist immigration legislation is likely to exacerbate populist racist tendencies. A third set of conditions relates to the issue of identities, especially national identities. Racism tends to embed itself in appeals for cultural and social homogeneity; it flourishes in periods where the nation either seems to be threatened or is in an expansive phase.

Immigration legislation has been and continues to be a particularly important aspect of the institutionalization of racism. In the USA and Europe, immigration legislation and rules may not have been couched in racially discriminatory terms, but they have had that effect. They either keep out certain categories of people or restrict the further entry of particular groups. As Goldberg has argued, these immigration restrictions 'though not for the most part racially explicit in formulation ... discriminatorily restrict entry or labour of members of those population groups considered undesirable – those who are identified, if only silently, in racial terms' (Goldberg 1994: 56). By banning the further entry to Europe of certain groups of post-World War II migrant labour, those same groups are officially branded 'surplus to requirements'. Whatever the measures that are then introduced to 'integrate' those already resident, and particularly the second and subsequent generations born in Europe, they have already been defined as a 'problem' and become the objects of racially exclusionary practice, even violence (Phizacklea 1994). When the freedom of movement provision of the single European market became operable in 1992 it also meant that the external borders had to be secured from what the British Prime Minister, John Major, described as the 'rising tide' of undocumented migrants and asylum seekers. As Stuart Hall has suggested, 'European prosperity is a strictly European affair, designed exclusively for what every self-respecting Euro-politician is calling "our populations"' (1992: 2). In the late 1990s, refugees and asylum seekers have become a major target of this kind of racism in Europe, portrayed as 'scroungers' and 'economic migrants' (Bloch and Levy 1999). These attacks have been particularly virulent in relation to asylum seekers from areas of Europe outside the EU, such as Albanians and Roma people from Romania.

In the accounts of migration inspired by Marxist political economy, which we briefly considered earlier in this chapter, racism was often viewed as an essential mechanism for the 'over exploitation of the so-called under-developed peoples' and for keeping the latter in a constant state of fear (Meillassoux 1981: 121). Such accounts, it was argued by some, ignored the social and cultural heterogeneity of migrant groups and 'the significance of the actor's perception of his situation, his orientation and perceptions were underplayed' (Khan 1977: 58). The focus of these critics was, instead, on the migrant as actor and as self-designated member of an 'ethnic' group that has self-maintained boundaries based on criteria of culture and ancestral descent. Khan, while admitting that understanding the internal dynamics of an ethnic minority group involved 'studying the process of interaction or reaction of these cultural preferences and patterns of behaviour with external determinants' (Khan 1977: 58), was criticized for not in fact doing so. A counter-attack developed that claimed that the position of ethnic minorities could not be understood primarily in cultural terms, and that the impact of class, racism and the activities of what was described as an 'authoritarian' state on the position of ethnic minorities were absent from these accounts (Bourne 1980; CCCS 1983).

Ethnicity and the culture of ethnic minority groups have often been seen in static and essentialist terms. Morokvasic (1983: 13) has argued that migrant women have been analysed in predominantly cultural terms in much of the migration literature and are seen as the bearers of tradition and many children. We prefer a more dynamic notion of ethnicity: ethnic groupings are constructed in relation to specific social process, in response to their interaction with those outside the group as well as to internal conflict. Resistance to racist exclusionary practice may take many forms: economic, such as the workplace, or cultural, in music or dress for instance. Brah describes how in Britain:

> African Caribbean and Asian young women seem to be constructing diasporic identities that simultaneously assert a sense of belonging to the locality in which they have grown up, as well as proclaiming a 'difference' that references the specificity of the historical experience of being 'Black', or 'Asian', or 'Muslim'. And all of these are changing subject positions. The precise ways and with what outcomes such identities are mobilized is variable. But they speak as 'British' identities with all the complexity, contradiction, and difficulty this term implies.
>
> (Brah 1993b: 26)

Phoenix's research with male and female adolescents indicates that while Black young people are overt in their positioning themselves as possessing a racialized identity, White adolescents are not. Few White youngsters presented themselves as possessing a 'White identity' and were quick to deny that colour of an individual was of any significance to them. Nevertheless, Phoenix argues that, at the same time: 'they gave accounts which were broadly essentialist, of Black people as the "other"' (Phoenix 1997: 111).

The relationship between ethnicity and 'culture' is often presented in essentialist terms in the burgeoning literature of so-called, 'ethnic minority entrepreneurship' and the use of 'ethnic ties' as a resource. A key question that this literature has addressed is why it is that certain migrant groups are more likely than others to become entrepreneurs. Edna Bonacich argued that certain groups (e.g. Jews, Chinese and Indians) are, regardless of context, more likely to concentrate in what she terms as a 'middleman' category. Seeing themselves as 'sojourners' they concentrate on trade and liquidatable lines, promoting hard work and risk taking and the retention of 'ethnic solidarity' (Bonacich 1973; Bonacich and Modell 1980). Other theories are more cultural in form arguing that certain ethnic groups have an elective affinity with business.

There are numerous problems with most of this theorizing: at worst it falls into an essentialist trap, at best it provides a gloss on what are complex situations. As we shall show in the chapter on employment, the much applauded hard work and risk taking of so-called 'ethnic minority' entrepreneurs is often nothing more than a hand-to-mouth survival strategy in the face of unemployment and could not function without recourse to largely unpaid female 'family' labour. While such businesses may simply represent a move from the 'lumpenproletariat' to the 'lumpenbourgeoisie', their existence viewed in traditional class terms contradicts the notion that migrants in Europe predominantly occupy an 'underclass' position. The more successful businesses on the other hand operate arm-in-arm with peripheral capitalism and do not become the spaces of resistance that the hybridity literature would lead us to believe (Mitchell 1997; Raghuram and Hardill 1998).

Ethnic minority business involves complex articulations between class, gender, racism and citizenship status. Apart from the small numbers of entrepreneurs who do make it from 'rags to Mercedes', most will occupy what Marx would have described as a 'petit bourgeois' class position. But this status means little if earnings are in fact less than they were in wage-earning days, if one's livelihood is dictated by under-cutting one's competitors in order to get orders from multinationals or the local hyper-market, and if one's working day is 18 hours. Few women are entrepreneurs, but many women work long hours, often unpaid, in family businesses. Social class categories that define women's position according to that of the (male)head of household are always unsatisfactory, but in this instance are virtually meaningless. The increasing importance of the 'ethnic economy' in Europe demands that we look more closely at the gender relations that underpin so many of these enterprises.

Conclusion

Gender roles, ideologies and practices are an integral part of all social structures and face-to-face encounters, and impact upon all aspects of transnational population movements. This element needs to be incorporated into every level of analysis if we are to provide a rounded and convincing explanation of international migration. In this chapter we have raised some of the problems that have arisen from gender blindness in the existing literature on migration, and from one field of scholarship being deaf to developments in other fields. One of the keys to understanding migration is the link between structure and agency. We therefore proposed a three-tier conceptualization of the migratory process in which the migratory institution mediated between the broader migratory regime and the individual migrant. We have also argued that the migratory process should not be seen in isolation from the formation of ethnic communities in the migration setting and from the social structures in which these take place.

Some of the relevant literature has been left out of our discussion: we have for instance paid scant attention to feminist work in development studies, which also forms a necessary element in a gendered account of migration. One of the most encouraging developments is the research and writing that is emanating from Asia, a major site of female migration. Asian women scholars are addressing issues around women's migration that are sensitive to the concerns voiced by migrant women themselves and to their everyday realities.

The growing literature on female migration has had little impact on policy makers, on mass media presentation, and also on the main body of migration literature where the male bias has continued to persist in spite of the growing evidence of women's overwhelming participation in migratory movements. Many questions of relevance to the theory of migration remain unanswered simply because they are never asked. Like Thadani and Todaro (1984) we are concerned with the efficacy of the research in altering women migrants' lived experiences.

In the chapters that follow we will develop the issues that have been addressed in this chapter in a somewhat abstract way. Chapters 3 and 4 will be primarily concerned with the migratory process and conditions of entry to Europe, whereas Chapters 5–7 address the conditions under which migrants are able to live, work and act collectively within the country of migration. In doing so we hope that we can move from a critique of existing theories towards a better understanding of key dimensions of migrant women's experience in Europe.

Chapter 3

European migratory regimes

As we have discussed in previous chapters, feminists have criticized the absence of women and of gender relations in the major models that purport to account for the development of international migration in Europe. The prime omission is women as labour migrants in their own right and as active subjects. Most of the mainstream analysis of European immigration has tended to assume a dominant guest worker regime that postulates a linear evolution from the primary migration of male workers in the initial stage to a subsequent stage in which women enter as partners. In contrast, we demonstrate below that women were present almost from the beginning of post-war migration both as primary migrants and working alongside male partners. In highlighting women's presence as active subjects, it is necessary to take into account the significance of different 'migratory regimes' operating in the post-war period until the general stoppage of mass labour migration in the mid-1970s. Unlike the single regime adopted by most writers, we propose a classification that takes account of the extent and availability of colonial labour in different European states. These differences generated distinctive gendered patterns of immigration and had implications for rights of settlement and access to citizenship. Effectively, three regimes can be discerned in post-war western Europe: the guest worker, colonial and hybrid. Hence in this chapter we seek to recover a diversified history of gendered immigration, a history that seems to have evaporated in a kind of collective amnesia.

In the past two decades the distinctiveness of these regimes has lessened, partly because of harmonization and convergence between European Union states, but also as a result of the ending of privileges enjoyed by colonial populations. Scandinavian countries have also become more significant places of destination, especially for asylum seekers. During this period, too, southern European states (Greece, Italy, Portugal and Spain) have been transformed from societies of emigration to immigration and have bypassed a stage of relatively organized labour migration. They have been seen as easier places to enter and find work, often in the large informal sectors, than in northern European countries. Unlike in northern European states, recent immigration legislation in Italy and Spain recognizes the need for economic migrants and these countries have a high rate of female employment, especially in the domestic sector. The Iberian countries have also maintained a number of privileged relationships with their former colonies in Latin America and Africa. Portugal, in particular, still receives the vast majority of its migrants from Portuguese-speaking Africa and Brazil.

Despite the convergence of migratory policies and regimes, different states still bear the imprint of their earlier regimes. For example, Germany has in the 1990s reinstated a rigorous guest worker or contract system that does not permit eventual long-term settlement. In the UK there has been some continuity despite considerable tightening up of privileged rights of settlement of Commonwealth citizens and the shift of migratory flows away from English-speaking countries to the European Union. The development of inter-governmental policies regulating asylum seekers has been the foremost terrain for the harmonization of European Union policies in the past decade.

In the first section of this chapter we outline the three principal migratory regimes during the period of mass migration and draw out some of the implications for the nature of female migration. In the second, we move on to the period of transition and the emergence of new phases of immigration that now encompass the whole of western Europe as a result of increasing harmonization and convergence. Three main migratory flows, for which distinctive regulations have been implemented, are studied in greater depth. First, primary labour migration continues in northern European states despite claims of a total stoppage, whereas in southern Europe it has constituted the major element since the 1980s. Second, family migration, which has become the dominant form of entry in northern Europe states since the 1970s and especially since the early 1990s, has been growing in southern Europe. Third, the increasing flows of refugees and asylum seekers since the mid-1980s, which have also come to the fore in state and European agendas of migratory control and management.

Migratory regimes

We have taken as the starting point for our discussion Bohning's[1] influential stages model of migration (1984). This model is based on a 'guest worker' regime, but has generally been presented as having universal applicability in Europe. Castles and Miller (1998), for example, reproduce it virtually intact. The core principle of guest worker regimes is based on the rotation of labour migrants, whose rights to work and residence are closely tied to the economic situation prevailing in the host country.

The stages, based upon the maturation of migratory streams, form part of what Bohning sees as the sociology of self-feeding migratory process. In his outline, the four stages exhibit distinct gender and age characteristics that unfold as migration deepens and extends in time and space. Schematically these stages are:

- Stage 1: migration of young single men
- Stage 2: predominantly male migration continues, with slightly older, often married men
- Stage 3: men bring their marriage partner and children to stay, i.e. family reunion. Women work to supplement the family income
- Stage 4: enlargement of immigrant population through increasing length of stay and family reunion. Emergence of ethnic institutions and employers and intervention by politicians

In Bohning's short first stage, young single males supply the labour needs. In stage 2, as emigration becomes more common older married men without their spouses and children join the flow of migrants. It is assumed that employers recruit only male labour in industries such as heavy manufacturing, construction and mining. For Bohning, stage 3 arises from the continuing maturation of migration. Male workers stay longer and wish to accumulate as much savings as possible. Hence the solution was to bring in wives and children to supplement household income. This led to a rapid expansion of women and children entering as family migrants and the likelihood of permanent settlement increased. Wives and older children were sent out to work, but their labour was secondary to that of mens. Multicultural networks develop and foreigners start to open businesses during this stage. In Bohning's fourth stage, the older waves of immigrants are joined by newer flows from more peripheral regions. As the duration of residence grows and ethnic communities become established, secular and religious leaders are brought in and ethnic businesses and institutions are set up. At the same time, political unrest over the issue of immigration emerges and politicians intervene, resulting in polemical discussions within the mainstream political agenda.

A number of problems arise from the way Bohning conceptualizes these stages and his widespread application of the guest worker regime to European states. The marginal position of women in his model has all too frequently become the abiding view of migration in the post-war period (Kofman 1999). The assumption that migrant women did not work or, if they did, it was a secondary consideration, reflected the position of German women at the time. They had relatively low levels of participation in the labour force during these years, for the corporatist welfare model was based on the male breadwinner model, the assumption that male workers earned adequate wages to maintain a family (see Chapter 6). In fact, a number of states actively prevented women who entered as part of family reunion from gaining access to the formal labour market. For instance, official employment was denied for such women in Germany from 1973 to 1979. Women were, however, a significant minority of labour migrants during the earlier period.

Writing in the early 1980s, Bohning justified the restriction of his detailed analysis to three countries with guest worker regimes (France, Germany Switzerland) on the grounds that migration to other countries had either been too small, undocumented and heterogeneous (Netherlands, UK); or had too chequered a history (Belgium, Sweden, UK). France, on the other hand, was deemed to conform to a guest worker model simply because there existed a plethora of work and residence permits. We would argue that France does not conform to this model although elements of it were present. From the onset of large-scale post-war migration, permanent settlement in France was far more significant and immigration policy initially shaped by pro-natalist concerns. Furthermore, different nationalities were treated differently; some were seen as more readily assimilable and therefore encouraged to settle permanently (Italians, Spanish, Portuguese). As in other countries with colonial and favoured populations, such as the United Kingdom, France permitted a fairly free movement, at least until the 1970s, of citizens from North Africa and West Africa. It also encouraged labour and family migration from its Caribbean territories that had been granted an overseas department status in 1946.

We have argued that state practices are crucial to an understanding of gendered flows and experiences; these practices are an integral aspect of migratory regimes. Not only does the state determine the general conditions of entry, work and residence, but it also differentiates between migrant groups through the application of different regulations. This does not mean that women did not face similar policies in different regimes, but that the nature of the regime did have a bearing on their entry and subsequent status. We would therefore suggest that there were three principal migratory regimes, defined in terms of the mode of entry, rights of residence and status of migrants, in the initial post-war period of immigration until the mid-1970s. These were:

- *guest worker regimes*: represented primarily by Germany and Switzerland premised on the rotation of workers
- *colonial regimes*: typified by the United Kingdom, where migrants from outside the Commonwealth and Ireland were in a minority, especially during the peak immigration years from the mid-1950s
- *hybrid regimes*: represented by France and the Netherlands, which combined colonial migrants (who had relatively easy rights of entry until the late 1960s and early 1970s) with non-colonial migrants who had to apply for work permits and guest worker migrants, usually from Mediterranean countries

The presence of colonial and ex-colonial migrants is highly significant in relation to citizenship status. For certain groups of migrant women, this has usually meant a higher proportion employed in professional occupations, such as nursing, teaching and the lower echelons of the civil service. It also resulted in a more substantial proportion of family migrants even in the early years of immigration.

Our typology of regimes is largely based on the period of mass labour migration and the initial transitional period. This is not to say that a migratory regime was unified or did not combine different elements. In our discussion, the operation of each regime will be exemplified by a particular country. Though Switzerland represents the purest form of guest worker regime in western Europe, we have chosen to focus on Germany as the country that has attracted the largest number of migrants in the post-war years. The UK has been selected as an example of the colonial regime, although, as we shall see, it also experimented with controlled European labour migration for a brief period immediately after the World War II. The hybrid form is exemplified by France, a state that combined colonial populations, who themselves had different migratory statuses, and labour migrants from its Mediterranean neighbours.

Migratory regimes and their gender implications

A guest worker regime: Germany

Although at the end of World War II the Federal Republic of Germany no longer possessed colonies as other major European states, it did receive a large-scale immigration of ethnic Germans from eastern Europe and the Soviet Union, including people who had been expelled and citizens of the German Democratic Republic. By the early 1950s, twelve million ethnic Germans had migrated from the eastern parts of the former Reich and east-central Europe. Between 1953 and 1987 this flow dwindled to about 37,000 per annum, primarily from Poland and Romania (Munz and Ulrich 1998: 28). Foreign labour only became significant from 1960–1 after the construction of the Berlin Wall. A series of bilateral agreements were signed between the mid-1950s and the end of the 1960s on the basis of a guest worker agreement. The majority of migrants (70 per cent by the late 1960s) passed through the state agency (*Bundesantalt für Arbeit*) that recruited and placed foreign labour. In the beginning, work permits were negotiated for a specified job and a defined time period.

A gender breakdown of labour migration statistics and dependants is available from 1962. Initial migration was indeed mainly male, but after the early to mid-1960s (Abadan-Unat 1980), and especially after the recession of 1966–7, women were recruited preferentially in the expanding electronics industry (Goodman 1987: 209). In a period when family values were being stressed, German women were not encouraged to participate in the labour force (Munz and Ulrich 1998: 34). Women came as workers in the

1960s because this was the easiest way of entering the country in the absence of a family reunion policy (Castles and Kosack 1985).[2] An increasing proportion of migrant women were employed in the manufacture of consumer goods and services from the late 1960s. Two-thirds of women, with the exception of Yugoslav women, were in four manufacturing groups (textiles and clothing, metal production and engineering, electrical goods and other manufacturing). The recruitment of female labour migrants varied considerably between nationalities. Starting from 173 registered Turkish migrant women workers in 1960, the figure rose to 159,984 in 1974. Abadan-Unat (1980) notes that Turkish women, often from rural backgrounds, were sent ahead by their male kin during these later years. Female labour formed a higher proportion in migration flows from Spain until 1967, and from Greece and Yugoslavia until the early 1970s (Booth 1985: 19). Female workers were less affected by the recession of 1966–7 and relatively few of them left after 1973. This differential propensity of males and females to return to the home country, and not just the increase in family reunification, contributed to the greater female presence after the mid-1970s (Zlotnik 1995). Married women too entered as labour migrants, since this was the easiest means of migrating during a period of high demand for labour from sending countries (Castles and Kosack 1985).

There were often substantial differences in educational levels between women and men. For example, amongst Turkish migrants, ten per cent of men compared with seven per cent of women had not attended school at all; 38 per cent of men but only 21 per cent of women had a higher educational level (Abadan-Unat 1980: 140). A minority of Turkish migrants had professional qualifications. Women teachers and nurses left in the 1960s, often in search of a different and less oppressive life in Germany, to find that the only employment was in sectors typically associated with female migrant labour (Seyhan 1997). Some went on to recount in autobiographies and novels their difficult working experiences in remote and hostile provinces and their subsequent move to Germany, sometimes as political asylum seekers. By the end of the 1960s, married men with wives in Germany were the largest single group followed by married men who had left their wives behind.

Hence in what forms Bohning's second stage, women actually represented about a quarter of labour recruitment. Women workers were willingly taken on as long as familial responsibilities were not brought with them into the country. The number of children left behind and the percentage of families who did so varied according to nationality. German statistics (probably from the early 1980s) showed that about a sixth of migrant families from Spain, Italy, Portugal and Yugoslavia had children in the country of origin, whereas amongst the Turkish population this figure was almost two-fifths (Charbit and Bertrand 1985: 13).

Booth (1985) confirms that family reunion was well under way before the suspension of mass labour migration. It was only officially recognized by the government in 1972, but it was already used amongst Greeks, Spaniards, Italians and Yugoslavs. Family reunion, on the other hand, was slower to take off amongst the Turkish population, but in contrast to the European groups it gained pace after 1974–5. One of the major reasons for the rapid recourse to family reunion, especially amongst the Turkish, is likely to have been the change in tax law, which now stipulated that only those with children living with them in the country could be paid child allowances (Abadan-Unat 1980: 153).

Despite the stoppage in recruitment in October 1973, the total number of immigrants did not drop drastically, and by 1976, the annual numbers entering were beginning to increase. Family reunion came to represent the main legal channel of entry, although, from 1973 to 1979, the German government prevented dependants (women and older children) from entering the labour market by giving them temporary residence permits. The reason given was that foreigners were not admitted for purposes of employment and so permission to work would side-step the ending of labour recruitment (Bohning 1984: 44). After this most restrictive and illiberal legislation was challenged by civil and human rights groups, and overturned by administrative and constitutional courts, the government still retained a period of residence and, therefore, dependency, before the spouse was granted entry to the labour force (Hollifield 1992, 84). It is estimated that about half of the immigration in the 1970s and 1980s was derived from family reunion (Veiling, cited by Munz and Ulrich 1998, 42).

A colonial regime: the United Kingdom

In the early post-war years several groups of Europeans were encouraged to settle or enter Britain as contract workers to fill severe labour shortages. First, many Poles who had fought in World

War II, totalling about 120,000, opted to stay. Second, about 100,000 displaced persons, mainly from Baltic and eastern European countries, were brought in under the European Voluntary Labour Scheme between 1946 and 1951 (Miles 1990). They were given work permits for only one year, and after 1947 were not allowed to bring in dependants. Later, European migrants (Austrians, Germans, Italians and Spaniards) classified as aliens, faced less stringent conditions (Rees 1993: 95). The Irish continued to form, as they had done for over a century, the largest single group of immigrants. Irish women, in search of work and freedom from a highly patriarchal society where their opportunities were limited, had since the late nineteenth century constituted over half of Irish immigrants (McLaughlin 1997; Sales 1997).

Under the 1948 British Nationality Act, Commonwealth subjects from the Caribbean and the Indian sub-continent were able to enter Britain, to settle and bring their families. The gender balance of migrants varied considerably. After an initial period of male immigration, Caribbean women soon joined male partners, often leaving their children behind. By the mid-1950s women from different class and educational backgrounds were often initiating the migratory process, which would in time lead to their own complex circulatory movements between the UK and the Caribbean and those of subsequent generations (Chamberlain 1994). European groups, such as Germans and Spaniards, were dominated by women. Male surpluses were, on the other hand, registered for Asian populations, especially Pakistani immigrants. The 1961 census (a 10 per cent sample) indicated a substantial percentage of women in skilled occupations. Among Irish women (152,660), of whom 33.9 per cent were economically active, 20.1 per cent were professional and technical workers, 15.9 per cent clerical workers and 50.2 per cent in other occupations. For Caribbean women (31,540), who constituted 35.2 per cent of the economically active, 22.6 per cent were in professional and technical occupations because of the large number in nursing, 11.8 per cent clothing workers and 51.9 per cent other (Patterson 1969).

The early politicization of immigration resulted in a series of laws, beginning in 1962, which limited the right of settlement and introduced work permits for those not born in the UK or holding UK or Irish passports. Work permits were initially divided into three categories depending on level of skill. Within the dependant categories, 'wife' was interestingly extended to those living in permanent relationships, even if not married, whilst 'child' encompassed adopted and 'illegitimate' children. A husband was eligible if he were coming to join his wife who was ordinarily resident in the UK. The number of dependants rose steadily after 1962 and eclipsed holders of employment vouchers. In the period from mid-1962 to 1966, children comprised just over 60 per cent of dependants. This development was a precursor to what would happen in other European countries in the mid-1970s. The rising number of dependants almost immediately became a major topic of discussion and led to the tightening of controls in the Commonwealth Immigrants Act of 1968 when the third skill category was also removed. The influx of skilled labour from developing countries at that time constituted an early version of the 'brain drain'.

The initial system of employment vouchers for Commonwealth citizens came to an end in 1972, and from 1973 those seeking to enter Britain had to have work permits. Exceptions to this regulation were 'patrials', that is, persons who had a least one grandparent born in the UK; those on working holidays; citizens of the European Economic Community and a few shortage areas in the health sector such as doctors and dentists. Special quotas were fixed for the hotel and catering industry, resident domestic workers and nursing auxiliaries, which were all sectors of high or exclusive female employment at the time. In the 1960s nearly half of the aliens admitted on work permits were women, although it fell to only 20 per cent for Commonwealth women. Male permit holders could bring in dependants who had the right to work; female permit holders could not (the challenge to this sexually discriminatory legislation is discussed in Chapter 4). Migrant women were thus treated as in a guest worker system and could not bring in their spouse or dependants (Bhabha and Shutter 1994: 167). By the mid-1970s, the majority of work permits were allocated to skilled categories originating from the United States, Japan, South Africa and Switzerland. Amongst patrials and those on working holidays, primarily from the old Commonwealth countries, especially Australia and Canada, there was a high proportion of female migrants and sojourners. For many, work in Britain formed a kind of rite of passage between school or university and settling down. This was also a period when the percentage of women entering higher education and pursuing a career was expanding.

A hybrid regime: France

The Office National d'Immigration (ONI) was set up in 1945 in France to deal with the conditions of entry, work and residence of foreigners. Initially it was strongly shaped by populationist thinking in favour of immigration as a means of making up the demographic deficit. The distinctiveness of French policy was its encouragement of family migration, which fitted with the desire to see migrants settle and contribute to demographic growth (Granotier 1979). ONI was unable to cope with the expansion of immigration after 1955, so that French policy resorted to the regularization or legalization of those who had already entered. By 1967, 80 per cent of migrants entered outside the framework laid down by the ONI and were subsequently legalized.

No single policy applied to all foreigners. There was a bewildering complexity of regulations (six forms in all), ranging from the existing colonies, which in the course of the 1950s and 1960s gained their independence, overseas departments, which to some extent were still treated as colonies, privileged countries in the Mediterranean, with whom bilateral agreements were signed, to a variety of other arrangements. Until 1962, Algeria was considered part of France, but even after its independence any Algerian with an identity card could enter France without needing a residence or work permit. Agreements were signed with Tunisia, Morocco, Portugal and Spain. Until 1974–5, those from France's ex-colonies in Africa could enter relatively easily with an identity card and work contract. In 1961, Bumidom (Office for Migration from the Overseas Departments) was set up to channel and manage an annual flow of migrants from France's overseas departments in the Caribbean (which were given this status in 1946) to fill labour shortages in metropolitan France, particularly in the lower echelons of the public services (post offices and hospitals) and to siphon off demographic pressure in the islands. But for this group, although they escaped 'the worst excesses faced by other immigrants, their French nationality only offered superficial protection from poor conditions of work and housing and exploitation in the early years' (Condon and Ogden 1991: 521). Female migration was almost from the beginning of considerable significance in domestic labour and hospitals (Anselin 1990; Condon and Ogden 1991).

In general, the early stages of labour migration were heavily male, although French officials did not even bother to note the sex of the partner (Tapinos 1992). Where only the head of household is taken into account, this imbalance is likely to be exaggerated. Subsequent labour migration contained substantial numbers of female workers, as was the case of Yugoslavs. The origin of migrant women, their working and family lives and expectations were very varied (Lévi and Taboada-Leonetti 1978; Morokvasic 1975). The first job in the labour force for many migrant women was in the domestic sector, although increasingly many moved into manufacturing jobs (Morokvasic 1975). An account by a Spanish female migrant from a traditional peasant background (Arondo cited in Morokvasic 1975) traced how she became increasingly aware of the disparity between the legislation in force and the actual conditions French and migrant women faced as domestics and how, in joining Jeunesse Ouvrière Catholique (Catholic Working Youth), she began to fight for improved conditions. Many Portuguese, one of the largest migrant groups in the late 1960s and early 1970s, came as couples. Women commented that they were now being monetarily compensated for previously unremunerated work and could lead a far easier life with two incomes and various allowances (Lévi 1975: 156).

France's demographic concerns meant that family immigration was encouraged; this included not only the possibility of being joined by family members but also being accompanied by the family (Tapinos 1992). There was an increase of family migration in the 1960s; 41,000 on average from 1960–4, rising to 55,000 per annum from 1965–9. The significance of family migration varied enormously. It was high amongst the Italians and Spaniards, and later in the 1960s, the Portuguese, but there were few Yugoslavs. Over 70,000 people entered as family migrants in 1972 and 1973, a higher figure than in subsequent years. Family migration, as in Germany, became the major source of official immigration with the stoppage of mass labour inflows, although it should be noted that some exemptions for purposes of labour migration were granted to Tunisians and Moroccans. However, the policy after 1974 fluctuated wildly from one Secretary of Immigration to another. In 1976, Paul Dijoud declared that the government wanted to facilitate family migration. The following year (1977) Lionel Stoléru, the new Secretary, announced its suspension for three years. The government's initial compromise in response to opposition to this measure was that spouses entering under family reunion could not initially seek employment. Interestingly, more women than men were granted work permits between 1976 and 1980. The attempted curtailment of family reunification was rejected by the State Council after a case brought against the government by *Groupe d'information et de soutien des travailleurs immigrés* (GISTI), an organization campaigning for migrant rights. The State Council found against the government, but upheld its right to lay down the conditions regulating family reunification.

Towards convergence and harmonization: the transitory period and new phases

As we have seen, from the mid-1970s onwards immigration regulations fluctuated considerably, and the return migration of unemployed workers, for example in France and Germany, was encouraged. Attempts to reduce immigration and the numbers settling have been made through limiting access to citizenship, for example, the new British Nationality Act passed by the Conservative Government in 1981. The impact of this Act was to deny automatic entry to subjects of Britain's remaining colonies and abrogate *jus soli* (the right to citizenship based on birth within a state: see Chapter 4). In France, a more voluntaristic nationality code was proposed in 1986, but was not adopted until 1993–4.

The distinctive migratory regimes began to break down as European states implemented similar restrictions on labour migration and adopted similar responses to the changing composition of migrant populations. Exceptions were made in all countries for shortage areas of employment. As Mediterranean societies shifted from emigration to receiving immigration, they became more like north-western societies of immigration. Their geographical positioning meant that they received a large number of migrants from the Maghreb and Egypt as well as from their former colonies in the case of Portugal and Spain. Former emigrants also began to return as authoritarian regimes made their transition to democracy and experienced economic growth. Colonial connections and diasporas also shaped the new patterns of return migration. The inflow of ethnic Greeks from the former Soviet Union was considerable but has now slowed down. Spain's links with Latin America can be seen in patterns of immigration and citizenship (see Chapter 4). Portugal, in particular, has sought to create a world-wide network of overseas communities and in 1996 established a Council of Portuguese Communities to advise the government on policies for emigrant communities (SOPEMI 1998). This is the culmination of a shift over several decades to a more positive Portuguese attitude towards emigrants (Feldman-Bianco 1992). There is a gendered dimension to the desire to return. Interviews with Portuguese women in France have revealed a marked reluctance to return compared with their husbands (Leandro 1998). The reasons they gave for wishing to remain were greater freedom and staying with their children who generally did not want to accompany them. On the other hand, many Caribbean women in the UK have left upon retirement, often citing racism in Britain and the existence of kin in their society of origin (Chamberlain 1994).

Nordic states, which previously had few migrants from outside the region, saw the numbers of migrants and asylum seekers, especially from the developing world, rise during this period. After Sweden put a stop to labour migration in the mid-1970s, the main external flows came from family reunion and especially refugees. It accepted one of the largest numbers of asylum seekers. Taking into account naturalized migrants, the biggest groups in Sweden were Yugoslavs, Poles, Chileans, Iranians and Turks (Alund and Schierup 1993: 101–2).

European migratory flows became more diversified within countries, whilst there was greater similarity between countries. A significant factor was the gradual withdrawal of privileged status for colonial subjects while members of other states within the EC acquired privileged access and rights of settlement. Migrants who had been heavily concentrated in one or two countries had now extended their migratory spaces, for example, Turkish migrants were now settling in France and Denmark and, by the 1990s, they formed the largest single group in the latter country. The bilateral

Table 3.1 Family reunion and formation in France: 1990–95

Year of entry	Family R	Spouse of French	Parent of French child	Family refugee
1990	36,949	15,254	3080	3200
1991	35,625	18,763	3146	1246
1992	32,665	19,045	2986	1065
1993	32,421	20,062	2834	1778
1994	20,645	13,145	1749	776
1995	14,360	13,387	1921	749

Source: Lebon (1995/7)

agreements of the 1960s and 1970s (with North African countries and later Turkey), which provided for non-discrimination between workers with respect to working conditions and social benefits, have now been reinforced and applied throughout the European Union. The granting of entry for different categories of migrants, remain, however, the prerogative of individual states.

In the mid-1980s a number of inter-governmental agreements and institutions, such as Trevi and Schengen, were developed in relation to clandestine immigration and asylum seekers. From the late 1980s an increasing number of asylum seekers entered European Union states, which led to stricter controls agreed in the Dublin Convention in 1990. The geopolitical fallout from the dismantling of the East–West divide had particularly strong repercussions in Germany where ethnic Germans from the ex-Soviet Union and eastern Europe came to settle. A disproportionate number of refugees from the Yugoslavian conflicts also sought refuge in Germany, leading to a peak net balance of 788,000 migrants and asylum seekers in 1992 and a population of seven million foreigners (Munz and Ulrich 1998: 51). The outcome was that the previously liberal asylum laws passed after World War II, and which did not necessarily require proof of individual political persecution, were made far more rigorous. In 1993, Germany's laws were brought more into line with the Geneva Convention and those operating in other European countries. In 1991, new European Agreements were signed with a series of eastern European countries (SOPEMI 1998: 72–4).

In regulating clandestine migration and the entry of asylum seekers, European states have begun to put into place a regional system of governance of migratory spaces. This does not mean that policy differences or the legacy of past migrations have entirely disappeared. Germany, for example, has revived a guest worker system with the explicit aim of preventing any future settlement. The UK has a complex set of regulations that, though more discretionary in its application than other countries, may also offer more flexibility. Southern European countries continue to practise regularization programmes with criteria generally favouring those who can prove they are in employment. As a result, large numbers of resident foreigners have been added to the official migrant populations. Italy has instituted a number of regularization programmes, the latest of which was promulgated in 1998. Those applying for regularization had to meet several stringent conditions in relation to housing, employment and lack of a criminal record. The numbers who fulfilled these conditions (250,000 out of the 308,000 who applied) went well beyond expectations (Farine 1999). Portugal's amnesty in 1997 resulted in 259,000 permits being issued whereas, in Greece, 374,000 applications had been received in the 1997–8 programme. Although without any such programme for over a decade, challenges to the highly restrictive measures, especially relating to family migration, forced France into announcing two programmes in the mid-1990s. Of the 150,000 applicants in the latest round (operating from June 1997 to May 1998), 85 per cent of residence permits (23,450 up to January 1998) have been granted for family-related reasons (SOPEMI 1998: 60), of which a high percentage went to women.

Therefore, it is important in the context of convergence to look at the regulations of entry, residence and work for different forms of migration (Kofman and Sales 1998). In the following section we shall examine the evolution of different types of migration and their gender implications.

Current types of gendered migration

Labour migration

As northern European states closed their doors to mass labour migration, a number of southern European societies – including Greece, Portugal and Spain – underwent political transitions that encouraged the return of their citizens as well as new migratory flows from outside Europe. Hence the reduction of intra-Western European migration was paralleled by an increase and diversification in migration from developing countries in the 1980s. The difficulty of acquiring work permits in northern European states oriented labour flows into southern European states, which until then had been states of emigration and had not yet clearly defined immigration policies. Labour migration in northern European states had not simply come to an abrupt halt in the mid-1970s. Exceptions were made for shortage areas in unskilled work, such as domestic labour and hotel and catering, as well as highly skilled work. The UK, for example, still issued work permits in the mid-1970s for a wide range of occupational categories and skills. The sharp reduction in permits issued for unskilled work, which did not reflect the real situation in these sectors, has encouraged illegal employment.

The rapid decline of heavy manufacturing and mining in the 1980s, the increase in contracting out and the shift to services began to change the pattern of demand for labour. Demand has increased in areas where female labour has predominated as well as in new openings. In southern European states, the increasing participation of women in the labour force and the shortfall in the provision of welfare services encouraged the use of migrant labour in the household. In Italy this phenomenon goes back to the late 1970s when Filipina women began to fill shortages in domestic labour. Today, in major cities such as Athens, Barcelona, Madrid and Rome, which have large numbers of well-off households and of women working in professional and administrative employment, a highly stratified labour market has become established (Chell 1997; Escriva 1997). In both Italy and Spain, the recognition of the continuing need for economic migration in recent immigration legislation means that there will be opportunities in the future for female migrants. Spain has set quotas for work permits since 1991, originally as part of the regularization programme. Well over half

Table 3.2 Acceptance for settlement in the United Kingdom: 1985–96. Dependent spouses

Year	Female	Male	% of male spouses	Total spouses acceptances of all categories
1985	17,990	6680	27.1	55,360
1988	15,120	7950	34.5	49,280
1991	19,010	11,160	37.0	53,900
1993	19,100	12,000	38.6	55,640
1995	19,940	12,680	38.9	55,480
1996	21,520	12,450	36.6	61,730

Settlement, or indefinite leave to remain, may be granted in several ways: upon arrival, after a year's probationary period of marriage, after a four-year period of work permits, on gaining full refugee status, and after seven years of exceptional leave to remain granted to asylum seekers.

The rise in numbers in total acceptances in 1996 is because of the increase in wives and children, and especially those not recognized as refugees but granted exceptional leave to remain, who have come to the end of the seven years required for the right to permanent settlement.

Source: Home Office, 1997

the permits were given for domestic labour, most of whom were of Dominican, Moroccan, Peruvian and Ecuadorian nationality (Colectivo de IOE de Madrid 1998). In Portugal, however, there has been less substitution by immigrants in this sector because of the ready supply of local labour (Oso and Catarino 1997).

The trend towards the use of labour in the private sphere, although more clearly developed in southern Europe, is not absent from northern European states, where welfare provision is increasingly privatized and pushed into the home, especially services connected with the care of children, the disabled and the elderly (Kofman and Sales 1996). However, many northern European states are unwilling to admit that there exists an unfulfilled demand in sectors employing migrant labour (Anderson and Phizacklea 1997). The informal conditions of work in this sector mean that many recent arrivals and those who are undocumented seek employment without any security. The number of undocumented workers has been swollen by those who cannot fulfil the requisite conditions of family reunion and people whose applications for refugee status are rejected, but who remain in the country and are very likely to find work in domestic labour or contracted-out services. Family reunion in many states does not permit immediate entry into the labour force, while asylum seekers are generally prevented from working for several months (Liebaut and Hughes 1997).

The new international division of labour produced by economic restructuring and the Structural Adjustment Programmes of the 1980s has exacerbated unemployment in developing countries, generating increased flows towards Europe. More than ever, women from developing countries accepted unskilled work well below the level of their qualifications. Migrant women are now more educated and tend to originate more and more from urban areas (Tribalat 1995). Deskilling, or what some have called 'brain waste' (Morokvasic and de Tinguy 1993) or 'occupational skidding' (Morawska and Spohn 1997: 36), has especially characterized women from the Philippines and Latin America, and more recently, eastern Europe (see Chapter 5). Their caring skills intended to be utilized in the public sphere, such as nursing, are often transferred into the private sphere of the household. Many women from these regions have at least secondary school qualifications. Even in the new waves of Irish migration to the UK in the 1980s, young women who form some of the most highly educated in London are unable to find jobs reflecting their education and skills (Kelly and Nic

Giolla Choille 1990: 180). In eastern Europe, the effects of market transformation have hit women hardest (Einhorn 1993). In a study of Polish women in Germany, Friese (1995) recounts the experiences of women with degrees in subjects such as agricultural economics and who speak several languages, but are forced to work as domestics, frequently for a number of different female employers. She notes an accrued polarization between women, with the input of migrant women enabling professional German women to continue their training and gain a career foothold.

The end of the old East–West division led to the settlement of ethnic Germans (Aussiedler), a group in which women comprised over half. Little attention was initially paid to them, but subsequent studies have shown the degree to which they have faced discrimination because of their gender and migrant status (Quack 1997). They have been pushed into a rigid German system of professional qualifications, where their diplomas are also not recognized to the same extent as those of men. There is also an unwillingness to give them access to specialist linguistic courses and they are required to find child care before being allowed to take up training courses. The situation of ethnic German women highlights their subordinate treatment in gaining access to educational and training provision and the expectation that they will fit into the mould of the carer and part-time worker. As a result of all these obstacles they are more likely to join the ranks of the unemployed. With the reduction of the budget allocated to integrating ethnic Germans, their exclusion from the work place is likely to become more prolonged.

New forms of circulation have emerged most strongly between eastern Europe and Germany. Dispensing with visas for central European countries (Poland, Czech Republic, Hungary and Slovakia), which are due to accede to the European Union in the first decade of the twenty-first century, has opened new migratory spaces based on regular circulation rather than settlement. The latter is officially impossible except for ethnic Germans and recognized refugees. Thus Morokvasic and Rudolph (1997) suggest that the novelty of the present migratory system lies in the quality and diversity of migrants. They are now of urban origin and far more highly qualified than the earlier guest workers. Furthermore, many of these flows are highly feminized because women in eastern Europe have often found themselves the losers in the marketization of the economy and society. Informal and transnational networks have become more important with the tightening up of official recruitment. Mobility rather than a definitive dichotomy of emigration and immigration characterizes the new movements, whether they be Russian scientists, transient sellers or frontier commuters. The strategy of these new migrants is 'to leave in order to be able to remain at home' (Morokvasic and Rudolph 1997: 25). Technically, however they are treated as tourists with the inevitable facile distinction of false and real tourists (Morokvasic 1997: 121) proclaimed by the media.

What then might be the gender dimensions of these strategies of spatial and social mobility? Firstly, women tend to undertake personal services, caring, and hospitality services, and are less likely to fall foul of police controls. They often earn more than men who are more likely to work in building and construction (the poorly paid and uncertain subcontracted sector), and as mechanics. Some women have set up regular support networks, a far less common situation among men. For example, Morokvasic (1997: 146) describes the operation of a network in which several Polish nurses from Cracow alternate in their care of an elderly German man in Berlin. Each of them is housed and fed and earns 100 Deutsch Marks per day, the equivalent of one month's salary in Poland. Their regular movements between the two countries thus enable them to return home to look after their own families.

Another principally female migration, which certainly existed before the removal of East–West borders, is sexual trafficking and prostitution. There have been several waves of trafficking. The first wave was composed of Asian women (mainly Thai and Filipinas), the second of South Americans (Dominicans and Colombians), the third of Africans (Ghanaians and Nigerians) and, since about 1992, central and eastern European women. The Dutch non-governmental organization (NGO), STV, reported that two-thirds of the 168 cases it dealt with in 1994 involved women from this area (IOM 1995: 9). Of those who sought assistance from NGOs, such as PAYOKE in Belgium and STV in the Netherlands, many had been employed in their country of origin. In Belgium, it has been estimated that about 10-15 per cent of the foreign prostitutes from poor countries are victims of trafficking (IOM 1995: 12). The majority of the trafficked women could keep little of their earnings and many, especially the young ones, were not even paid. Many were deprived of their papers and effectively treated as hostages. The International Organization for Migration (1995: 2) stated that the 'violence and exploitation endured by these women often goes beyond the exploitation suffered by other migrants'. These women do not always enter illegally: many countries issue visas for entertainers. Huge profits can be made out of the international transportation of women seeking work, whereas traffickers are rarely prosecuted. Far more likely is that the women themselves will be deported if they manage to lodge a complaint. Few countries have any explicit policy to combat trafficking other than to deport the victims.

Some recent policy measures have been introduced such as tightening up on entertainer contracts so that they are given to the women rather than the employer in Belgium/Netherlands. The contract has to state explicitly the amount of payment, and the women are given booklets stating their rights and conditions as well as addresses to which they can turn for help. The Netherlands was the first country to introduce a temporary residence permit in 1988 for victims of trafficking. Belgium has also introduced a 'rest period' of 45 days before a women is deported, during which she can decide to make a statement against the traffickers, for which she may in return be able to obtain an indefinite residence permit on humanitarian grounds. Unfortunately, very few have been granted it (IOM 1995: 26). Most women from east and central Europe, though not from developing countries, return to their countries of origin

Not all women take up unskilled employment in the course of international migration, although both European women and third country nationals remain largely invisible in studies of skilled employment (Ackers 1998; Kofman 1998; 2000). In Chapter 5 we shall explore the possible reasons for this invisibility. For the moment, we should note that there is evidence from immigration and emigration statistics that the proportion of skilled female has been rising. In the UK, for example, the proportion of work permits issued to non-EU citizen women rose from about 16 per cent in the mid-1980s to 20 per cent in the early 1990s. The figure was even higher for those from the old Commonwealth. The feminization of professional emigration is confirmed by Australian studies (Hugo 1994). We also need to bear in mind that a good number of migrants from the old Commonwealth who find employment in the welfare sectors often come in their early to mid-twenties on working holiday schemes or are patrials who do not require work permits. Colonial ties continue to shape skilled employment patterns in southern Europe too. For example, many Brazilians in Portugal are to be found in teaching, health and other scientific and technical professions (SOPEMI 1998).

There have been relatively few comparative studies of female labour migration. Some analysts maintain that Europe has no need for less skilled labour, claiming that there is only demand for selected shortages caused by inadequacies in education and training in northern European countries. We have shown that there exists a strong demand for female labour, skilled and unskilled, across a number of sectors. Labour migration, far from ceasing, has become more diversified and increasingly feminized.

Family reunification and formation

Family reunification and formation became the dominant form of legal entry to many European states from the late 1970s, although, in Mediterranean states, the absence of a tradition of immigration meant they were slow to legislate in this area. In the mid-1970s NGOs, especially Church-based ones, and international organizations (UN and the ILO) voiced concern about the difficulties migrants encountered in maintaining family life across states and set out a series of recommendations (Dumon 1976). Though many NGOs treated family reunion as a human right, the relevant clauses in international conventions were weakly enunciated, simply requesting that states take all possible measures to facilitate the family life of migrants. Some of the key issues raised then still remain highly pertinent today. These included the lack of comparative data and understanding. There have been few substantive studies of family reunion and its changing composition and strategies. In the absence of such evidence, it can nevertheless be claimed that levels of education and the labour market skills of people currently making up the family-reunification streams from the Mediterranean countries seem to be as low as they were during first-generation flows (Kuijsten 1994: 33).

A number of questions need to be addressed. For example, to what extent do family reunion migrants enter the labour market; what has been the effect of the masculinization of family reunion; what specific problems do those wishing to bring in a family member face and how do men and women attempt to overcome them? One of the main reasons for the lack of interest in exploring these issues stems from the conceptualization of family migration as secondary, in contrast to primary labour migration. Its mostly female composition is also a factor. The assumption is still that female migrants, if they happen to work, do so for pin money or to supplement the household's income (Werner 1994).

As we have shown previously, family reunion began before mass labour migration ceased, even in guest worker regimes (Mehrlander 1994) and it was a prominent feature in colonial and hybrid regimes. Its significance obviously became more apparent with the steep decline in labour migration, as can be seen in French data. Labour migration (177,377) and family reunion (81,496) both peaked in 1971. By 1974 when labour migration drastically fell to 64,462, family members numbered 68,038 (cited in Dumon 1976: 56).

As soon as it became obvious that reducing labour migration would not in itself diminish total immigration, states tried to halt or impose strict conditions on the rights of dependants, at that time primarily women and children, to enter. One of the classic strategies in the 1970s was to deny the right of work to dependants either for a specified period or indefinitely. In France and Germany these measures were challenged so that by the 1980s this regulation was abolished in France and shortened to three or four years after entry in Germany. This attempt undermines the view that women do not wish to enter the labour market. In fact, the original German ruling in the 1970s was on grounds that allowing dependants to work gave them an unfair advantage over labour migrants and German nationals who, according to the Constitution, benefit from national preference in employment (Bohning 1984).

What family migration clearly reveals is the dependency that women are forced into upon entry and which may continue to determine the rest of their lives. We shall look more systematically in the following chapter on citizenship at a number of issues that arise from women's dependent status and the struggle for personal autonomy.

In the 1980s, the numbers entering under family reunion increased and then stabilized in many European states (Lahav 1996). It has been estimated that about 50 per cent of Germany's immigration in the 1980s stemmed from this source. The use of family reunion, or in reality family formation, by children of migrants has been particularly discouraged in Germany; for Turks in both Germany and the Netherlands, it is the main form of family migration. Germany is particularly severe in the conditions stipulated for entry of family members. It has brought down the age at which children can join parents to 16 years, which is lower than the norm of 18 years that prevails in other European countries.

Policy changes have been extremely important in determining the levels of family migration and the gender balance. British policy from the late 1960s until the mid-1980s embodied profoundly sexist assumptions, with the male breadwinner expected to determine the place of familial domicile. Male migration was also considered to pose a threat to the labour market. The opposite applied to women, especially those from the Indian sub-continent who were expected to follow their husbands and were assumed not to enter the labour market (Bhabha and Shutter 1994: 73). When the government was forced to remove its discriminatory practice against women born overseas after a case before the European Court for Human Rights in the mid-1980s, it responded by levelling down the regulations for both sexes. This led to a changing gender balance of spouses, with more men entering (see Table 3.2). Other immigration rules, such as the primary purpose rule introduced by the Conservative Government in 1980, created a climate of suspicion about the reasons for marriage by British citizens of migrant origin. The rule stipulated that one cannot use marriage in order to gain admission, even where the marriage is accepted as genuine. Bhabha and Shutter (1994: 70) commented that the use of 'primary' is telling for it also indicates the status of male migration. The legislation was eased in the 1990s, again because of several challenges to the European Court, and the ruling was abolished by the new Labour Government in 1997. Restrictions continue to be placed on those seeking to remain in Britain as a result of marriage. The Immigration and Asylum Act of 1999 includes provisions to prevent what are termed 'sham marriages'.

In the Netherlands, the Bogus Marriage Preventive Act passed in 1994 could be seen as a version of the primary purpose rule. In effect it is applied most forcefully to marriages with third country nationals who are suspected of using marriage to bypass immigration legislation (de Hart 1999). A large age gap between partners can be considered an indicator of false marriage and the partners have to prove that they have not entered marriage for any motive other than affection and love (Lutz 1994).

States have tended, in contrast to the recommendations of international conventions, to impose a number of conditions on those seeking family reunion, such as period of residence, steady income of the sponsor and adequate housing often at the standard of the indigenous population. These conditions have become stricter, rather than more liberal in recent years (Kofman 1999) as states seek to limit as far as possible family reunion without actually abrogating the right (Lahav 1996). For example, the years of residence required to qualify for family reunion may be lengthened, or the income required may be increased and, as in France, not allowing certain benefits to be included as income. The impact of the legislation brought in by Charles Pasqua (Minster for the Interior in the right-wing government in France elected in 1993) is demonstrated in Table 3.1, which shows a dramatic fall in the numbers entering for family reunion. Those eligible for admission as family members have been influenced by the age at which children are considered to reach adulthood: this is now generally 18 years rather than 21 as it was previously. The EU draft guidelines on family reunion, tabled in 1993 and still to be adopted, would in fact make the conditions more restrictive in some states. For example, Belgium currently does not have a minimum period of residence prior to the submission of an application for family reunion, but the guidelines would impose such a period.

Entry conditions for family visits have also become stricter. The mere suspicion of intent to remain with one's family has led to the refusal of tourist visas. In the UK, a large percentage of certain nationalities, such as Jamaicans, have had their applications rejected, or worse not been allowed to enter the country after making the journey (JCWI 1990). Close relatives, who may be crucial in times of family pressure such as illness, may have to leave at the end of their prescribed tourist visa. In Germany, children under 16 years have once again required visas to visit their parents (*The Guardian* July 1997).

Structural conditions interact with policy changes in determining the numbers and composition of family reunion migration. Increasing levels of unemployment or scarcity of steady jobs prevent migrants from bringing in family members. The decline in social housing also affects the ability to meet the requirements and this, as in the past, is one of the major obstacles to family reunion (Dumon 1976). It is undoubtedly more difficult for women, who wish to bring in family members, to meet all the necessary conditions, especially if they cannot call upon their family to contribute resources. Those employed as live-in domestic labour may not have adequate independent housing. For example, in Italy few women have availed themselves of the right to family reunion since the legislation permitting family reunion was passed in 1986 (Campani 1997), although the longer-established Filipina women who have achieved some social mobility have brought in husbands (Chell 1997).

The complexity of the strategies women use in relation to family reunification and formation needs to be recognized. Migrant women with citizenship or the right of permanent settlement are a valuable means for a man to gain entry to a country. Marriage to a professional man or someone with resources may represent social mobility for the women and her family. Although arranged marriages may be dismissed disparagingly, women have often thought carefully about the advantages of importing someone from the homeland rather than someone socialized in the country of settlement. In Autant's study of Turkish girls in France, several explained that they are able to gain the upper hand for a time by bringing in a husband from the homeland, and thus be free from the dominance of parents-in-law (Autant 1995). Algerian migrant women described how marrying an emigrant allowed them to achieve their desire for a different way of living. As with the Turkish women, they welcomed the ability to live away from the mother-in-law in a nuclear family, something that would have been more difficult to establish in Algeria in the face of social pressure. Several recounted how they had rejected offers from men in Algeria, who were socially their equal, in order to marry men who were often less educated and from a peasant background (Boulahbel-Villac 1994). Marriage may thus be a means of gaining a degree of freedom and, as we have discussed in Chapter 1, women are more likely to migrate for social emancipation, especially from strongly patriarchal societies (Stalker 1994).

One significant development in family reunion and formation since the mid-1980s is its masculinization (see Tables 3.2 and 3.3). This is caused by the impact of the increase in the numbers of daughters from migrant families who marry husbands from the homeland on the one hand, and the willingness of men to move to the abode of the wife on the other. Social norms have also changed in countries of origin. In the UK, there is the additional factor of less discriminatory legislation since the mid-1980s for women wishing to bring in spouses.

Greater mobility has also brought about an increase in international marriages between non-migrants and nationals of another state but there has been little interest in bi-national or mixed marriages (de Hart 1999). De Hart argues that mainstream research in the Netherlands tends to assume that migrants marry exclusively within their own ethnic/nationality groups In the UK, as elsewhere, many of those initially entering the country for short periods apply subsequently to extend their stay or to settle permanently on the grounds of marriage (Haskey 1997: 14). In the Netherlands, Dutch born men tended to have a propensity for marrying Polish, Dominican Republic, Thai and Filipina women. However, more than 50 per cent of mixed marriages with Nigerians and Egyptians were with Dutch-born women. Marriage with a partner from a developing country is not without its problems, for immigration officials often view those bringing back husbands and wives from developing countries suspiciously. A thriving industry has developed in 'mail-order brides' in some countries such as Germany, where men are often looking for wives from Latin America, Asia and now eastern Europe and the former Soviet Union, who they believe will be less assertive than German women. Thai women in Germany, many of whom have entered as mail-order-brides, have become totally sexualized and regarded with utmost suspicion. Yet we should be wary of categorizing all mail-order brides in the same way (Humbeck 1996). Bi-national marriages have often generated a negative image; in the case of a woman she is assumed to be naïve and uncritical, for the man that he is the abuser (de Hart 1999).

International migration forces individuals who wish to remain together to get married unless they have managed to acquire an

Table 3.3 Gender division of family reunification and formation: France 1990–95

	Male	Female	Total	% Female
Spouses in family reunification				
1991	3745	12,765	16,510	77.3
1992	3741	11,417	15,158	75.3
1993	3540	11,341	14,881	76.2
1994	2245	7538	9783	77.0
1995	1451	5829	7260	80.3
Spouses of French citizens				
1991	9449	9314	18,763	49.6
1992	9632	9413	19,045	49.4
1993	9556	10,524	20,080	52.4
1994	5719	7426	13,145	56.5
1995	6154	7233	13,387	54.0

Sources: Lebon (1995/7)

independent status in the country of destination. Whilst the European Convention of Human Rights is increasingly recognizing cohabitation in its deliberations, 'marriage has become, more than ever, the backbone of legal entrance to the EU' (Lutz 1994). With a few exceptions, such as Denmark and Sweden, most states do not accept cohabitation as grounds for granting residence status to non-nationals. The Netherlands regards it as equivalent to marriage for its own nationals. Though cohabitation in European societies has become common, immigration rules have been moving in the opposite direction in some states. In the UK, formal provision for the entry of cohabiting partners was abolished in 1985 and this has remained highly discretionary. The Conservative Government in 1996 ceased allowing cohabitation as a reason for entry, simply because numbers had risen from 400 in 1991 to 900 in 1996. The convoluted nature of the present ruling introduced by the Labour government in October 1997 will not help cohabiting couples to meet immigration regulations.[3]

Refugees, even more than settled migrants, face almost insurmountable problems in fulfilling conditions for family reunion. Only those granted full refugee status under the Geneva Convention are generally able to bring in close family without satisfying the income and housing criteria. The far greater number granted temporary or 'tolerated status' must wait for several years and then comply with the normal conditions. A recent study in the UK showed that many of those granted Exceptional Leave to Remain were refused family reunion because of inadequate income and/or housing (Citizens Advice Bureau 1996). The narrow definition of the family poses particularly acute problems. In many instances, refugee families may have been split between different countries and be living in refugee camps (Cohen-Emerique *et al.* 1998i). Support networks are frequently wider than the nuclear family but cannot be activated within the restrictive definitions of the family applied to migrants and asylum seekers in European states (Rezai and Wihtol de Wenden 1998).

Asylum seekers and refugees

In the 1970s several major waves of asylum seekers were received and settled in European countries. In the Chilean case, refugees were welcomed in the UK for several years after the coup of 1973, but only after Labour returned to office in 1974. The resolution of the internationalized Vietnam conflict, in which the UK had supported the United States, and France had links from its colonial past in Indochina, led to these two countries taking a number of 'boat people'. It should not be forgotten nevertheless that a number of southern European migrants left their countries for political reasons in the 1960s and 1970s, whether this meant fleeing conscription in Portuguese colonial armies, the Colonels' coup in Greece (1967) or repression in Spain against renewed political resistance and student movements. Many political activists entered as labour migrants or enrolled as students. For many Turkish workers in Europe, opposition to political repression at home was a factor in their migration.

The relative openness of the earlier years and the organized settlement of refugee populations, as with the Vietnamese in the 1980s, did not last as the balance of asylum seekers shifted towards spontaneous refugees and Cold War imperatives to accept those fleeing from Communist countries came to an end. Changing attitudes on the part of governments and the failure of the West to keep refugees at a distance in the source regions also produced a change in language, with refugees increasingly labelled economic migrants. As numbers grew (see Table 3.4), the humanitarianism of the 1970s, even if at times reluctant, had been replaced by complacent xenophobia and self-interest in the 1980s (Robinson 1996). By the 1990s and the outbreak of civil war in Yugoslavia, countries of asylum sought to exclude as many as possible from gaining entry, and actively deter those who had gained entry from

Table 3.4 Number of asylum claims submitted in selected European countries, 1983–91: 1992 and 1998 in thousands

Country	1983–91	1992	1998
Austria	19.8	16.2	13.8
Finland	2.0	3.6	1.3
France	43.8	28.9	21.8
FRG	146.1	438.2	98.7
Italy	10.2	2.6	4.7
Netherlands	15.6	20.3	45.2
Sweden	25.9	84.0	13.0
Switzerland	25.9	18.0	41.2
UK	21.6	32.3	57.7

Sources: 1983–91: Cited in Kiujsten 1994; Secretariat for Inter-Governmental Consultations on Asylum, Refugee and Migration Policies in Europe, North America and Australia 1992, 1998: SOPEMI 1999 settling by reducing the rights and welfare benefits of those awaiting decisions. Asylum seekers were also increasingly detained and the principle of non-refoulement flouted.[4]

Germany has succeeded in stopping a large number at the border after it ended its long-standing principle of accepting refugees in 1993. In other countries, recognition rates have dropped dramatically and a growing proportion are given conditional or tolerated status. For the first time, states moved away from unilateral action on admission to concerted efforts of harmonization of the conditions of entry. One of the first of these measures was the Dublin Convention of 1990, which restricted applications to one country only. Since 1985, the Schengen Accord countries have expanded from five (Belgium, Luxembourg, the Netherlands, France and Germany) to nine, which now encompass the southern states of Greece, Italy, Portugal and Spain. Within this Schengen space, which became fully operative in 1997, a policy of open movement for citizens has been implemented, accompanied by a common visa policy to keep out non-Europeans. Around this inner circle or 'Fortress', outer countries, who aspire to become future members of the EU (Czech Republic, Hungary, Poland), serve as a buffer zone.

During these different phases of the refugee regime, women's experiences were largely ignored until the 1980s (Indra 1999). They found it more difficult to gain recognition as refugees in their own right. The process of claiming refugee status is ostensibly gender neutral, but the law does not recognize or respond specifically to women's experiences. Politics is seen as public and predominantly male. Women's political activity, particularly in states where social norms restrict women's movements, is often in informal social movements not always recognized as 'political'. Women are thus rarely seen as political actors in their own right and therefore as potential Convention refugees.

Women entering as dependants have often found their needs neglected, and overshadowed by those of male partners who may have spent periods in prison. They were also marginalized in the development of programmes and given little opportunity for participation in decision-making (Lopez Zarzosa 1998; Camus-Jacques 1989). On the other hand, much research has suggested that women refugees have found it easier than men to adapt to life in the new country, and have been able to adopt more flexible strategies towards securing income and social rights (see Chapter 6).

The focus on the conditions of women refugees goes back to the Copenhagen conference held in 1980 in the middle of the UN Decade for Women Equality, Development and Peace (1975–85). It became concerned with the abuses meted out to women refugees and children whom it was recognized formed the bulk of refugee populations (Osaki 1997: 12), though, as we saw in Chapter 1, statistics on the gender composition of refugees are particularly poor. Awareness by the UNCHR of women's situation grew in the mid-1980s and 'Women's rights as human rights' was chosen as a theme of the World Conference on Human Rights held in Vienna in 1993.

In Europe there was a slow recognition of gender persecution in the implementation of refugee law during the 1980s as a result of international and domestic pressures. In the early years of the decade a number of Iranian women had their requests for asylum rejected. They had claimed that they faced persecution because they refused to respect the strict dress code and had demonstrated against the regime. Dutch, German and UK adjudicators considered their persecution too slight and not necessarily incompatible with human dignity. The specificity of gender persecution was acknowledged by the European Parliament in 1984, which called for states to recognize women who transgressed social norms of their society and that they should be treated as a 'particular social group'. During the 1980s, judicial authorities began to recognize gender persecution as a valid reason for the granting of refugee status. With the collapse of Communism and the rise of fundamentalist Islamic regimes as the scourge of Western foreign policy, governments were more prepared to question state sovereignty of Islamic systems (Bhabha 1996: 18–19).

Advocates of women's human rights in Canada campaigned for gender guidelines, which were adopted by Canada in 1993 and subsequently in Australia and the United States in 1996. Though no European state has actually adopted such guidelines, some progress has been made in creating more gender-sensitive practices within the refugee determination process (Crawley 1997). Sexual violence is recognized as a form of persecution by France, Germany and the Netherlands, whereas abortion, sterilization and genital mutilation can be treated as forms of torture in the UK (Kuttner 1997: 18).

The 1951 Geneva Convention guarantees the right to seek asylum to people 'who owing to well-founded fear of being persecuted for reasons of race, religion, nationality, membership of a particular social group or political opinion, is outside the country of his nationality.' Persecution on grounds of sex is not included, and to gain refugee status, women must claim that they have suffered rape, sexual assault or other violations as a result of membership of one of the Convention categories. Some campaigners have argued for women to be classified as a 'social group' for asylum purposes. Adjin-Tettey (1997) argues that applicants would need to show they had suffered serious harm as a result of their sex in the same way as applicants basing their claim on membership of other social groups. Others have rejected this call, claiming it is 'inappropriately comprehensive' (Crawley 1997). Most countries interpret the Geneva Convention in terms of individual persecution, making claims of belonging to a social group difficult to sustain. Sweden, for example, grants a lower degree of protection for refugee status granted under the social category. The courts have sometimes recognized more narrowly defined 'social groups'. A British judge ordered an Immigration Tribunal to hear the case of a woman who feared stoning for adultery on the grounds that she was a member of a social group (women accused of adultery) within the meaning of the Convention (Refugee Council 1997: 5).

Although it may still take some time to get gender guidelines onto the European agenda, it should be noted that with some organized mass groups of refugees, for example of Kosovan refugees in the UK in 1999, women and children have predominated. They are thought of as needing more protection, but are also considered more likely to want to return home to their menfolk as providers and heads of family. These aspects are likely to play a part in the preference for the admission of women and children.

Conclusion

Overall, the trends we have outlined in this chapter point to an increasing number of undocumented migrants. First, a short-sighted attitude to labour migration, which fails to recognize the real shortages in unskilled labour, will tend to encourage an increase in undocumented migrants. Only skilled and designated labour is officially permitted entry into northern European states. In southern European states this kind of policy will inevitably be more difficult to police because of the larger informal sector. Second, whilst maintaining the principle of family reunification, future

European guidelines will implement restrictive conditions in line with the existing regulations currently practised by major European countries. Third, a reinforced hierarchy of exclusion is being designed to segregate the majority of asylum seekers (Fekete 1997; *The Guardian* 1998). The hardening attitude of European states to the regularization of undocumented migrants, the vast majority of whom are from developing countries, thus points to the permanent exclusion of many from the citizenship of nation-states and hence the European Union. This will be one of the key themes developed in the next chapter.

Notes

1 Bohning was the Chief of the Employment Branch for International migration at the International Labour Office in Geneva.
2 Castles and Kosack (1973) clearly demonstrate the key role played by women in the labour market. Yet, subsequent writing, for example, Munz and Ulrich (1998:42) maintains the fiction that it was mainly young males who migrated for the whole of the period of labour migration in Germany until 1973–4.
3 The change in regulations in the UK in October 1997, which resulted primarily from a campaign to recognize same-sex couples, has made it less discretionary than under the Conservatives, but it now stipulates that cohabitation is only to be recognized as grounds for granting leave to remain in the UK when marriage is not possible. Couples must demonstrate a sustained and stable relationship for two years before the partner enters and for two years after entry before being allowed to remain permanently.
4 The principle of non-refoulement means that refugees should not be returned to a state where they may be in danger.

Chapter 4

Citizenship, rights and gender

Since the late 1980s, and at a time when entitlements have been severely restricted for many, the issue of citizenship has re-emerged on academic and political agendas. Entitlements and obligations, and the shifting boundaries of inclusion and exclusion have become central themes of these discussions. After an initial preoccupation with models of nation–state citizenship and comparisons between them, recent writing has sought to decouple citizenship from its traditionally close association with the nation–state. The exclusionary practices of citizenship have been recognized as being ill-equipped to deal with an age of large-scale and heterogeneous migratory movements. Many theorists and activists have therefore advocated a more internationalist and multi-layered global governance whereby rights are delivered and guaranteed at different levels, ranging from the local, national, and international. In particular, it was hoped that international human rights law would 'provide a tool for sculpting a more inclusionary model of citizenship' (Lister 1997: 60) transcending nation–state boundaries. Whilst this aspiration is shared by virtually all those concerned with migrant rights, major differences arise over the degree to which economic, social and political rights of migrants really are covered by an international regime.

Despite the burgeoning literature on citizenship, modes of incorporation and the recent development of European citizenship, there has unfortunately been little interest in examining different outcomes for women and men (Baubock 1994a,b). Yet we know that women in general were excluded from citizenship until well into the twentieth century, and then often only incorporated as dependants with derived rights. Although feminists have massively invested in the debate on how to make citizenship more inclusive, migrant women and their specific situation have been largely neglected in these discussions (Kofman 1995).[1] Still today, crossing borders often reinforces dependency for third country and EU migrant women (Ackers 1996, 1998). EU policy gives primacy to labour migrants, who are assumed to be overwhelmingly men. One area of concern for many decades, not just to migrant women but also to nationals who married non-nationals, has been the right to retain and transmit citizenship. The blatant gender inequalities were often not rectified until the 1980s, as in the Netherlands (1985) or the UK (1983).

In this chapter, we firstly examine a set of related issues concerning access to and exclusion from the rights bestowed by nation–state citizenship, the implications arising from the emergence of European citizenship and the degree to which European and international conventions are able to complement or overcome discrimination and lack of rights not covered by citizenship entitlements. Gender considerations play a major part and will be discussed in relation to the different forms of citizenship and international conventions. In the second part of this chapter we turn to the ways in which different nation–states have related to and sought to incorporate minorities and migrants, whether it is through the development of imperial, ethnic, republican or multicultural models. In many instances, a hierarchy differentiating groups, capable and incapable of fully belonging to and integrating into a society, has been established. These models shape and are shaped by gender relations.

Citizenship and rights

Discussions of citizenship in the modern era have traditionally centred on the acquisition of rights and the exercise of obligations, and how rights served to forge attachment to a particular society, generally equated with the nation–state (Barbalet 1988; Turner 1990). The nature of these rights, the time of their acquisition and the groups entitled to them have varied historically and between states. The tendency in the principal traditions of citizenship was to emphasize the inclusionary dimension operating within the boundaries of the nation–state. The liberal tradition of rights, whose main theorist was T.H. Marshall (1950), based it on the British experience. He argued that individual members of the society progressively acquired civil, political, economic and social rights, the latter primarily as strategies of class abatement. The civic republican tradition, most fully developed in France and derived from the principles of the French Revolution, is concerned primarily with citizenship as participation in the polis; it has tended to pay less attention to the resources required to be able to take part in the public sphere. Issues of disadvantage, exclusion and belonging, especially of outsiders and the marginalized, and the Europeanization of concepts and practices associated with citizenship, have broken down some of the stark differences between the models. On the one hand, the writings of Marshall were discovered by those working within the civic republican tradition, on the other, the notion of social exclusion, as opposed to narrower concepts of poverty and deprivation, and adopted by the European Commission in the 1980s in its social programmes, has been incorporated into British thinking on these topics (Samers 1998).

In both traditions, the attendant rights and obligations of citizenship were contained within the nation–state, which was itself conceptualized as culturally and morally homogeneous. They also paid little attention to issues arising from the admission of outsiders to a society and how they might alter the basis of citizenship as membership of a bounded community expands and new potential members enter. Similarly, the development of dual and transnational citizenships and the impact of international human rights conventions that might complement citizenship rights were not taken into account. Today the plurality of communities and the degrees of citizenship, enjoyed by different categories of individuals, and creating new hierarchies of civic stratification, have generated more complex discussions over the multiple meanings and practices of citizenship. The relationship between the public and the private had also been taken for granted, i.e. citizenship was concerned with the enjoyment of rights and obligations and desirable behaviour in the public sphere. Yet feminist and gay critiques of degendered narratives of the emergence of the modern citizen (Carver 1998; Pateman 1988) questioned the unproblematic relationship of the public and private, and the unquestioned marginalization of the activities, resources and socio-sexual relations located in the private sphere.

In relation to migrants, it was the growth of settled immigrant communities in Europe that led to several political theorists voicing concerns over the disenfranchisement of substantial minorities of long-term legal residents, sometimes called denizens, and the consequences for democratic institutions (Costa-Lascoux 1987; Hammar 1990). By the 1980s, the introduction of long-term residence and work permits, as in France and Germany, had given a growing number of migrants greater security. In 1981, the socialist government in France granted a renewable ten-year work and residence permit. In Germany, the shift from temporary to more stable permits also facilitated the ability to change employment, although this did not necessarily lead to the hoped for social mobility (Caglar 1995; Goldberg *et al.* 1995). Denizens had thus acquired considerable economic and social rights as a result of their increasing embeddedness in national societies (Brubaker 1989; Soysal 1994). Political elites, especially in states based on civic republican or ethnic models, where citizenship is acquired through kinship, tended to resist more forcefully the extension of political rights. In the UK, this aspect has been far less significant because the majority of the post-war migrants from former colonies and Ireland had formal citizenship (Piper 1998).

Scholars, however, often tended to concentrate on the extension of formal rights, but did not adequately consider the continuing significance of various forms of discrimination, which could undermine their substantive reality. Direct and indirect discrimination bear upon the migrant's actual position in the labour market: welfare and social conditions and the need to be taken into account in the exercise of rights and the quality of life. For the children of migrants, education and training loom large in their prospects for better living conditions and acceptance by the wider society. Discrimination may even be sanctioned by the state (Lochak 1993; Aukerman 1995), and has by no means been overturned by international conventions, which retain respect for state sovereignty. For example, the right to reserve employment in the public sector does not contravene international conventions. In many states, this covers a wide range of protected sectors such as education, health and the civil service, and may extend to state services such as the post office and railways. In France, it is estimated that in the 1990s almost a third of employment is not open to non-citizens (CERC 1999). In Germany, and this has been a sticking point in its unwillingness to sign the 1975 ILO convention for migrant workers, national preference is enshrined in labour law. Lutz (1994) notes that this discriminatory regulation makes it particularly difficult for qualified women migrants to find employment outside ethnic niches. Indirect discrimination may also profoundly alter the life chances of migrants. For example, children of Turkish migrants in Germany tend not to be directed to vocational training or to stay on at school and therefore find themselves disadvantaged in the workplace. Employers often apply stereotypes in refusing employment to migrants, such as their wish to return to their homelands, lacking requisite linguistic knowledge, etc. which persist well after the reality of these conditions has evolved (Goldberg *et al* 1995).

One of the consequences of focusing on the extension of denizen rights is that it overlooks two significant axes along which states attribute rights and create a hierarchy of citizenship entitlements. These are, first, the entry status of migrants that excludes some migrants from specified rights, if not permanently then at least temporarily. Second, there is the legal status of migrants (permanent, legal temporary and undocumented) and the possibility they have of moving from a less to a more secure status (Baubock 1991).

Temporary and more conditional forms of entry, associated with more contingent rights, have also become increasingly common. Examples of these are contract and fixed-term labour, and asylum seekers and refugees with temporary or humanitarian status, whose rights are at best limited, if not refused. In particular, contract and seasonal labour, as in Germany, are not given the possibility of converting short stays into permanent residence (Schmidt 1998). For these migrants, social rights are severely constrained and closely tied to employment. Since the mid-1980s, some migrants, especially those entering through family reunion, have had their right to settle made dependent upon the condition of no recourse to public funds (Williams 1995: 144). For example, in the UK, the range of public funds has been augmented from unemployment benefits to include child and disability benefits. Refugees attributed humanitarian status and asylum seekers do not have any immediate right to family reunion. During the initial period after entry, and whilst their cases are being heard, the latter may find themselves severely curtailed in their activities and dependent on the most basic and meagre resources. One of the major consequences of stricter controls for entry and higher refusal rates for asylum seekers is that an increasing number of migrants circumvent the regulations for entry or overstay beyond the period they may have been granted on a tourist visa. This leads to different kinds of illegality, which vary between countries (Wihtol de Wenden 1990: 30). It ranges from those who enter illegally; to those who enter legally for a temporary period but overstay their period of original residence; individuals who are legally employed on a restrictive contract and work beyond its expiration; and those who have permission to stay but not to work and who take up unauthorized employment. Women with family reunion status in certain states frequently fall into this category in the initial years. Current state control mechanisms have focused on illegal presence of foreigners and encouraged a number of ambivalent situations. In Germany, a number of indications show that the majority of persons defined by the state as illegal entered legally, but subsequently lost their status (Wilpert 1998). According to German law, being illegal is a greater crime than undertaking unregulated employment.

In the past, some countries let migrants shed their clandestine status and acquire legal status through regularization programmes that enabled those who were on the margins of welfare provision to have access to social rights. Though open to large numbers, these programmes could be less favourable to women if they stipulated regular employment as a basic condition. A French survey of the 130,000 successful applicants in the 1981 regularization programme revealed participants were young and unmarried and had often entered as tourists and overstayed. It also found that women and young children were over-represented, suggesting that many had entered as family members without authorization (Wihtol de Wenden 1990: 31). Although for many years France resisted implementing further mass regularization programmes, campaigns and protests nevertheless pushed the government into granting an amnesty to a substantial number of undocumented migrants in the wake of the *sans papiers* movements in the mid-1990s, in which many women have been prominent (Lloyd 1997). Interestingly, despite the large number of single applicants, many of those regularized have been family migrants (OECD 1998). Mediterranean countries have had several regularization programmes since the mid-1980s, but on the whole states have sought to curtail these programmes. Other countries, such as Germany and the UK, have refused to implement general amnesties. The absence or cessation of regularization programmes has serious implications for an eventual accession to citizenship. Without a legal status, migrants and their children are barred from applying for citizenship. Changes in nationality laws may reinforce this aspect. For example, until the 1981 British Nationality Act, children born in the UK automatically acquired citizenship. Since its implementation in

1983, only children of British citizens or those who have a settled status, i.e. permanent status, obtain this automatically. The children of asylum seekers no longer qualify for citizenship at birth, though they may apply at ten years of age.

Feminist perspectives on citizenship

Feminist engagement with citizenship debates has tended to focus on the gendered nature of access to economic, social, civil and political rights associated with citizenship. These critiques have highlighted the masculine assumptions that underpin the model of the citizen and the difficulties women face in achieving the conditions required in order to benefit fully from the rights ascribed to the citizen.

Given that historically women were exiles from citizenship and then incorporated partially, it is not surprising that a number of feminists have been highly critical of the idea and practice of citizenship. Men's fraternal contract at the time of the French Revolution was gained at women's expense, particularly their exclusion from the political sphere (Pateman 1988). As men were politically enfranchised in the mid nineteenth century, women saw their civil rights diminished. This was the peak of private patriarchy in which women were confined to the private sphere, and married women were firmly placed under the tutelage of male protectors, unable to exercise rights over their bodies and dispose of their property (Walby 1990). Extensions of political citizenship in the mid-nineteenth century to all British men, and not just members of the propertied class, took place in the context of broader discussions about who was to be included and excluded from citizenship. Women and colonial peoples continued to be excluded from participation in the political arena. The resulting stratification resembled a family in which each person had his or her role and where the White male was the head of household (Vogel 1988). Despite the political confinement of women, there was some loosening up of the patriarchal hold over their economic and social lives. As from 1882, women could dispose of their own salary and wealth. The history of women's, especially married women's, right to independence varied historically between states. In France, for example, similar civil and social rights came later than in Britain, at the end of the World War I.

Nonetheless, the concept of the citizen was still predicated in the twentieth century on the male worker, his support of dependants, his independence, and the integrity of his body. So too was the right to defend one's country and sacrifice one's life for it reserved exclusively for men. Although modern warfare has made it necessary to bring large numbers of women to service and sustain far-flung military operations, they remain barred from active combat on the front-line (Enloe 1989). We are not arguing that women should be incorporated into the military. Whilst women made gains in civil, civic and political rights in the twentieth century, they lacked the key qualities that gave men full citizenship and continued to be treated as citizens with a difference. Principally they lacked the resources from the labour market (e.g. pay, pensions, full-time work), that would enable them to be autonomous and realize their self-development, while welfare policies assumed they were dependent on men (see Chapter 6). Their weaker economic position cannot entirely explain their exclusion from the political sphere, especially in France, where relatively little progress had been made by the mid-1990s in the proportion of women at national level, i.e. around 6 per cent from the time they first obtained the vote in 1944 (Mossuz-Lavau 1996). The recent campaigns for *parité* in France thus construct gender divisions as the remaining key inequality to be overcome in the political domain without taking into account the diversity of women's resources and interests.

So, despite the numerous critiques of dominant conceptualizations of citizenship in the early 1990s (Phillips 1991a,b; Lister 1992), scant attention has been paid to migrant and ethnic minority women, their treatment under immigration law and the problems they faced in acquiring citizenship. Lister (1997) argued that earlier discussions of citizenship had emphasized its inclusionary potential, but that recent radical critiques have taken up its propensity for exclusion and the need to deconstruct the unitary woman as the bearer of citizenship rights. This shift has highlighted the gendered and racialized nature of citizenship. Black, and subsequently lesbian, disabled and older feminists, challenged the universal construction of womanhood.

As we have stressed, migrant women cannot be treated homogeneously. Their access to citizenship and exercise of rights will vary according to the tradition of citizenship, entry status, residence status, marital status, class and country of origin. This will determine the degree to which they enjoy substantive rights and are eventually able to acquire citizenship. Even those with citizenship often encounter discrimination in employment, housing and welfare. Some of the most weakly positioned, in relation to claiming rights, are migrant women who are forced into dependency by nationality and immigration law. The boundaries of inclusion and exclusion reinforced by the nation–state in an age of migration have remained outside the 'agenda of Marshallian theories of citizenship' (Yuval-Davis 1991: 61). Yet as we have seen, their complex stratification means we cannot in turn construct a unitary migrant.

In the subsequent sections, we shall examine some key issues, for migrant women with different statuses in relation to developments in national and European citizenship. In particular we shall focus here on the specificities arising from the process of migration. Discrimination in employment and welfare applicable to new and long-established migrants will be dealt with subsequently in Chapters 5 and 6.

Migration, gender and citizenship

Worlds Apart (1985) was the first book to analyse comprehensively the differential treatment of women and men under British immigration law and the implications of nationality policies. The authors hoped that 'a successful outcome might inspire feminists in other European countries to undertake a similar task', but this had not yet eventuated at the time of the book's second edition (Bhabha and Shutter 1994). Our discussion will therefore inevitably draw heavily from the British situation, although we shall make comparisons with other states.

Interest in gender, nationality and citizenship emanated from a concern for the unequal treatment of women, who in marrying non-nationals, themselves became aliens or even stateless persons. In the nineteenth century this situation prevailed in most European states. As from 1870, British born women lost their citizenship upon marriage with a foreigner (see previous section). France, probably because of its high rates of immigration and inter-marriages in the years after World War I, restored to women in 1927 the right to keep their nationality after marriage to a foreigner (Sohn 1992: 109). Although this issue was considered at the Hague Conference, convened in 1930 to discuss conflicts in nationality laws in different states (Bhabha and Shutter 1884: 24), no positive steps were taken to redress women's unequal treatment resulting from loss of nationality and associated citizenship rights. So whilst marriage represented a crucial rite of passage for the majority of British women in their enjoyment of basic civil and social rights, it was even more salient for those who transgressed the boundaries of the nation and therefore lost their right to be part of it (Klug 1989: 22). Being dependants, British women could also not bring in foreign-born husbands as dependants of their own: a situation that was only dismantled in 1985 following a judgement of the European Court of Justice (Klug: 1989: 27). Nor, until recently, did many states allow women to pass on citizenship to their children. In the Netherlands and the UK, this situation was not remedied until the 1980s. As we saw in Chapter 3, the Primary Purpose Rule, which came into force in the UK after 1979, made it difficult for prospective husbands from developing countries, and especially the Indian sub continent, to gain entry.

For new migrant women today, the shortfall in citizenship lies in the probationary period imposed on spouses following entry and the various forms of dependency derived from their specific status. The nature of their entry, residence and work statuses will be crucial in determining their formal access to citizenship and, in particular, the dependency they may be forced into. Our discussion focuses on the vast majority who enter through family reunion or as dependants in male-headed households. Where a couple apply for entry, it will be the man who will be classified as the head of household. Neither category of women has an independent status or independent status at the time of entry. In terms of access to citizenship and its social rights, there will therefore be additional hurdles to overcome.

Legally, the rights of dependent migrant women are derived from the male in the first few years after their entry; sometimes this may last for the whole of their lives in the host country. Very few countries give the spouse full residence and employment rights immediately upon entry. The rights of dependants are tied to the status of the primary migrant. In the 1980s when migrants increasingly acquired more secure forms of settlement and long-term residence and work, the situation of dependants also improved.

On the whole it has become easier for spouses to enter the labour market. However, although outright restrictions were eased in Germany in the early 1990s, when a year's waiting period was lifted, the issuing of a work permit still depends on the state of the labour market during the following five years. The rights of Turkish spouses are governed by an association agreement (1980) whereby they have the right to work after three years of legal residence and complete freedom after five years. Similarly, the Irish impose conditions that make participation dependent on the state of the labour market. Inevitably these regulations push women into the informal sector and more precarious jobs.

Most countries impose probationary periods of marriage during which the partners have to stay together. This may apply not just where both partners are migrants, but also to a national marrying a non-national (see Chapter 3). The fearful reactions generated around marriages of convenience has led to longer periods being imposed on the duration of a marriage before the spouse is able to gain an independent status. In France, this was extended by the Pasqua laws to two years, but has been subsequently restored to a year by the socialist government since the new legislation of 1998. In Germany, the probationary period is even longer: three years for Turkish women and four for other third country nationals (Boyd 1997). For some women this may leave them in the straitjacket of a violent or deeply unhappy marriage. Southall Black Sisters in the UK dealt with 755 cases of threatened deportation because of marriage breakdown in an 18-month period from January 1995. The current Labour Government is unlikely to abolish this probationary period, but has now allowed women driven out of violent marriages to be able to stay permanently rather than face deportation (*The Guardian* 1999). The level of evidence (court order or police cautions) they will have to provide is quite severe. As we shall see in Chapter 7, there are a number of on-going political campaigns in European countries striving to get rid of or reduce the probationary period.

Another aspect relating to marriage is polygamy, which although encompassing a small number of women, has become a major issue in France in recent years. In 1988, the UK ceased to recognize the right to constitute polygamous relationships although by then only 25 applications of this kind had been registered (Bhabha and Shutter 1994: 65). In France, the situation is far more complicated because, since the Montcho case in 1980 when the second wife had her status regularized, it was permitted by French authorities (Rude-Antoine 1997). Thus for over a decade France recognized the validity of different systems of international private law. Since 1993, however, only one wife in a polygamous relationship may be admitted. It is not simply a matter of immigration, but of social rights that have long been denied to the second wife in France. Whilst mistresses of French men, or what might be called 'informal polygamy', may be covered by the latter's social security arrangements, wives living in polygamous relationships have no such right. In effect, even in the past, although polygamous families could be legally constituted in France, men often did not have sufficient resources to bring in wives through the official channel of family reunion. This meant that many women entered on tourist visas and stayed without any residence, employment or social rights. Some managed to get themselves regularized as mothers of children born in France, but others remained forever 'without papers' and have effectively become non-persons without any identity (Poiret 1996). As a result of the growing number of migrant women without independent status, campaigns for such a status to be granted upon entry, irrespective of marital status or the nature of their husband's permit (Rajfire 2000), have become more prominent.

European Union citizenship

Since the principle of European citizenship was enacted in the Maastricht Treaty in 1993, the gap between EU citizens and denizens has widened. One of the principal advantages conferred on European citizens, but denied to denizens from third countries, is the right to mobility within the European Union. The implementation of the European Union has widened the circle of preferences to nationals of other member states. Erstwhile migrants from Mediterranean countries have become privileged EU citizens. In practice, European citizens too face a hierarchy of rights that have developed based on notions of social contribution and family relationships. At the apex are full, independent workers, followed by citizens with derived rights via marriage and whose entitlements depend on their spouses being in employment, and finally by those with no social rights, such as the unemployed, students and pensioners, who may not become a burden on the social assistance system of the member state (Ackers 1996: 320).

The worker is defined by the EU as someone who performs a task derived from an economic purpose, so that voluntary work and informal care are outside this conceptualization. Community law is permeated with a male breadwinner model where the rights of spouses are dependent ones. Married women migrants are less likely to receive positive returns from migration (Lichter 1983).

and suffer from migration-induced dependency whose effects may become extremely severe should they become separated or divorced The 10 per cent of migrants who cohabit are also not covered by the social entitlements of their partners.

The issue of third country nationals has been frequently raised since the mid-1980s, especially by the Commission and the European Parliament, but their calls for action in equality of treatment and socio-cultural integration between EU and non-EU nationals have generally been blocked and ignored by member states. The Treaty on European Union (1992) simply dumped the situation of this group of migrants into the Third Pillar of inter-governmental co-operation, where they share the agenda with issues of combating illegal immigration, police co-operation for the prevention and combating of terrorism, and drug trafficking. The Treaty of Amsterdam, which came into force on 1 May 1999, does at least transfer immigration policy to the First Pillar where the Commission and the Parliament have more authority. It is not yet clear what shared guidelines will result. For the moment, third country nationals do not have the right to move freely within the community. At a time of unemployment, the right to move in search of better employment prospects may yield considerable benefits both for the skilled, as in the health sector (see Chapter 5) or those in hard-hit primary sectors, such as mining (Rea 1995). Furthermore, the European Court of Justice has reiterated that foreign spouses of EU nationals do not have rights of their own and only derive them from the worker moving to another member state (Guiraudon 1998: 659).

Equally of concern are the differences in access to citizenship in European states, which remain a matter of national sovereignty and subsidiarity. Hence, there exists enormous inequality between states in the possibility of becoming a European citizen for women and men within the European Union. Although some convergence has occurred in migratory regimes (Chapter 3) and systems of incorporation, the disparity between states in the conditions of naturalization for first generation migrants is nonetheless substantial. At the moment there is no likelihood of the replacement of national citizenship by European citizenship, a position reiterated at the 1997 intergovernmental meeting in Amsterdam (Hansen 1998: 754). For the children of migrants there has generally been some convergence around a cross-European entitlement to citizenship (Hansen 1998).

International conventions and rights

So far we have considered the implications of national and European policies relating to the enjoyment of different kinds of rights and the possibility of acquiring citizenship. In this section we raise the question of the extent to which national citizenship has been displaced by an international regime of human rights that gives migrants a high degree of protection and benefits. A number of European and international conventions have been adopted, although not always ratified by European states in the post-war years. For example, the European Convention for Human Rights (ECHR), which bestows rights on individuals rather than citizens, deals primarily with civil and political rights rather than economic and social rights, and is only incidentally concerned with aliens. All other European Conventions, such as the European Convention of the Legal Status of Migrant Workers (adopted by the Council of Europe in 1977) and covering the rights of migrant workers, only apply to members of contracting parties. Internationally, the ILO, founded in 1919, has been the main body concerned with migrant rights. The ILO pushed through a number of Conventions against discrimination of migrant workers, such as Convention 97 in 1975, which was signed by some southern, but no northern European states. After a decade of protracted negotiation, the International Convention for Migrant Workers and their Families (United Nations 1991) was passed in 1990 under the auspices of the United Nations.

Since the 1980s, the rights of intra-European migrants have been vastly expanded, but as we have shown, those of third country nationals have been left behind in the drive to European integration. Yet some scholars (Soysal 1994, 1996) suggest that migrants, including third country nationals, now participate in a post-national membership, where the acquisition of rights no longer depends on formal citizenship but on personhood. In addition, Soysal contends that the codification of ideologies and instruments of human rights have been particularly important for immigrants, so that the major difference today between denizens and citizens is the latter's right to vote. Sassen (1996a) also claims that immigrants have diluted the meaning of citizenship, noting in particular the territoriality of social security regimes based on residence rather than citizenship status. She in particular cites the adoption of the 1990 International Convention for Migrant Workers, which no European state has so far ratified, despite being exhorted by the European Commission to do so in order to demonstrate a commitment to the large numbers of third country nationals in their societies.

In contrast, Joppke (1997: 68) has characterized international conventions and treaties as 'toothless fair-weather declarations'. Ghai (1997) commented that the West has been reluctant to recognize the equality of migrants with nationals, and that 'migrant rights have been something of a Cinderella in the family of human rights'. For Baubock (1993) consideration of migrant needs and the transnationalization of entitlements have not kept pace with the globalization and diversification of migratory movements. The International Convention for Migrant Workers and their Families might at least have indicated a sign of willingness by receiving countries to guarantee a minimum set of rights for the documented and undocumented (who had been employed for a specified period). However, not only was its negotiation a protracted process, but its impact has been more symbolic than substantive. Twenty states world-wide are needed for its ratification for it to enter into force – so far only nine, none of which are major receiving countries, have done so. The reasons for the vexed negotiations and abysmal record of ratification lie in the jealous guarding of state sovereignty and identity of states, and the refusal to acknowledge rights for undocumented workers. It should be noted that the stipulation of a period of employment for the undocumented has profound gender implications in that most family migrants have been women and they generally tend more than men to be pushed into employment in the informal sector.

Overall, it is hard to sustain the notion that a post-national citizenship for migrants has become a reality in the European Union, although some cases have invoked the European Convention for Human Rights. Applicants to the ECHR have based their challenges to national immigration laws and practice on Article 8 (respect for family and private life), Article 12 (right to marry) and Article 14 (principle of non-discrimination). One major case that was referred to the ECHR had far reaching consequences for British immigration law. A 1985 ruling by the European Court of Human Rights found that the British government was in breach of two articles (8,14) of the ECHR in relation to the rights of non-British women to bring in their husbands, a right that non-British men had. The response of the British government was to equalize downwards so that women and men were subjected to the same restrictions (Bhabha and Shutter 1994: 76–8). Concessions to the primary purpose rule were also wrenched grudgingly from the British government in 1992 as a result of several appeals to the European Court of Justice on grounds of the breach of rules of free movement within the European Community. The change meant that those who had been married for five years, or who had a child, had the right of abode in the UK (Bhabha and Shutter 1994: 85–7). As a result of this ruling, the number of husbands allowed to enter rose substantially as from 1992.

Guiraudon (1998: 661) emphasizes the fact that jurisprudence relating to third country nationals was not initially based on human rights considerations but on freedom of services or association treaty provisions that a number of states had previously signed with Turkey and North African countries. The impact of external legislation has been variable, gradual and belated. In effect, the extension of rights, resulting from the embeddedness of migrants in the 1970s and 1980s in countries such as France, Germany and the Netherlands, arose primarily from constitutional principles (Guiraudon 1998). For example, the right to family reunion was protected by French and German courts in the late 1970s and early 1980s. Today, although adhered to in principle, family reunion has been severely limited in practice and will probably continue to be so under any future EU common guidelines. In Scandinavian states in recent years, legislation against ethnic discrimination has been passed partly in response to pressures from international agreements.

According to Stasilius (1997), diametrically opposed conclusions in immigration and citizenship debates about whether liberal democracies are becoming more or less inclusive of migrants and non-citizens reflect the instability in immigration, refugee and labour market policies, pro- and anti-immigrant politics, state and non-state narratives, bureaucratic interventions, and juridical rulings. Far from signifying a globalizing trend towards post-national rights, there is a growing convergence among affluent countries to regain control of their borders through more restrictive immigration and refugee policies as well as through a general withdrawal of civil and human rights for certain categories of non-citizens. The growing number of undocumented migrants and refugees with temporary status therefore makes the earlier preoccupation with denizens limited in any discussion of access to rights and full citizenship.

State sovereignty largely reigns supreme in the elaboration of immigration policies that should be kept distinct from integration policies directed towards legally resident migrants. Those who believe that international regimes are actually being applied tend to emphasize the extension of rights of the lawfully resident but ignore the growing number of those who remain relatively defenceless and legally unprotected by both international and national legislation. The divergence in the conclusions reached also stems from differences in the range of rights that are deemed to be influential in migrant lives. Sassen and Soysal emphasize, above all, the territorial principle of social security, the increase of rights over time, i.e. principle of embeddedness, and a gap between citizens and non-citizens that is primarily constituted by the absence of political rights.

Whilst we would not dispute the extension of social rights, especially in guest worker regimes, there are several aspects that have not been sufficiently taken into consideration. An evaluation of the actual gap in the rights of denizens and citizens cannot be limited to an enunciation of abstract and formal principles. Although many European states, including Germany, have ratified the International Convention on the Elimination of all forms of Racial Discrimination (passed in 1966) and Convention 97 of the ILO (passed in 1975), which also obliges states to prevent discrimination by all suitable means, only the Netherlands, Sweden and the UK have passed special legislation giving migrant workers protection from discrimination. A number of reports undertaken by the French trade unions and state authorities since 1997 are leading to new measures against discrimination being enacted. Many studies tend to consider formal citizenship rather than discriminatory practices shape the reality of substantive citizenship as in the German case (Kolinsky 1996). Children of migrants in Germany, who have not gone through the German educational system, are counted as part of the foreign population for purposes of the foreign entry quota to German universities (Ansay 1991). Even where formal exclusion is absent, it is necessary to determine the actual position of migrants and the possibilities for organising collectively as an interest group. In most states non-European migrants have far higher rates of unemployment (see Chapter 5). In Sweden, these groups lag behind in income. They and their children are also in a disadvantaged position compared with native Swedes in terms of place of residence, access to higher education and health (Graham and Soninen 1998: 527).

The position of migrants in the labour market is of particular concern for it has profound consequences in relation to concrete benefits arising from the formal rights of citizenship or denizenship (Graham and Soninen 1998). Although explanations in terms of structural reasons, linguistic competence and lack of suitable qualifications have been proffered, there is also evidence of direct and indirect racial, ethnic and national discrimination. Demands for cultural competence are deemed understandable, as in a recent Swedish report on *Employment for Immigrants*, which uses arguments that would not today be acceptable for excluding women from male-dominated work and professions (Graham and Soninen 1998). Various studies of employment practices in Germany (Goldberg *et al.* 1995), Denmark (Diken 1998) and Sweden (Graham and Soninen 1998) demonstrate that employers invoke a wide range of cultural and social reasons to discriminate against migrants. Migrants are weakly represented in unions, which, in turn, fail to represent their interests (Graham and Soninen 1998). Furthermore, the state still continues to have the right to discriminate between citizens and non-citizens (Lochak 1993), especially in relation to public sector employment. As a Danish study indicates (Diken 1998), the principle of priority for citizens in employment retains much support. Though varying in entitlements between states, we would conclude that citizenship still confers a host of rights in employment, housing, welfare, and the right to pass on one's own citizenship.

Gender and international conventions

As we have seen, a number of European and international conventions have been adopted, but are either primarily applicable to European citizens or have not been ratified by European states. However, one advance that should be noted has been the explicit recognition for first time of the active involvement of women in migration in the International Convention for Migrant Workers and their Families (Hune 1991). Article 2(1) explicitly stated the principle of equal treatment. Part III has several articles that could be used against the extreme vulnerability of women in areas of sexual exploitation, physical abuse and forced prostitution, although none of these has been specifically enunciated. It sought to ensure that migrant women would be less dependent and were no longer placed in jeopardy in case of death or dissolution of marriage, which is of considerable relevance to migrant women in Europe. The Convention, however, does not address the special situation of migrant women, such as the unequal position and segregation of women in the labour market, their sexual exploitation and victimization. These are issues of growing concern in Europe (Leidholdt 1996), but have so far only resulted in extremely weak measures, except in Belgium and the Netherlands (IOM 1996). The EU has adopted sexual trafficking as an issue and funded studies with the aim of achieving greater co-operation through its Daphne Programme, where it is closely associated with the need to combat criminality (Uçarer 1998).

It has taken several decades for the situation of women migrants to be taken seriously in international conferences and conventions. Their marginal position was clearly expressed in the single paragraph that appeared in the recommendations drawn up at the World Conference of the International Women's Year in 1975 in Mexico. By the 1985 Nairobi Meeting several new concerns, such as sex tourism, violence against women, forced prostitution, international transportation, exchange and sale of women, had been added to those of women as workers and their families, which was raised in the Copenhagen meeting of 1980. The International Organization for Migration (based in Geneva) has been especially active in promoting the empowerment of migrant women, drawing attention to the fact that many fora did not give migrant women the prominence they deserved and that references to them were scattered.

Models of incorporation

Having previously outlined issues concerning gender, citizenship and international conventions, we turn in this section to issues concerning models of incorporation. This concept is wider than individual economic, social and political rights, which we discussed earlier in the chapter, and includes collective identities and rights of minority groups. By incorporation we mean the ways in which migrants and minorities are treated in relation to the wider society and the degree to which the identity of groups is recognized. As with citizenship, models of incorporation represent ideal forms; different states may combine elements of several models. Official state rhetoric of assimilation may not capture a more dynamic reality, as Zincone (1998) comments in relation to France, one of the most assimilationist states in Europe. We should also recognize that divergent attitudes towards migrant and minority identities exist within the nation state. It is quite common in many European states to find different policies and levels of support for the expression of migrant identities at national and local levels. In many states the local level may be more responsive to migrant identities and the pursuit of anti-discrimination policies. There may also be significant differences between provincial and municipal authorities, especially in decentralized states, such as Germany, and those where the concrete application of policies is left to lower levels, as in Italy.

There is also no single available classification. We shall follow that outlined by Castles and Miller (1998), which links incorporation into the nation–state with the acquisition of citizenship by migrants and their children.[2] Their typology covers four main models: imperial, ethnic, republican and multicultural. As with other systems of classification, gender considerations are generally overlooked. Whilst there is a solid literature on the gender implications and critique of multiculturalism (Martin 1991; Saghal and Yuval-Davis 1992; Yuval-Davis 1997), there is very little to draw upon for the other models.

Each of these models has implications for the ways in which migrants can become members of the society, the extent to which in doing so they are able to retain their cultural identity, and the possibility for migrants of organizing autonomously and representing themselves. The latter includes the formation of associations for the pursuit of the rights of women migrants. European states differ in the number of years of residence and conditions migrants must fulfil to obtain citizenship. One of the key indicators of a willingness to incorporate migrants has been the ease with which children, who have either been born or educated in a country, may acquire citizenship and not be treated as migrants for the rest of their lives. They may acquire citizenship through *jus sanguinis*, which refers to citizenship passed on through kinship or *jus soli*, which is citizenship acquired through birth within a designated territory. In effect *jus domicili*, whereby children of migrants can make a simple declaration at an adult age following a specified number of years of residence, has become a common means of acquiring citizenship in states that do not admit of *jus soli*.[3] As we saw previously in chapter three, the situation is constantly changing and generally moving towards greater harmonization.

With calls for gender equality, both women and men have been able to transmit citizenship and this has contributed to greater prevalence of dual citizenship, which is in practice increasingly accepted by European states, even if not in principle.[4] For our purposes, we shall focus on the tensions and contradictions in the models and the implications they have for the role and treatment of women. For each of the models we have taken particular states as representative of the principles of a model, although, as noted above, we should be aware of disparities between local and national levels.

First, the *imperial model*, though no longer operative, has left its mark on several European societies. Its objective was to bring together ethnically and racially differentiated subjects of an Empire. Metropolitan powers, in particular France and the UK, initially denied citizenship to subjects deemed to be racially inferior, such as Muslims in Algeria. In the UK the 1914 Nationality Act removed any distinctions between inhabitants of its colonies and Britain, whereas the 1948 Nationality Act, gave all citizens, formerly subjects, the right to enter and reside in the country. The rights derived from marriage were quite different for women and men. The 1948 Act did not allow alien women married to British citizens to become citizens themselves. At the same time, dominions such as Canada declared their own citizenship. As colonies became independent states, their citizens ceased to be British citizens while the imposition of immigration restrictions undermined free entry to the UK. So by 1962 the imperial model effectively ceased to apply. However, for certain citizens of its White settler colonies, privileges, though much diminished, were maintained. Patrials (see Chapter 3) still have right of entry to the mother country. The French response has been slightly different. In some colonies, right of entry was halted because of hostilities; in others they were permanently incorporated as in the case of the French West Indies.

Second, the *ethnic model* is one in which the national community is passed on by descent, thereby excluding new minorities from citizenship but allowing automatic access to those with cultural links who live outside state borders. Citizenship is based on the principle of *jus sanguinis* and consequently difficult to acquire. It requires a relatively long period of residence, demonstration of a degree of assimilation and good knowledge of the language. This is the case with Germany where the hundreds of thousands of ethnic Germans from eastern Europe, who have settled since the late 1980s, have automatic access to citizenship. In contrast, children of immigrants do not become citizens through being born in the country. Although the laws were eased for children in 1991, they nevertheless must have undergone a number of years of schooling in the country and wait until adulthood before acquiring citizenship. The change in the German government in 1998 had led initially to the promise of further major change in Germany's citizenship laws to enable third country nationals, especially the large Turkish population, to become citizens after eight years of residence. As a result of a setback in the regional elections in September 1998, the SPD–Green government has backtracked. Children will have to choose between nationalities at the age of 23 which means that once again dual nationality is not permitted. It is thought this is one of the most significant factors dissuading the Turkish population from taking up citizenship. According to research conducted by the Turkish Research Centre in Germany, half of German Turks would take out German citizenship if they could retain their Turkish citizenship (JCWI 1999: 12).

The ethnic model made it more difficult for new minorities to establish independent associations and to achieve their own voice (Joppke 1995), although, over the years as they have become embedded in the host society, migrants are able to found their own bodies free from the tutelage of indigenous officials. In the earlier years, special welfare provision was usually delegated to charitable organizations linked with churches and labour organizations (Castles and Miller 1998: 229). Even today, the Commissioners for Foreigners generally have little power and act mainly as consultative bodies, although there is a wide divergence between cities, with socialist and Green councils being the most liberal towards migrants.

It is no accident that Germany should have some of the most restrictive family reunion policies and prolonged periods of dependency for spouses before they can obtain their own right to residence and employment. As we highlighted in the previous chapter, it was thought that preventing women from entering the labour market would serve to dissuade family reunion. The subordination of migrants, even in organizations set up to meet their specific needs, meant that migrant women found it difficult to create their own associations. However, migrant, and especially

Islamic, women are generally seen as bearers of tradition and part of the problem (Kolinsky 1996). This may be compared with policies towards migrant women in France where their potential as modernizers is played upon by official authorities (Kofman 1997).

Third, the *republican model* is one where the nation is defined as a political community to which newcomers are admitted providing they accept the political norms and national culture. In principle, it does not recognize the right of minorities to make claims for cultural recognition and social rights on the basis of their group identity. In France, the emphasis on cultural assimilation of earlier decades has been challenged by academics and migrants alike. It is also unstable to the extent that the state, especially at the local level, no longer pursues an undifferentiated cultural model or refuses to recognize ethnic affiliation. In the 1980s, the state encouraged the establishment of Muslim organizations. There now exist umbrella migrant and anti-racist associations as well as more nationally-oriented groups, including a range of groups representing women migrants (Mahé 1992; Quiminal 1997).

The acquisition of citizenship for first generation migrants does not necessitate a lengthy period of residence. Pasqua's legislation in 1993 had forced children of migrants to confirm they wanted to be citizens. The return of the socialists into power in 1997 reintroduced automatic citizenship at the age of eighteen years for those born in France of migrant parents who had lived in France since the age of eleven (Farine 1998). What may be as significant a change is the flurry of activity and discussion about the pernicious effect of discrimination confronted by migrants and racialized populations (CERC 1999; Haut Conseil à l'Intégration 1998; Hommes et Migrations 1999). If an independent Commission is set up and sanctions against discrimination on the basis of origin are strengthened, then this will bring France closer to countries practising multicultural policies who have set up anti-discrimination legislation across a wide range of sectors (see below).

Concern with assimilation and integration in France has influenced policies towards women migrants. Seen as caught between tradition and modernity, women have received attention from successive governments since the early 1980s in their potential role as vectors of integration (Kofman 1997). In recent years, funding has been made available for training and maintaining women as mediators (*femmes-relais*) for new migrants and their contact with the welfare and educational bodies (Bentchicou 1997).

Official funding has been provided to a number of migrant women's organizations, especially at the local level where it is felt they are most effective. Research programmes were developed to study gender and generational relations in neighbourhoods and the distinctive role of young women, especially of North African origin (Gaspard 1992).

Fourth, the *multicultural model* is based on the idea that the nation–state contains a degree of plurality that allows migrants to retain their cultural identity provided they adhere to the political norms. This does not negate the existence of a dominant culture. Variants of a multicultural model have been adopted in the Netherlands, Sweden, and the UK. Multiculturalism has a number of aspects so that policies may shift over time. It may involve the recognition of cultural pluralism or provision for the specific economic and social needs of ethnic and national groups, which may take on responsibilities for the welfare of their communities. Multiculturalism may also include the demand for economic and social equality between migrants and the wider society, thus leading to the establishment of anti-discrimination policies accompanied by sanctions. Multiculturalism is not always an entirely positive development because, in practice, it may encourage and fix essentialist and static views of migrant identities, as has increasingly been highlighted in the Sweden case (Alund and Schierup 1993; Alund 1998).

Most states professing multicultural policies have developed anti-discrimination and anti-racist policies backed up by sanctions. The first to be implemented was the Race Discrimination Act of 1976 in the UK. In Sweden, indirect policies with the aim of guaranteeing access to general social programmes, and direct policies concerned with special needs (multilingual education, information services) have been implemented. Although associations are generously funded, the government determines which ones are worthy of being funded, and is thus able to exert considerable social control. It tends to encourage organization by ethnicity at the local level, thus making it difficult to build bridges and migrant political alliances across these differences. Alund and Schierup (1993: 140) speak of 'prescribed multiculturalism' whereby immigrants and ethnic organizations are co-opted into the corporatist state and politically marginalized. On the other hand, it has taken many years for specific legislation banning ethnic discrimination to be passed. To some extent the pressure to do so arose from Sweden's ratification of international conventions and growing experience of discrimination by the second generation and new refugees (Graham and Soninen 1998). It also took until 1994 for the Netherlands to introduce an Employment Equity Act and in 1995 a General Law on Equal Treatment covering race, ethnicity and religion (Penninx 1996).

Criticisms of an excessive emphasis on difference, to the detriment of shared problems and a more combative anti-racist stance, have been made in several countries. The Netherlands Minorities Policy was altered in response to the critique of its emphasis on cultural aspects. Just as in other models of incorporation, official rhetoric does not necessarily correspond to the reality of migrants' lives nor their acceptance by the wider society, which may demand a high degree of conformity to dominant values. Such has been an increasingly vociferous critique of and disillusionment with Swedish multiculturalism, which has left migrants with unequal rights and leading segregated existences (Alund 1998).

Multicultural citizenship, as we have noted, runs the risk of essentializing and freezing timeless cultural differences within the boundaries of homogeneous ethnic groups. Feminists, in particular, have levelled critiques against the patriarchal nature of multicultural policies that support male leadership and the persistence of traditional values (Martin 1991; Yuval-Davis 1997).[5] They have questioned who is empowered to interpret and impose cultural norms. State and other institutions may accept cultural norms that communities have transplanted from home society, such as the conduct of women in private and public, without any real considerations of the changes in the economic and social environment in which a custom is practised. This has been the case of polygamous marriages in France (pp. 87–8). There may be little reflection about the interplay of social forces between particular cultures and the wider society. Multiculturalism may represent a more liberal tolerance of what goes on in the private sphere of different migrant groups but this can leave intact gender inequalities and repressive practices towards women. The case of domestic violence exemplifies the tolerance of practices in the private sphere on grounds of non-intervention in the customs of others. Social workers may therefore fail to intervene in cases of domestic violence.

At the same time, there has been more discussion and activity between ethnic minority, migrant and indigenous women, especially in the UK. The fact that ethnic minority feminists have generally been citizens, some of whom are employed in professional occupations, has undoubtedly played a part. Feminist movements have raised issues around the interplay of racism and sexism; which has also been addressed by official bodies (Equal Opportunities Commission 1995). By the mid-1980s, ethnic minority women began to challenge the dominant concerns of White women over the meaning and role of marriage and housework (*Feminist Review* 1985). Ethnic and migrant women have also been able to organize autonomously (Sudbury 1998).

Not all countries can be easily slotted into the above models. New countries of immigration, such as Italy and Spain, have only recently developed policies towards immigration and models of incorporation (Danese 1998a,b). Although these countries are some of the few European countries who were signatories to key international conventions passed by the ILO in the 1970s and incorporated them into their constitutions, the large proportion of undocumented migrants does not mean these conventions give protection to many of their migrant population. Both countries have a strongly developed policy towards territorial minorities, such as the Basques and Catalans in Spain, but the development of multicultural policies in respect of migrant minorities has been slower. Recent Italian legislation on immigration (European Coordination 1998) has left the implementation of social and cultural policies in the hands of local authorities.

Conclusion

Despite the proliferation of international conventions and human rights instruments, citizenship still determines to a large extent the rights that different categories of migrants are able to exercise. The establishment of European Union citizenship has widened the gap between citizens and third country nationals. What we have highlighted is the significance of gender roles and relations in determining the impact of international conventions on individual rights. We saw that women who married outside of their national communities or crossed borders were deprived of some of the most basic rights of citizenship and that since the 1980s these radical differences have generally been erased. However, migrant women, whether of third country or European origin, have still to attain independent rather than derived citizenship rights if they move as members of a family. Even where these rights are the same as those of male migrants, women may find that their weaker economic position may make it more difficult to exercise certain rights, as in family migration.

In the second part of the chapter, we outlined the different models of incorporation and the ways in which gender relations are raised and dealt with in each of them. Despite critiques levelled at multicultural models of incorporation, the greater openness of these societies to debating and enacting legislation and acknowledging differences has also meant that gender relations and equal opportunities issues are easier to raise.

Notes

1 By this time British feminist literature did encompass a Black and ethnic minority, which, it was assumed, were formally citizens but whose status fell short of full substantive citizenship because of racial and sexual discrimination. The situation in other European countries has been varied, but one could generally say that ethnic minority and migrant women have been ignored in discussions of citizenship. The failure to address racial discrimination until recently and enact effective legislation by the European Commission has not helped to advance a more widespread consideration of migrants and women.

2 Different definitions, Soysal's for example, actually include a number of elements such as economic, social and political rights, that are normally discussed in conceptualizations of citizenship.

3 Sweden, for example, allows young people aged between twenty-one and twenty-three years, if they have lived in Sweden for five years before they were sixteen years old, and are still in the country, to make a simple declaration to obtain citizenship. Similarly, in Germany, as from 1991, young people between sixteen and twenty-three years old, with eight years of residence and six years of schooling, may apply for citizenship.

4 A number of states signed a Convention in 1963 to simplify multiple citizenships and reduce the extent of dual citizenship. However, with greater mobility, objections to it are more than ever divorced from the reality of migrant aspirations and situations. Many children of mixed marriages now have dual citizenships. The effects of the German reform facilitating the acquisition of citizenship by children of migrants has been blunted by the refusal to recognize dual citizenship by the German authorities, although Turkish authorities are now willing to give back citizenship more readily. On the other hand, the international norm is being undermined by a number of European states, which no longer require renunciation (Belgium, Greece, Ireland, Portugal, the UK). The new European Convention of Nationality (1997), while not abrogating the 1963 Convention, allows states to permit dual nationality if they wish. One of the main rationales for this changed position was to enable spouses to take the nationality

of the other and encourage the unity of nationality within the same family (Koslowski 1998: 742–3).

5 Many of the most trenchant critiques have emanated from feminists in countries where multiculturalism has been practised for several decades and where ethnic organizations are used to sustain welfare provision, as in Australia.

Chapter 5

Migration and women's work in Europe

Since the onset of migrant labour demand in the post-war period the economies of Europe have undergone massive re-structuring and change, changes that not only tore the heart out of the traditional centres of labour intensive and extractive industries in north western European economies, but virtually decimated the traditional labour movement. We have witnessed the continuing rise of women's paid employment and a continuing decline in full-time male jobs (Eurostat 1997) leading many to talk of 'the feminization of the labour force'. This phrase not only refers to the increased numbers of women in paid employment but also to a deterioration in the terms upon which both men and women are employed in the pursuit of 'flexibility' in the workforce. With the imposition of deregulated working practices, to varying degrees in different countries, an increasing number of employees are no longer protected by the level of social security they would have previously enjoyed. Although the UK led the way in the timing of deregulation, France and Germany too had by the mid-1980s begun to loosen the regulation of work contracts. Fewer employees can now expect the kind of permanency, and security or employment protection, that characterized so much of male employment twenty-five years ago.

Despite increased integration into European labour markets, women are still on average paid about 20 per cent less than their male counterparts (European Commission 1996). These inequalities become heightened among migrant women who face a 'double set of sexist relations' to those internal to the migrant group and to those of the dominant group and the state (Anthias 1993: 165). Thus, the average earnings of migrant women in Germany were just 48.4 per cent of that for German men (Reitz *et al.* 1999).

Furthermore, the patterns of disadvantage vary with country of origin with some ethnic minority groups, as for example the Turks in Germany, receiving lower wages than other foreigners.

There is also evidence of a much greater polarization in women's work, with low paid highly routinized service work at one end and better paid managerial and administrative jobs at the other. Some of the discussions of this polarization have focused on the experiences of 'global cities' such as London, Paris and Amsterdam, with migrant women servicing the more highly paid transient migrant workforce, which is disproportionately male (Sassen 1991). Women in particular have taken up part-time and temporary jobs, many of which are not accompanied by full social entitlements. Deregulation is not necessarily the cause of growth in part-time employment, as for example in the UK, where part-time employment is extremely common (Bruegel 1999). However elsewhere it has increased: in France, Germany and Ireland by between 10 and 11 per cent from 1985 to 1991 with even more spectacular increases in Belgium (20 per cent) and the Netherlands (40 per cent).

There are thus large intra-European national differences in the nature of the labour market and in the employment positionings experienced by women within the European Union. Some are citizens of member states, some are not, some enjoy the privileges that 'whiteness' confers and some experience racialized discrimination, whether or not they are citizens, some women have documents allowing the right to reside and to employment within the EU, others do not. The range of diversity is endless. Besides, women's position also shifts with time, leading to complex patterns 'in which legal entries can generate illegal overstayers and – subsequently – legal migrants, all within a two- or three-year period' (Cross 1998: 247). Women migrants also follow different occupational trajectories during their life course, which particularly influences the 'life-chances' of the next generation. But as we shall in this chapter, women's migration into Europe reflects the polarization of women's jobs more generally. Migrant women do not enter European labour markets on equal terms. Apart from the highly qualified it has become progressively more difficult for so-called 'economic' migrants to enter the European Union and work legally in the last twenty-five years. This has not meant that men and women have stopped entering Europe for purposes of finding employment, but it does mean that they often work for a number of years, at least, without documents. Added to this we still have a situation in many countries where women who enter as spouses have to wait for up to four years to enter the labour market legally.

The scale and pace of economic and political change world-wide has changed the nature of migration, with new refugees, asylum seekers and undocumented migrants displacing labour migrants as the numerically significant group of migrants to Europe. A continuing concern remains over the fate of those millions of men and women in Europe of all ages and generations who continue to experience racialized discrimination at work, whether they are citizens or non-citizens of member states. Most countries in Europe have now come to realize that racialized discrimination is endemic in European labour markets and that some form of legislation is necessary to combat it, but progress on this front is uneven (see Chapter 4). When we consider the kinds of low skill, low paid jobs that migrants entered in the post war European boom we would expect to see by now a real improvement in occupational mobility, but this has been limited and uneven. For many it has been a case of moving horizontally, in some cases into self-employment of a precarious nature.

In this chapter we begin by looking briefly at the positioning of migrant and ethnic minority women within the context of changing European labour markets over the last 30 years. This analysis concentrates on Britain, France and Germany initially and then goes on to take account of migration in southern Europe, which only took on numerical significance in the 1990s. We go on to consider four case studies: domestic work and sex work, which currently constitute the main source of employment for incoming migrant women from outside the EU, and clothing production and small businesses. The latter industries also constitute important sources of employment for migrant and ethnic minority women alike. In the final section, we examine reasons for the lack of attention paid to skilled migrants and how skills are socially constructed.

Changing labour markets

Looking back to the early 1970s we can see how certain patterns of employment for migrant women became established. A report published by the European Commission argued

> Working women in the community countries eschew employ-
> ment in domestic and servile jobs in preference for service

occupations in which a greater number of openings has become available. There is thus room at the bottom of the ladder for the women immigrants to tackle the 'women's work'.

(Delacourt 1975: 103)

In comparison to Germany, Britain and France have very similar migrant labour histories, both drawing on colonial and ex-colonial labour as well as labour from the European periphery, and doing so in a way that was not, in the main, officially organized. Both countries have also had a long history of recruitment of migrant women for domestic work; even in the nineteenth century Irish women migrated to escape poverty and hunger to work in British households, a migration that became officially encouraged in the twentieth century. In the immediate post-World War II period Irish women in domestic work were joined by Italian, Spanish and Portuguese women, the latter requiring work permits at that time (MacDonald and Macdonald 1972). The 1950s and 1960s saw the entry into Britain of African Caribbean and Cypriot women workers, neither of whom prior to 1962 needed a labour voucher to work, nor if they entered as a spouse after that date. Many women from the Caribbean came as independent workers, not as part of a process of family reunion (Phizacklea 1982). In contrast, few women from India, Pakistan or Bangladesh came to Britain outside of a family reunion or marriage context. None of the women who were drawn from different parts of the old British empire could be legally channelled into specific parts of the labour market, but the reality was that by 1971 they were already over-represented in the lowest paid, although not necessarily the least skilled, sectors of the British labour market. In contrast, foreign workers from outside the 'new Commonwealth' were subject to the work permit system and special quotas were set aside for the recruitment of domestic workers in hospitals, hotels and private homes. Filipino and Malaysian women took up the largest share of permits in this category. In 1980, the special quota for domestic workers was abandoned and replaced by a concession that allowed employers to bring their domestic workers into the country as a type of 'chattel'. The domestic worker was tied to that employer and if for any reason he or she left the employment of the named employer he or she could be subject to deportation. As we shall see in the domestic worker case study the concession was widely abused by employers over the eighteen years of its existence.

By 1971, the clustering of Caribbean, Irish, Malaysian, Mauritian, West African and some Filipino women in the 'professional' category was somewhat misleading. The vast majority were in fact located either in nursing or allied medical services and in the least desirable sectors of nursing (*Department of Employment* 1976). The other industries in which migrant women were over-represented in 1971 were engineering and allied trades, and clothing production (Department of Employment 1976: 121).

A very similar picture was evident in the 1975 census in France. Whereas 30 per cent of foreign women were located in non-market services (read domestic workers), by 1975 only 1 per cent of French women were left in this category. Just as we shall see in the case of Italy later, French natives had shunned domestic work. In fact foreign women's share of unskilled work in France rose sharply between 1962 and 1975 (Singer-Kerel 1980). Where Britain and France differed greatly from Germany at this time was that family reunion was possible for many migrant groups and women from predominantly Muslim backgrounds who had low economic activity rates. For instance, only 16 per cent of Pakistani women were deemed to be economically active in Britain in the early 1970s, and 28 per cent of Tunisian women in France (BELC 1976; Smith 1977).

Germany was very different, the 'guest worker' system discouraged family migration so that even amongst Turkish women the economic activity rate was 44 per cent (*Bundesansalt für Arbeit* 1980). In June 1969, 70 per cent of foreign women in Germany were located in manufacturing: this was before the big push in Germany towards a relocation of labour intensive manufacturing work to low-wage countries. A decade later the number of foreign women in manufacturing had fallen to 57 per cent, paralleled by a big increase of their share in hotels and catering (*Bundesansalt für Arbeit* 1980). In other words, we see more clearly in Germany the way in which the employment structure for migrant women was already changing by the end of the 1960s. Decreased demand in manufacturing reflected global changes in the location of manufacturing work and increased demand in the service sector. The major difference between migrant and German women's employment is that this shift did not represent an improvement in the type of work carried out by migrant women as they remained concentrated in the manual sectors of service work.

Finally there is the question of whether or not migrant women were more vulnerable to job loss than women as whole. The short answer is yes, in all three countries. Not only were migrant and ethnic minority women experiencing higher levels of job loss and bouts of unemployment than women generally, but by the early 1970s these levels were higher than those experienced by ethnic minority men and men generally.

Moving on a decade to the late 1980s comparisons between the three countries become more difficult for a number of reasons. In Britain, the categories of 'White' and 'ethnic minority group' were used in the Labour Force Survey, but for the purposes of European-wide statistics anyone without British citizenship had become classified as a 'foreigner'. French principles of universalism mean that a person is either a French citizen or a foreigner, and officially the category of ethnic minority is not recognized. In Germany, the restrictive nature of nationality law means that it is very difficult to become a German if one is not born 'German by blood'. Thus indicators provide a very imprecise picture over time and across generations. Despite these problems, it is apparent that certain patterns continued to characterize the employment of migrant and ethnic minority women in the three countries.

In Britain, as early as 1982, the Third Policy Studies Institute Survey of Ethnic Minorities was beginning to show a closing of the gap between the job levels of ethnic minority women as compared with women generally (Brown 1984). Nevertheless, the much higher rates of unemployment amongst ethnic minority women led the authors of this survey to conclude that the apparent bridging of the gap was largely illusory. Ethnic minority women in the poorest, most vulnerable jobs were becoming unemployed whereas those in the better jobs were as a result becoming a larger proportion of all those in employment. In addition, ethnic minority women were far more likely to be working full-time (40 per cent as against 27 per cent of all women). When full-time jobs are disaggregated, there remain continuing concentrations of Caribbean women in nursing (but not health administration) and Asian women in clothing production. Full-time work lifts many women out of low-pay ghettos, but this is less true for ethnic minority women in Britain. The 1982 survey showed that in all types of households the earned income per person was lower among Caribbeans than the population as a whole, and even lower in Asian households (Brown 1984: 231).

By the early 1990s, the ethnic minorities were becoming more mobile but suffered from much higher unemployment rates. The Fourth PSI National Survey of Ethnic Minorities in 1994 revealed more pronounced disparities between minority groups, which was substantiated by detailed statistical evidence on job levels and earnings. Hence Modood (1998) suggested that what needs to be explained is both racial inequality and ethnic diversity. In terms of relative improvement in employee job levels, Caribbean women had made the most progress closely followed by White and African Asian women since the Third Survey in 1982. Chinese women were in the best position of all women. In terms of the earnings of those employed full-time, the average earnings of ethnic minority women were better than for White women, especially amongst Caribbean, Indian and African Asian women. Modood (1998: 62–3) comments that the general progress in job levels (men and women) and earnings may be a sign that they are returning to their pre-migration occupational levels. Migration for many represented downward mobility as those of professionals origin failed to secure posts and the petit bourgeoisie were proletarianized. For others, such as the Pakistanis and Bangladeshis, they have remained amongst the most disadvantaged in the labour force.

In France, exactly the same pattern of aggregate data was evident by the end of the 1980s. While on the one hand, the gap between French and 'foreign' women's job levels had shrunk, on the other hand, 'foreign' women were still more likely to be found in manufacturing than French women, twice as likely to be unemployed and less likely to be found in the more 'desirable' sectors of 'women's work (INSEE 1989). There were also significant inter-ethnic variations in unemployment, with Turkish women having unemployment rates as high as 48 per cent (Salon 1996, cited in Samers 1998). On the other hand there were also intra-ethnic variations, with 75 per cent of the Antillais immigrants in Sarcelles (a northern suburb of Paris) in the early 1990s being women (Veillard-Baron 1994, cited in Samers 1998).

In Germany, foreign women took the brunt of manufacturing job losses in feminized sectors in the early 1980s, but by the end of the decade there had been a considerable rise in employment for women generally in Germany. Nevertheless foreign women were still over-represented in manufacturing compared with women generally (42 as against 24 per cent) and more likely to be located in the manual sectors of 'women's' work (*Bundesanstalt für Arbeit* 1990).

In Sweden, while there was an increase of 14 per cent in employment rates for foreign born women between 1960 and 1990, closer inspection of these figures reveal that this increase did not keep pace with the rise in employment rates for Swedish women (Bevelander 1999). Besides, there were large variations between different groups of migrant women, with migrants from Nordic countries and Germany having higher growth rates in the early part of this period. In the 1970s and 1980s, of the larger immigrant groups, employment rates increased for Chilean women but decreased for Iranian women (Bevelander 1999).

Migrant women are often educationally disadvantaged, both within the secondary education system and in further training opportunities, and this limits their labour force participation. For instance, among Italian and Greek migrants to Germany, the proportion of those who lack both schooling and vocational training is 25 to 32 per cent for men, but 35 to 60 per cent for women (Reitz *et al.* 1999). Nearly half the disparities between labour market returns of migrants and nationals in Germany arose from their lower educational status. Furthermore, even those who obtain training find that their employment opportunities are restricted. Goldberg *et al.* (1995) found that only 66 per cent of young women were employed in the professions that they had learnt, although this percentage drops to 42 per cent for young men. An ILO study in the Netherlands revealed that 28 per cent of job applications by Surinamese female applicants for jobs in the retail trade and service sector were rejected immediately, after the applicant revealed their surname (Bovenkerk n. d.). However, the same study went on to show that the extent of discrimination in hiring practices declined for jobs requiring a college education.

Discrimination may also be age specific with unemployment particularly affecting those at either end of their working lives. In Germany, unemployment has particularly affected those in the twenty to thirty years age bracket, although the figures do not vary much between men and women in this age range (Goldberg *et al.* 1995).

Despite mounting evidence of discrimination, migrants may also find themselves without formal labour rights. In Germany, some of the fundamental rights are reserved solely for Germans, as for instance, the right of access to public authority (Article 33, Section 2). Migrant workers are also not eligible for protection against discrimination, although it has ratified Convention no. 97 of the International Labour Organization under which Germany is obliged to prevent such discrimination (Goldberg *et al.* 1995).

Both in the Netherlands and Sweden, increasing unemployment rates among migrant women also arise out of the increase in labour force participation of indigenous White women who have pushed migrants out of work, especially in the service sector (Samers 1998; Bevelander 1999). As a result of all these factors, undocumented employment has become an increasing reality for many migrant and ethnic minority communities throughout Europe, as it has world-wide. The 1998 SOPEMI country report for Germany includes the following paragraph:

> The illegal employment of foreign labour persists, despite numerous efforts to combat the entry of illegal foreign immigrants. Criminal trafficking organizations are developing, especially those smuggling workers in from the central and eastern European countries. Since 1994, some 30,000 foreign nationals have been apprehended each year after entering the country illegally, most frequently via the borders with Poland and Czech Republic. Breaches of labour legislation on the illegal employment of foreign workers have risen sharply (86,800 in 1996 compared with 79,500 the previous year).
>
> (SOPEMI 1998: 110)

Any discussion of undocumented migration is politically sensitive. Although social scientists may often have not addressed the issue of undocumented migration, as in Germany (Wilpert 1998: 269), far right parties (and others) in Europe have however made a great deal of political capital from exploiting the issue. What has come to be called the 'migration industry' (individuals and organizations involved in the transportation and often job placement of persons without documents, traffickers, etc.), and unscrupulous employers have at the same time made a great deal of financial capital out of the most vulnerable group in any labour market, the undocumented.

The use of the word 'illegal' rather than undocumented is favoured by the political right because it conveys criminality. The reality is of course that it is nation states or groups of nation states (e.g. The Schengen Group of states in Europe) that define the legal status of migrants through immigration controls and rules. Processes of globalization, including transnational flows of capital, trade and investment, global communication systems and transportation, in themselves result in social change and dislocation. Political transformations and the continuing and widening gap in living standards between the North and the South have also led to an acceleration in migration. Immigration controls do not stop people from migrating and the undocumented are many and varied, as we saw in Chapter 4. These and many other groups are invisible in aggregate data, but because of their need to earn a living do join the ranks of unrecorded workers.

In this respect it is important to see undocumented migrant workers within the context of a spectrum of unrecorded work encompassing many millions of people in Europe. Building workers who use the 'tools of their trade' to work at the weekends, homeworkers who make everything from clothes to security alarms, for example. The difference is that undocumented migrant workers may have no right to reside or only a derived right, and may be subject to deportation if they come to the notice of the authorities. For many migrant women entering Europe there is no option. A great deal is made of ethnic minority women's 'lack of skills', their 'language deficiencies' and in some cases, their irregular legal status. There is little doubt that employers have trotted out these standard phrases in rationalizing their payment of low wages and poor working conditions (Phizacklea 1983b). What is often overlooked is the role of the state in shaping job status through immigration policy and rules. At one extreme are those workers who find themselves in an irregular status often caused by factors outside their control (as we shall see in the case of domestic workers who become overstayers). Then there are those workers who are tied to a specific form of work by the work permit system. Finally there are those migrants who enter as spouses under regulations permitting family reunion, and who in some countries require a minimum period of residence before they can enter the labour market. Families are thus forced to settle without access to welfare, pushing many into poverty and, for some, unregistered work.

Sex work, domestic work

In the late 1970s in Europe there still existed a demand for labour throughout most sectors of the economy. Migrant women could, for instance, be found in most feminized sectors of manufacturing as well as most service industries. But more recent migrant women find that, in Europe, apart from sex work or domestic work, the avenues for employment are almost closed to them. There is now widespread recognition that the restrictive immigration policies practised by virtually all states that receive migrant labour do not stop migration, they simply increase the number of migrants who are clandestine. This increase in clandestine migrant labour is not simply a feature of the traditional destinations for migrant labour such as the US and Europe, but now characterizes much of the migration within Asia – a region where migration has rapidly increased alongside lop-sided development and industrialization, some states experiencing wage rises and labour scarcity, others the exact opposite (Anderson 1997a: 2). Some of this industrialization has opened up opportunities for women in export-oriented industries, making clothes, electronics, toys, etc., but the work is low paid and precarious, and finding work abroad can present a more lucrative option. And there is no shortage of recruiters, the migration industry thrives: nine out of ten foreign placements for Asian workers are handled by recruiters in some form, with an increasingly high proportion of those recruited now being women. Official figures continue to show a higher proportion of men migrating for reasons of work than women (Zlotnik 1995); but as all the regularization programmes indicate in Europe, official figures provide a misleading picture. Lim and Oishi (1996) argue that official data are also based solely on figures relating to officially recorded overseas employment migration. These figures take no account of women who leave as tourists or students and then end up working in their destination country, nor those who use undocumented channels.

A high proportion of these women will find themselves working in either the sex industry or in domestic work in a private household because this is where the demand for their services rests. Truong (1996) argues that there are three main reasons for this. The first, is the withdrawal of state services for the young and the elderly. We would add that in the case of southern Europe, these services have never been particularly well developed and the regularization programmes in Greece, Italy and Spain reflect this. It is an admission of the inadequacy of these services. The second reason is the rapid increase of women in waged work without a commensurate change in attitude towards the traditional division of labour in the home. The third factor is the expansion of the 'hospitality' industry and the increased mobility of the male workforce whose needs must be 'catered' for. What Truong calls 'sex affective' services are being increasingly built into the corporate management apparatus: 'Once a corporation allows its employees to claim entertainment as business costs, entertainment enters the corporate management system and becomes repeated in different branches and locations' (Truong 1996: 36).

Over the last twenty years there has been a rapid increase in the sex-related entertainment industry in affluent and newly industrializing countries, in some cases it has become an integral part of the tourist industry in those countries. An estimated 50,000 Thai women and 80,000 Filipino women work illegally in the Japanese sex industry (Anderson 1997: 16). Even when women can avoid prostitution as legal 'guests', they may be forced into it as indebted overstayers (Anderson 1997a: 28).

Similar stories of indebtedness characterize Thai women's experience of being trafficked to Germany, but it is from central and eastern Europe that increased numbers of women are now coming. It is estimated that approximately two-thirds of the 30,000 migrant sex workers in Italy are from Albania. Newspapers in the East openly carry advertisements such as 'Erotic work. Knowledge of foreign languages an advantage' or 'Young girls needed for work in Italy' (*Guardian* April 25th 1997: 10). The same story reports how openly traffickers were operating in Hungary: one trafficker arguing 'they can get as much in an hour as they would in a month at home'. Poles can enter Germany on three month tourist or visitor visas, although these visas do not permit them to work. But NGOs working with Polish women in Berlin report the ease with which sex work can be found.

Many of the accounts of sex work are harrowing in the extreme, so why do women get involved? For many there is a high level of deception, recruiters may say that the work on offer is waitressing or domestic work. But Kempadoo argues that this is not always the case:

> Sex work is another resource that women rely on to support and shelter themselves and families . . . to buy a plot of land . . . or to more generally improve the quality of life for themselves and kin. The amount they can potentially earn in the sex trade on a temporary short-term basis can be an initial pull and can be a retaining force.
>
> (Kempadoo 1998: 128)

But she goes on to argue that while all migrant workers are vulnerable to exploitation because of their unfamiliarity with the migration setting, their lack of citizenship rights, their dependency on agents and racism in the migration setting, all of this is worse in the sex trade because of the outlawed nature of prostitution and the moral condemnation of commercial sex (Kempadoo 1998: 130).

It would be wrong to cast all sex workers as victims, as some will choose sex work over domestic work because it is better paid. But this assumes that the individual has at least some measure of control over the terms upon which they work and accurate information. Many, including children, have no idea what kind of work the village 'recruitment agents' have in mind for them. Psimmenos' work in Athens with Albanians indicates that the fourteen- to sixteen-year old girls and boys, much favoured for sex work, had all identity papers removed by traffickers once in Greece, who in turn had no use for them after seventeen years of age (Psimmenos 1996). Children who have been intercepted working in the sex trade without documents have in the past been simply deported, (in the year 1995–6, over 19,000 people without documents were deported from Greece (SOPEMI 1998: 115)). Policing authorities have been slow to recognize that simply 'bussing out' undocumented sex workers as 'undesirable aliens' is not the solution to trafficking, the traffickers go free and the workers are left unemployed and stigmatized in their home country.

Public reaction to the often harrowing evidence of conditions of work, of non-payment of wages, of debt and deceit experienced by sex and domestic workers as well as many others, is often 'then why do people continue to migrate?' Goss and Lindquist's excellent research in the Philippines suggests that the more institutionalized migration becomes, the more fraudulent and corrupt the system becomes. Despite this, individuals still seek employment abroad. The authors conclude that:

> Of course this is an indication of relative deprivation in the country but it is also the result of the selective flow of information through the migrant institution. Institutional agents control knowledge about the risks and disappointments of international migration, but it is obviously in their interest to hide these and to promote the advantages of overseas labour.
>
> (Goss and Lindquist 1995: 344)

The politics of sex work involves a wide spectrum of opinion, many arguing that the 'hype' around trafficking is unhelpful in aiding serious debate (Doezema 1998; Murray 1998). Murray (1998: 64) argues that it is 'important to distinguish different types of sex trade work. The situations that the anti-traffickers rail against, insofar as they exist, are a result of economic, political and gender inequalities and it is those inequalities which should be our central cause for concern.' As existing laws and Conventions cover the issues of slavery, non-consensual sex and the exploitation of children, then the issue, Murray (1998: 63) argues, is their ratification and enforcement by all states and the de-criminalization of prostitution. The problem remains that information about migration and sex work is patchy and often unreliable, relying heavily on journalism or very small-scale studies and is highly coloured by which side of the political fence you are positioned.

The other large growth industry world-wide for migrant women is domestic work. The demand for domestic workers world-wide has increased dramatically over the last ten years (Gregson and Lowe 1994). As the number of dual-earner couples has increased in the affluent countries so too has the demand for maids, very often a demand that requires the domestic workers to live with the family. Rather than couples questioning patriarchal household and work structures (such as the 'man-made' day) and re-organizing domestic labour and child-care on a shared basis, the preferred option has increasingly become one of buying in replacement labour for these chores. Macklin (1994) and Hondagneu-Sotelo (1994) both provide accounts of the demand for undocumented domestic migrant labour in the US, and research carried out by Anderson in five European countries in 1996 indicates that the practice of employing undocumented migrant women to carry out a wide range of domestic tasks is also widespread (Anderson and Phizacklea 1997; the research is reported in full in Anderson 2000). Not only are we looking at a situation in Europe of improving educational and employment opportunities for female European Union citizens, we are also looking at a situation of an increasingly ageing population (Walker and Maltby 1997). In southern Europe, welfare services are poorly developed and whereas in the past women in extended families would have been obliged to care for the elderly, the breakdown of the extended family and the obligations that went with it are leaving a very large gap. Countries, such as Italy, Greece and Spain, recognize the demand for domestic work by either regularizing large numbers of undocumented domestic workers at frequent intervals or actually setting aside a certain quota of work permits every year for this occupation. (In Spain, the annual quota of 9000 work permits for domestic workers has historically been used to regularize the position of women already working in Spain in an undocumented status.) There is widespread admission that migrant workers are carrying out work that EU nationals are no longer prepared to do (such as live-in domestic work).

There are many forms of domestic work and although migrants dominate domestic work, some better paid, more secure, higher status categories of domestic work continue to employ indigenous men and women. For instance, Cox (1999) found that the au pairs in London whom she interviewed were largely European, mother's helps and nannies were either British or from the old Commonwealth, whereas housekeepers, cleaners, cooks and maids were from a variety of nationalities, particularly from Portugal, Philippines and Spain.

The case of Italy and the demand and supply of domestic workers to that country is instructive here. On the demand side, the increased number of Italian women in employment (particularly in the north), the reluctance of Italian nationals to engage in domestic work and even in politically progressive regions such as Emilia Romagna, a dearth of welfare provision for the elderly and disabled has resulted in an increased and continuing demand for migrant domestic workers (Hoskyns and Orsini-Jones 1994: 11).

On the supply side, domestic work is an area of employment increasingly shunned by Italian nationals and in turn increasingly regarded as 'migrant women's' work. In January 1996 there were 991,419 third country nationals residing legally in Italy. One of the largest nationality groups with work permits are Filipinos who, at the end of 1993, numbered 46,332, of whom 70 per cent were female (Ministero dell'interno 31.12.93, quoted in Iris di Rimini 1995 statistical annexe: 7).

The migrant labour force in Italy is heavily segregated by ethnicity and gender, for example Filipinos are predominantly women and predominantly domestic workers, whereas Moroccans (the largest non-EU national group in Italy with work permits) are predominantly male and clustered in construction and agriculture.

Andall's historical analysis of the migrant domestic workforce in Italy traces the demand for such workers back to the late 1960s. She argues that Italian domestic workers had become increasingly reluctant to work as live-in domestic workers and by the early 1970s were working largely on an hourly basis; 'This left a specific gap in the market for live-in domestic work, which migrant women would be forced (institutionally) and encouraged (informally) to fill' (Andall 1996: 10). Andall's argument is that while the Italian government aimed to discourage the employment of migrant domestic workers by the late 1970s, its earlier decision to confine migrant domestic workers to full-time work probably contributed to the attractiveness of non-Italian national workers for the Italian employer (they were not allowed entry to work on an hourly basis like Italian nationals). In 1979, their employment situation was limited further by tying their entry to a specific employer. Andall's research clearly indicates that employment within the sector at this time was equally available to documented and undocumented labour.

In 1986, the Italian government suspended the issuing of labour permits for domestic workers altogether, but provided for a regularization of undocumented immigrants. During the regularization period, which lasted until 1988, approximately 118,000 non-EU citizens received a residence permit. Another 'amnesty' took place in 1990 leading to a further 204,000 non-EU citizens being regularized, the largest numbers being from Morocco, Tunisia, Senegal and the Philippines (Groenendijk and Hampsink 1994: 48). The overwhelming majority of Filipinos regularized were female domestic workers.

In 1991, a special decree was passed that allowed for the hiring of foreign domestic workers on a temporary basis; in 1993, the majority of the 20,000 non-EU citizens granted an employment permit were domestic workers (Groenendijk and Hampsink 1994: 51). In addition, the Martelli Act 1990 eased the restrictions on working hours for migrant domestic workers and the ties to a specific employer.

In Italy, as in many other countries, immigration policy has increasingly become a political football. In November 1995, the caretaker government of Lamberto Dini gave in to pressure from the Northern League and introduced a decree (usually referred to as 'the Dini decree'). On the one hand, it allowed for the deportation of illegal immigrants and made employers who hire them liable to a two- to six-year prison sentence and, on the other, introduced provisions for the regularization of immigrants currently in Italy if their employer declared that they had been in the same job for four months and was prepared to pay social insurance contributions in advance for them (IRR European Race Audit 17 January 1996: 14).

Not surprisingly by the middle of December the police reported real difficulties in deciphering the decree; few employers were taking the steps to regularize their employees and there was a reluctance to carry out deportations (IRR European Race Audit 18 March 1996: 11). It was only amongst the employers of domestic workers that any real interest in regularization was forthcoming in the initial period, the more usual reaction being to sack immigrant workers.

But despite the initial confusion, by November 1996 (when the Dini decree could no longer be renewed) it was estimated that 220,000 foreigners had received a residence permit under its criteria. The regularization process indicated that about 25 per cent of Italy's foreign population was undocumented with Filipinos representing the largest nationality group (*Migration News Sheet* June 1996 and January 1997).

These kinds of calculations provide us with very rough and ready estimates of the gender and ethnic composition of contemporary transnational movements, but it is important that we make that effort. The point that is being made here is that unless we examine the gender and ethnic composition of the undocumented as well as the documented migrant labour force we say very little about the degree of 'feminization'. For instance the OECD migration country report for Greece in 1994 argues that one in twelve employed persons in Greece is a foreigner:

> Most foreigners who work in Greece do so illegally. Immigrants without work permits can find jobs despite high unemployment. Their wages, perhaps three to six times more than they can earn at home, are half the market rate in Greece ... foreign labour is used by many households for the care of small children and older people ... the large size of the informal economy and established networks that assist newcomers with information and accommodation contribute to the continuing flows.
>
> (SOPEMI 1995: 93)

In February 1997, Italy's General Accountant declared that over the next 50 years Italy would need at least 50,000 immigrants per year to balance the social security budget and support the economy in the face of a stagnant birth rate.

It is of course a state of affairs that recognizes that there is a two-tier labour market, one for EU nationals and one for nationals of 'third' countries who provide cheap and flexible labour power. But examining the social relations that characterize the employment of migrant domestic workers suggests reasons other than purely financial considerations.

Domestic work represents the commodification of highly personalized and emotional relationships, yet the employment of a third country national seems to mean for many employers the opportunity to treat the worker with less respect. And just as in sex work, there is a racial hierarchization of domestic work, with Black women earning less than 'White' groups (although, in Italy, local projects working with sex workers suggest that Albanians are the most exploited).

The vast majority of migrant domestic workers interviewed in Europe suggested that they had no choice but to migrate in search of work, some suggested that this compulsion was more than economic, so that the lines between economic migrant and refugee can be very blurred. In some countries of eastern Europe, the transition from a socialist state to a capitalist system with a dramatically different employment system has nudged many women to migrate for domestic work. Barbi and Miklavi-Brezigar (1999) provide an example of this in their study of migration of Slovenian girls and women to Italian towns in search of employment within the domestic work sector. But for the majority, migration was the only way in which money could be sent back to an extended family at home, a family that in some cases is caring for the migrant's children. Remittances do constitute an important economic contribution to governments and families alike, but, increasingly, migrants themselves are saddled with debts to intermediaries. For instance, many women in London and other European cities had originally found work through employment agencies who 'loan' the women the airfare and the fee and who keep their passports in the migration setting until the 'loan' is paid off, which means prolonged absence and vulnerability in the migration setting.

Nearly all research carried out in the migrant's home country indicates that it is neither the poorest nor the least well-educated that migrate. The very poor are the least likely to have the means to reach large cities as 'jumping off' points nor have the access to agents facilitating overseas migration. What this means is that often those who migrate are seriously underemployed (see research carried by LIFE in Rome and Milan 1991). Research carried out in Spain in 1996 indicated that Filipina women were the preferred nationality group as maids in families with children, precisely because they could teach the children English. Chell's research (1997) in Rome confirmed this. Their bi-lingual skills were taken for granted and there was no additional financial reward for the provision of this specialized skill (Anderson and Phizacklea 1997).

As with sex work, many of the accounts of domestic work are very grim from both a physical and emotional viewpoint: long hours of arduous work often involving emotionally demanding work with children and the elderly. But it would be wrong to paint a picture of the migrant domestic worker as victim. We think it is vital to also look at the migratory experience as a process of empowerment in a number of ways. Most women are able to send home remittances and most will work towards improving their situation, particularly to regularize their legal status. On 23 July 1998 the UK government announced that it intended to regularize the position of migrant domestic workers who entered under certain immigration conditions and who had become overstayers due to no fault of their own. Specifically, those conditions related to a concession introduced by the Thatcher government in 1980, which allowed foreign employers to bring in their domestic workers with them, but which tied those workers irrevocably to those same employers, who had no immigration or employment status of their own. The system was widely abused with one agency alone handling over 4000 reported cases of imprisonment, physical and sexual abuse, as well as widespread under and non-payment of workers by their employers. The workers' usual means of redress was simply to run away from the abusive employer, which immediately alters the conditions under which they were admitted and many through no fault of their own became overstayers. In short they joined the ranks of undocumented workers in the UK.

Ongoing empirical research by Anderson and Phizacklea indicates that being granted permission to regularize is only the first step in what has become an intricate, expensive and lengthy process for thousands of workers in London. But each step is also a process of empowerment. When asked 'what are you most looking forward to when regularized', one worker responded, 'not feeling panic when I see a policeman'. Yet many women have already had to pluck up courage and report their passports as 'missing' (meaning their original employer refuses to give them back their passport), to the police before their embassy will even consider issuing them with a new passport, the second step towards regularization. They must provide evidence of employment from employers who are often extremely reluctant to admit to the employment of a domestic worker. The obstacles are many, but tackling each hurdle is in itself part of an empowerment process for each individual.

No one interviewed so far had ever dreamt the day they left home that they would end up as an overstayer through no fault of their own. Few of them fit cosily into the classic household strategy of a migration model, which assumes that households make rational decisions about who should migrate in order to maximize household returns. Most informed other members of households of their plans only after detailed arrangements had been made (usually through a recruitment agency for work in the Gulf States if they come from Asia) because, for a range of reasons, they knew there was no alternative but to migrate. Bringing a better life to their families is pre-eminent, sending home money to their families is their priority, but their own aspirations for the future are not just a better paying, legal job but the prospect of moving out of domestic work altogether. For some women, a permanent return home is unlikely, they have left a failing or failed marriage and all the shame that comes with that admission in their home country, yet their responsibility to their children's welfare remains their priority. None of these women is a victim in the sense that she ever passively accepted her 'lot in life', each one left her home, her family and everything that was familiar to sell her labour on the global market place, and that takes great courage.

Why are migrant women preferred as domestic workers and sex workers? The answer is not just about money, that they are cheaper and more easily exploited. There are additional reasons that relate to racialized assumptions about the sexual and domestic nature of migrant women from 'poor' countries. It means that they can be treated differently, treatment which is conditioned by embodied racism, which cast them as 'exotic' or 'subservient' and which for many Europeans may be a way of restoring what they see as 'proper' relations between genders and 'races'.

In the next section we consider two other industries that have provided an economic niche for migrant women in Europe: clothing production and small-scale business.

Making clothes and doing business

By the late 1970s there had been a considerable shift in migrant women's employment in Germany (or what was then West Germany) from a concentration in manufacturing to a sizeable presence in the service sector. This shift reflected the speed with which German manufacturing firms seized the opportunity of further reducing labour costs by shifting their production to low-wage labour sites.

Although there were other incentives, such as tax holidays and restrictions on labour organization in those low wage countries who were keen to attract foreign employers, wages were deemed to be the single most important factor in attracting employers away from the higher wage unionized countries (Hancock 1983). Much has been made of the advantages to countries such as Germany of the guest worker system, such as paying nothing for the rearing or education of the worker, preventing costly family reunion and the fact that unemployment could be exported. But it did not turn out to be a clear run for German employers. German trade unions (nor most other western European unions) were not prepared to see a 'dilution' of wages in those areas of manufacturing that they represented and nor were migrant workers on the whole happy about being treated differently. Trade union organization and collective bargaining agreements and/or minimum wage legislation largely denied employers the opportunity of using migrant workers to undercut wages. In addition, the competition for migrant workers in the advanced industrial countries of Europe had led to many concessions being made on issues surrounding, for instance, family reunion. The attractions of 'off-shore' sites were compelling, particularly in industries such as clothing production where 80 per cent of costs were in garment assembly, and where the risks of mechanization were deemed too high.

The relocation of manufacturing production in industries such as clothing has not stopped over the last thirty years, but there have been and continue to be large national differences, which to some extent can be explained by the coincidence of changing markets and immigration policy.

One study carried out in West Germany indicated that by 1975 relocation to low wage sites had been adopted as a strategy by the majority of textile and clothing firms. Industries such as clothing had been major recruiters of female migrant labour in Germany, with 12 per cent of the total workforce in clothing in 1969 being drawn from the major countries of foreign recruitment. British clothing firms were also faced with serious problems of international competitiveness in the 1970s, and while both countries adopted a strategy of technological gradualism and a continued search for cheap labour, their pursuit of the latter took remarkably different forms. In Britain, clothing firms off-loaded their high-risk, unpredictable sectors of demand, and maintained flexibility by increased subcontracting domestically to the many small, inner city firms dominated by ethnic entrepreneurs and labour. In contrast, in Germany, manufacturers began to exploit the labour cost advantages of the new international division of labour by subcontracting work abroad to low-wage countries, (Phizacklea 1987, 1990). There were a number of reasons for this difference in approach. Germany, compared with Britain at this time, was far more accepting of trade liberalization and a new international division of labour. Germany did not have a sector of small subcontracting firms to fall back on, the Jewish-dominated clothing industry in Berlin had been decimated in the 1930s and 1940s, and a new high productivity sector based in North Rhine-Westphalia and Bavaria had taken its place. It was to these factories that migrant women had been drawn in the 1960s, but who had become increasingly surplus to requirements by the mid 1970s as cheaper labour was to be found in eastern Europe and further afield. Finally, what were then very different attitudes to immigration in the two countries influenced the pattern of subcontracting. The guest worker system in Germany recruited workers for specific jobs for which they were issued specific types of work and residence permits, the latter generally stating that the holder was not permitted to set up independently and family migration discouraged. In Britain, migrants from the new Commonwealth had originally the right to enter freely, as did their spouses and dependants who also had the right to enter the labour market. Manufacturing job losses hit migrant workers hard in the UK in the 1970s, but some workers were able to create alternative economic niches for themselves and their families, by using their small redundancy payment package and using skilled, cheap and flexible labour. A good example of how this transition took place was Coventry in the West Midlands. In the late 1960s there was no clothing production in Coventry, a city famed for its highly paid car production sector. Between 1975 and 1984, 74 per cent of all job losses in the area were in the engineering and metal manufacturing industries, which had been big recruiters of Asian male labour. By 1983, unemployment in areas of Asian residential concentration had risen to between 40 and 47 per cent (Gaffikin and Nickson n. d.). By 1994, clothing production had become the only manufacturing growth sector in Coventry with Asian entrepreneurs dominating ownership of the 80 factories located in the city. One study carried out in the mid 1980s reported that some manufacturers in London were quite happy for their assembly work to be transported up the M1 because it was cheaper than relying on London subcontractors (Phizacklea 1990). Most firms increased the flexibility in their labour force by employing homeworkers on a highly casualized basis, a practice that has continued into the 1990s (Phizacklea and Wolkowitz 1995; Felstead and Jewson 1999).

Thus, the fate of migrant women in the clothing industry in the two countries took a rather different form. In Germany, migrant women were pushed sideways into labour intensive service work, whereas migrant women in Britain (particularly Asian women) were readily absorbed into a thriving secondary sector of clothing production.

Homeworking also allowed women to combine their domestic responsibilities with paid work. For some migrant communities, cultural norms such as veiling also proscribe the limits to women's use of space, and homeworking may allow women to 'work' without transgressing these spatial boundaries. Yet an analysis of migrant women's participation in homeworking must also move beyond a focus on individual circumstances or cultural norms. Naila Kabeer revealed the ways in which Bangladeshi women's participation in this sector must also be seen in terms of bargaining with others within the household in the context of racism and social exclusion from the mainstream. As a result, community solidarity and networks become key symbolic resources for the Bangladeshi women and influence their bargaining powers within the household. Hence, the decision of Bangladeshi women to work as homeworkers is influenced by a range of factors: individual preference, cultural norms and the interaction of racism, community identity and gender relations (Kabeer 1994: 307).

Another route taken by those who were becoming unemployed was entrepreneurship, although this sector was dominated by men in Britain, France and the Netherlands (where similar 'ethnic economies' in clothing had developed). Women were rarely becoming the entrepreneurs: it was men who were bosses and women remained largely workers, at best supervisors in these small subcontracting firms (Morokvasic 1987; Phizacklea 1987).

However, more recent research has revealed that at least some women have used self-employment as a tool to social mobility by engaging in some of the more profitable ethnic niches, such as in fashion and food industries (Raghuram and Hardill 1998). As the children of some migrants have achieved social mobility and have increased their disposable income, a range of industries have come up to meet their specific demands. Raghuram and Hardill (1998) identified women entrepreneurs who owned firms that were selling antiques and fashion garments. In recognition of this increasing salience of Asian women in Leicester's economy, the Leicester Asian Business Association organized a day conference for Asian businesswomen. The women who attended the conference were engaged in a number of different enterprises where they used their diasporic networks to produce cheaply in their countries of origin and to sell in other parts of the diaspora. Other entrepreneurs provided a range of specialist services such as arrangement of Asian weddings and children's birthday parties, marketing of beauty products, etc.

Yet, this success has not been apparent among all ethnic groups, even in Leicester, with African-Caribbean business women still concentrated in sectors of low return such as hairdressing. Also, the ratio of self-employed men to women remains high, as for example among Turkish men and women in Berlin where it remains at 3:1 (Rudolph and Hillmann 1998). This may be partly explained by the relative ease with which Turkish women find employment in some other sectors such as sales and trade compared with Turkish men. Yet, overall, women do often remain in supportive roles in small businesses. It is interesting that commentators in the field of 'ethnic minority business' implicitly accept this sexual division of labour as 'normal':

> The 'captive' labour supply provided by immigrant wives, whose way of life keeps them largely separate from the wider society, is vital to the success of the enterprise, as is the interest of the potential entrepreneurs in accepting low wages for their work in return for gaining the experience which will equip them to set up their own in due course.
>
> (Mars and Ward 1984: 4)

The fact that the fringe benefit of entrepreneurship is reserved for men is not questioned. Research carried out in Birmingham, UK and Lyon, France in the early 1990s in the retail and service sector, painted a similar picture. Many of the ethnic minority male entrepreneurs indicated that self-employment and business start-up had been a 'fall back' position either because of unemployment or blocked opportunities in mainstream employment. These were very much family businesses, but a recurrent feature of the interviews conducted with proprietors in both countries was the unacknowledged or grudging admission of the role of women in the business: the following is a fairly typical comment made by a North African garage owner in Lyon:

> I take care of everything, well there's one thing I hardly touch at all and that's the paperwork, my fiancée does that, actually she's indispensable for the management side.
> Do you pay her?
> No! She does it for me because I haven't got the time. In fact she takes care of EVERYTHING.
>
> (Phizacklea and Ram 1996: 334)

Given the opportunity, the women in these 'family' businesses were very clear about their contribution to the viability of the business even though it was not registered in their name. Women's understandings of the 'firm as the family' should not be ignored, nor the ways in which predominantly female labour forces in ethnically homogenous businesses may negotiate their own 'women's' space, take pride in their work and recognize their crucial contribution to household income.

Making generalizations about the self-employed across Europe is difficult[1] . In Britain, ethnic minorities are twice as likely to be self-employed as Whites, but, apart from the Chinese, women's self-employment is on average only half or less than half that of men's (Modood and Berthoud 1997). Morokvasic produced an interesting study of ethnic minority and immigrant women in self-employment and business in five European countries. Given the strength and determination of the women interviewed in the research, she concludes that a major obstacle for migrant women who are self-employed is overcoming the stereotype of migrant women as 'problems' (1991b: 99). There are of course, very real legal and material obstacles to employment in some EU countries for non-EU citizens, which need to be lifted. For instance, in the Netherlands, entrepreneurs require permits in order to establish an enterprise and these permits are obtained through specific vocational training programmes, which may be harder for migrant women to access (Kloosterman *et al.* 1998). In addition, non-EU qualifications may not be given proper recognition and there is a need for migrant women to gain access to rights of residence and citizenship as individuals and not through relations with men as husbands or fathers.

Ignoring the skilled

The omission of skilled female migrants in the literature on international migration and the general silence on the degree of de-skilling experienced through the process of migration are questions that need to be addressed. These are issues that apply to female and male migrants although the former have also had to contend with the tendency to undervalue activities associated with so-called female occupations and construct their skills as being less worthy and demanding than those carried out by male workers (Phillips and Taylor 1980).

It is true that much of the work that is currently on offer to migrant women is confined to a narrow band of jobs that are traditionally viewed as appropriate to 'women's' caring and servicing roles and deemed to require little skill. But this does not explain the absence of research on skilled female migrants. Elsewhere, we have suggested there might be several reasons that contribute to such a partial picture of migrant employment (Kofman 2000), which underestimates the contribution of many of them, especially those from the developing countries.

Research in the 1960s and 1970s acknowledged the effect of the brain drain for both developed and developing countries (Oommen 1989) and its significance in a world labour market (Petras 1981). The subsequent expansion of trade, the development of an international division of labour and the growth of transnational corporations spurred, in the 1980s, an interest in skilled migration. These were the individuals who populated the heady summits of financial circles or had technological skills to offer (Findlay and Gould 1989; Salt 1988, 1992). They were inevitably men because women found it difficult to be sent on overseas assignments (Adler 1994).

As a result of this transfer of interest, the scientists and welfare professionals (education, health, social services) slipped into the background. In the early days, the gender balance favoured males, but as women participated increasingly in higher education and it became more acceptable to lead independent lives, the proportion of female migrants in the welfare sectors increased. In addition, new areas, such as cultural industries and computing, have emerged as significant sectors attracting a wide range of international personnel on short- and longer-term contracts. In particular, it has been global cities, and in Europe often at the same time post-imperial cities (King 1991), that have attracted a cosmopolitan population of intellectuals, students, artists and exiles. With some notable exceptions (Morokvasic 1991b; Bhachu 1993; Lutz 1993) feminist research too has neglected professional migration (Kofman 2000).

The groups mentioned above, however, often enter by different channels, e.g. recruitment agencies, professional organizations, familial and social networks, and individual efforts, rather than those moving within or between companies. In the traditional professions (medicine, law) migrants have also had to meet criteria set by regulating professional bodies (Iredale 1997). As we saw in Chapter 3, many female migrants from the former colonies staffed the lower echelons of health services or came to undertake postgraduate training. For instance, in the UK, only 72 per cent of doctors practising were born in the UK (Labour Force Survey 1996) and the inflow of doctors is becoming more feminized. In France, a quarter of all hospital doctors are foreign or naturalized, although they are concentrated in the least desirable specialisms (CERC 1999). Within the European Union, Scandinavian countries and the UK are countries with shortages of medical personnel. The UK continues to experience severe shortages of nurses, especially in the public sector, because of nurses leaving for better paid private sector employment in the UK and overseas (Buchanan *et al.* 1993). In other countries, such as Germany, nurses too are imported under contract from eastern Europe. In 1993, 21,000 medical workers left the Philippines, 79 per cent of whom were nurses (Lim and Oishi 1996: 93). Many others, who trained as nurses, left and subsequently entered unskilled jobs.

This raises another facet of the deployment of skills in the process of migration. There is plenty of evidence to show that women migrants are often desperately underemployed in the migration setting. Research carried out with Filipinas in Italy in 1991 indicated that half of the 101 interviewed had college education (LIFE 1991). Chell's study (1997) of Filipino and Somalian women working in the domestic sector in Rome also demonstrates professional background: one had trained as a doctor and others had nursing and teaching qualifications before emigrating. Deskilling and loss of career does not only affect the labour migrant. Women who accompany husbands migrating as expatriate managers, tend to be unable to find work whilst abroad (Hardill and MacDonald 1998; Wagner 1998), in effect they form the international trailing wife (Bruegel 1996).

Refugees, in particular, face enormous difficulties in pursuing their original occupation, often because their qualifications are not recognized, they lack the requisite linguistic knowledge and do not have the resources to retrain. And as Findlay and Gould (1989) noted, those who move for political rather than economic reasons are usually enumerated separately, and their skills not taken into account. At the same time we would caution against splitting off the economic, social and political as reasons for migration. Some skilled migrants who left oppressive regimes had sufficient resources not to have had to request refugee status, for example from the Middle East or South Africa. Some may maintain a close relationship with their homeland, but choose to spend the major part of the lives abroad in a more congenial milieu. What form of exile is open to an individual depends to a great extent on their economic and social capital, gender, racial background and country of origin (Heitlinger 1999).

Conclusion

Twenty-five years ago migrant women were distributed across the spectrum of 'feminized' jobs, but were largely confined to the manual sectors of 'women's' jobs or the least prestigious sectors of certain types of work, such as nursing. Their position has always been one of 'first to fire and last to hire'. Unemployment levels are still far higher for migrant women when compared with women generally (SOPEMI 1998). Nevertheless, when we talk about 'migrant women' in Europe today, we are looking at a different and diverse picture. There are older first generation women who have moved from manufacturing work into services and some into providing the backbone of labour in 'family' businesses. Often their daughters, having undertaken all of their education in Europe and sharing the aspirations of their peers, have moved out of these low-level jobs into more secure and better rewarded sectors. Nevertheless there is evidence of racial discrimination operating in mainstream labour markets and there continues to be a problem of citizenship rights in many countries. The 'new migrations' of women in the face of stringent immigration controls heavily restrict the opportunities for work, as we have seen many now report that sex work or domestic work are the only channels for employment for the recently entered. Contemporary migration flows therefore continue to paint a picture of increased numbers of European women, with the citizenship of their member states, abandoning or refusing to return to jobs that have traditionally been regarded as the domain of women and correspondingly underpaid and devalued. But the fact that these are jobs that apparently are suitable for migrant women, tells us a good deal about gender relations in Europe as well. The marriage bureaux, which function predominantly to put European men in touch with women from Asia and eastern Europe, make a good deal of how they can effect introductions to women who will make 'good wives'. It is all too easy to discuss migration in a clinical way without looking behind phrases such as 'demand driven'; migration in contemporary times tells us a good deal about changes in gender relations that go well beyond the labour market, and for feminists world-wide it raises difficult questions.

Notes

1   The extent to which migrants are able to set up in business varies by state. Business entry is allowed after 8 years of migrant status in Germany or in Italy for nationals of states with which bilateral agreements in this area have been signed (Tacoli 1999).

Chapter 6

Welfare and gendered migration

This chapter examines relations between migrants and 'welfare states' in Europe. The post-war period saw the development of a variety of welfare states, or 'welfare regimes' (Esping Andersen 1990) whose specific forms reflected national social and political traditions and internal class conflicts. The institutions and practices (Baubock 1993) established at this time were based on the nation state with national boundaries marking who belonged and, therefore, who had rights to welfare provision. Developing notions of social citizenship (Marshall 1950) gave ideological support to the identification of rights with membership of the national community. The notion that citizenship implies social rights, however, also implied exclusion against those deemed as not belonging, as 'outsiders' (see Chapter 4).

In practice, migrants have been incorporated into aspects of social citizenship within the country of settlement in a variety of ways. The extent and nature of this incorporation has depended on the particular state welfare regime, migratory regime and tradition of conferring citizenship, as well as on the citizenship status, class, length of stay and gender of the individual migrant. Social citizenship, unlike political and civil citizenship, defies 'clear cut institutionalized criteria' (Faist 1995: 178) and therefore the boundaries between citizens and non-citizens tend to be blurred. Some theorists have argued that, as non-citizens gain access to a wider range of social rights, the importance of formal citizenship status is diminishing. However, we have suggested that, in spite of the powerful forces favouring inclusion to which Soysal draws attention, formal citizenship status remains of crucial importance. European integration and the development of 'European Union citizenship' has paradoxically increased the importance of national membership and the gap between the rights of citizens and non-citizens.

Migrants' access to welfare services in the country of settlement has therefore been restricted through formal rules as well as institutional practices. The rights accorded to non-citizen migrants have changed with the restructuring of migratory regimes (see Chapter 3). In general social rights have been extended for those with permanent residence and curtailed for those with insecure residence.

Even where formal rights exist, however, the institutional structures of welfare states may mean that migrants' access to services may be restricted by discriminatory practices, especially along racial lines. Several studies have shown the differential treatment accorded to Black and White citizens by welfare services (Williams 1989; Klug 1993). Lack of knowledge of the local language and unfamiliarity with institutional structures may also mean that migrants need support in gaining access to appropriate services.

Migrants have, on the other hand, played a crucial role in the provision of welfare in Europe during this period, particularly in colonial regimes. Migrant workers, especially women, have been disproportionately concentrated in welfare services, both as professionals and in occupations deemed 'unskilled' such as catering and cleaning. Migrants now increasingly work within the domestic sphere (see Chapter 5) as the expansion of female paid employment has produced new demands for childcare and care for the elderly.

Problems of accessing mainstream services have meant that migrants have been forced to provide for their own welfare needs through the family and wider social networks, and through voluntary and community organizations. This phenomenon is not new: there is a long tradition of new migrant groups providing support from their own communities both in order to overcome exclusion from national services and to provide for specific cultural and religious demands. Examples include the Jewish Free School established in London in the early 1900s and the involvement of the Catholic Church in Spain and Italy in providing welfare to groups such as those from Cape Verde and the Philippines (Campani 1993c: 514). This need has been greatly extended recently as restrictions have been imposed on the range of benefits that can be claimed by groups without permanent residence. In Britain, for example, the removal of cash benefits from asylum seekers has meant that refugee organizations and voluntary groups have been forced to take on the increasing burden of supporting their own communities.

Women have tended to play a key role as providers of welfare for their families and community, generally through unpaid work. The restructuring of welfare states, with an increased emphasis on market solutions, which has occurred in varying degrees across Europe, has intensified this process. The emphasis has shifted from standardized public provision towards private provision and an increasing reliance on voluntary labour. Migrant women often have extensive networks of caring relationships, sometimes with family across national boundaries (Ackers 1998). At the same time, some migrant campaigns have succeeded in their demands for more appropriate services. This has led, particularly at local level, to initiatives aimed at extending access to particular groups. In this new environment, migrant women are often involved in formal roles as mediators between their community and the welfare services (Lutz 1993; Hoggart and Sales 1998).

The foundations of welfare regimes in Europe were based largely on the assumption of female dependence on the male wage, the 'male breadwinner model' (Lewis 1993; Colwill 1994) with women's access to social rights often channelled through men rather than directly to women in their own right (Lister 1997). Migration helped sustain the 'hegemony of the white male breadwinner model' (Williams 1995: 135) because by meeting some of the labour needs of post-war economies they filled a gap in the labour market that indigenous women might otherwise have been expected to fill. This process also served to divide women, with migrant women often constructed as deviant because of being unable to conform to the prevailing social norms of full-time motherhood.

During the post-war period European welfare states have moved away from this model to varying degrees: indigenous women have gained more independent access to social rights as female labour force participation has increased, whereas the 'traditional' family has declined in significance. The ageing population in Europe, combined with restrictions on publicly provided care, has also fuelled demand for care of the elderly. These processes have brought new, predominantly female, migration flows whose domestic labour has served to support the paid work of indigenous women. This also reflects a class shift: whereas in the post-war era it was working class women who were most likely to be in paid work, it is now middle class women – who are able to earn sufficient income to pay for domestic labour – and who are most likely to be in work, particularly full-time employment (Bonney and Love 1990).

In spite of the erosion of the notion of female dependence in Europe, however, official policy towards women migrants continues to treat them primarily as dependents. This applies in relation to the conditions of entry (see Chapter 3) and to their access to social rights. Different migration regimes create different hierarchies of rights for migrants according to their citizenship status, and also create specific positioning of women migrants. This chapter will discuss the role of migrants as providers of welfare to the general population and then migrants' own access to welfare, both through formal services and through their own work and that of a range of voluntary organizations. It will begin with a brief discussion of 'welfare regimes' and the implications of welfare restructuring in Europe.

Forms and provision of welfare

The definition of welfare is itself contested. The tradition of 'social policy' or 'social administration' has tended to view welfare as largely confined to formal policy and institutions that supplement or modify the operation of the market system. In this view, social policies can be broadly grouped into three areas:

1   income maintenance for individuals unable to support themselves through the market or family, e.g. unemployment benefit, poor relief, pensions;
2   public provision of services, e.g. education and health care, public housing, social work; and
3   regulation of working conditions, e.g. limitation of working hours, health and safety.

All have explicit or implicit gendered effects and differing implications for people according to citizenship status. The outcome of welfare transfers, for example, depends on the conditions of entitlement. Schemes in which payments are based on earnings tend to reinforce labour market inequalities and therefore disadvantage women who may be out of employment for long periods because of caring responsibilities, and migrants who have less time to build up payments. As Faist (1995) suggests, however, it may be easier for non-citizens to access these benefits than non-contributory benefits where entitlement is based on citizenship.

In general, regimes that emphasize services rather than reliance on cash benefits tend to be more equalizing in relation to gender. Provision of services, particularly childcare, is essential for women's entry into the labour force, whereas the development of welfare services has provided the major expansion of employment opportunities for women and is disproportionately a source of employment for migrant workers. Access to services, however, depends on being able to demonstrate eligibility. While in most European states all residents have a right to emergency medical treatment and children have a right to schooling, access to other services is dependent on legal status. In spite of the feminization of employment, the institutions of the welfare state tend to be characterized by a sharp division of labour both on gender and ethnic lines, with women and ethnic minorities largely absent from the structures of power and decision-making.

Labour market regulation has been the main element of European Union social policy, for example through the *Social Chapter of Workers Rights* (see below). This has focused mainly on setting minimum standards in employment and promoting equal treatment between men and women workers. This type of regulation, however, gives little protection to those outside the formal labour market, either the unemployed or those working in the 'informal sector' (Sales and Gregory 1996). The impact for migrants, who are disproportionately confined to unregulated work, may therefore be limited.

Non-gendered accounts of welfare implicitly assume a sexual division of labour in which the unpaid work within the domestic sphere on which the market system depends is predominantly female. Feminist analysis has challenged the separation of the public and private spheres at the root of liberal thought (Pateman 1988) arguing that male domination in the public sphere of employment and the state is based on the assumption of women's economic and sexual dependence within the family, and the provision of unpaid care. In the development of welfare states, women have been central as providers of both formal and informal welfare and as mediators on behalf of the family with welfare agencies. Women tend also to be at the centre of a network of obligations that include not just children, but parents and other relatives, neighbours and friends. These latter forms of welfare have been of particular importance for migrants. A more appropriate definition of welfare would therefore include not only formal services that involve some form of market transaction (through for example employment or the payment of benefits), but also informal welfare (in the family and community) for which no payment is made.

Welfare provision has always involved in practice a mixture of state, market and voluntary agencies, often working in combination. Recent policy changes have shifted the balance towards a greater reliance on the market and voluntary sectors. The dividing line between private and public welfare is blurred, particularly for migrants, whose survival often depends on a range of informal networks.

Welfare regimes

A considerable comparative literature has developed on European welfare states (Esping Andersen 1990; Cochrane and Clarke 1993; Taylor 1993), including feminist analyses (Lewis 1993; Sainsbury 1996). In this section we discuss briefly some of these studies, and then draw out some of their implications for immigration: an area that has not generally been incorporated into these analyses.

In an influential comparative study, Esping Andersen (1990) linked welfare provision to wider political and economic processes. He argued that a number of distinct welfare state regimes emerged in advanced capitalist countries in the post-war period, which he labelled liberal, conservative and social democratic. These are distinguished by the way in which access to social rights, particularly income maintenance, is gained. He suggests that the critical aspect of the benefit system is its capacity for 'decommodification', or 'the degree to which individuals, or families, can uphold a socially acceptable standard of living independently of market participation' (Esping Andersen 1990: 37).

The *liberal* regime is typified by English-speaking former colonies of settlement such as the USA and Australia, and Esping Andersen includes the United Kingdom in this model. Welfare provision is strictly means-tested, providing only very modest living standards. The middle classes therefore rely heavily on the market to supplement state provision. Although the 'sanctity of the market' (Esping Andersen 1990: 28) is paramount, 'the liberal dogma is forced to seek recourse in the pre-capitalist institutions of social aid, such as the family, the church and the community' in order to provide for care of those outside the labour market (Esping Andersen 1990: 42).

Conservative or *Bismarkian* regimes developed in corporatist states, such as Germany, France, Austria and Italy. Benefits are high but largely earnings-related with little role for private insurance schemes. Conservatism is also expressed in the promotion of 'family values', and there is a strict division between men as breadwinners and women as wives and mothers. The care of dependents is presumed a private family matter, falling mainly on women.

Social democratic regimes are exemplified by Scandinavia, where the benefit system is based on universalism and a high degree of decommodification. Support for high taxes is maintained by benefits and services sufficient to meet middle class aspirations, leaving little role for private provision. There is a high degree of socialization of family responsibilities with well-developed childcare facilities. These regimes depend on full employment of both women and men to maintain political support for high taxes and to finance benefits.

Leibfried (1991) developed a typology broadly corresponding to Esping Andersen's, but introduced a fourth regime type, the *Latin Rim* to characterize states of the southern European periphery (Spain, Portugal, Greece and, to a lesser extent, Italy). Leibfried classifies these regimes as *fundamental*: that is with relatively low state welfare provision. Like liberal regimes these stress residualization, but they can call upon older traditions of religious involvement in welfare as well as the extended family. The development and expansion of welfare systems in the 1970s and 1980s has greatly altered the character of these regimes. In Italy, for example, the welfare system has shifted towards a more universalist model, especially in the north-west and Emiglia-Romagna (Del Re 1993). The system remains characterized by clientism with the boundary between political and welfare systems blurred (Paci, cited in Chamberlayne 1992) and highly uneven provision of services (Bimbi 1993: 165).

Although these typologies have gendered implications, this is not the primary focus of these analyses and the exploration of the gender dimension is not systematic. Esping Andersen, for example, demonstrates the implications of caring responsibilities for women's labour market status, but does not link this to his analysis of decommodification. Indeed, as Lister (1997: 173) points out, he conflates individuals and families in his definition of commodification, thus avoiding the crucial issue of the gendered nature of decommodification.

Feminist critiques have shown how access to social rights is always gendered (Lewis 1993; Sainsbury 1996). The primary focus on decommodification through formal state transfer payments obscures the extent to which welfare, provided through unpaid domestic labour, is a necessary basis for the commodification of labour. For women, the increasing commodification of unpaid reproductive labour in the post-war period has been a precondition for greater social and economic emancipation. Langan and Ostner argue that:

> Men are commodified ... by the work done by women in the family. Women on the other hand, are decommodified by their position in the family. Thus men and women are 'gendered commodities' with different experiences of the labour market resulting from their different relationship to family life. [Women] ... protect the vulnerable in a market economy, that is those who cannot become fully commodified but that this in turn makes them vulnerable.
>
> (Langan and Ostner 1991: 131)

A number of feminist critiques have attempted to make gender central to their understanding of the differences in welfare states. Langan and Ostner take Esping Andersen's typology, drawing out the gendered implications of these regime types. The Scandinavian social democratic regimes are characterized as the 'universalization of a female social service economy', in which, although based on dual-income families, women's labour continues to be concentrated in servicing, whether in public or private sphere; the German Bismarkian model as the 'gendered status maintenance model', which is built on strongly differentiated roles of male breadwinner and housewife; and the Anglo-Saxon regime as the 'dualistic' model, which they argue applies increasingly to Britain, where the assumption of full equality in the market place coexists with the notion of female dependency.

Lewis (1992) develops a different typology based on a distinction between strong, weak and modified breadwinner states, i.e. the extent to which social policy maintains women's dependence on men.[1] Whereas Esping Andersen characterizes France, along with Germany, as a conservative regime on the basis of its social security regime, Lewis's focus on gender differentiates between them. She describes France as a 'modified breadwinner regime' on the basis of its comprehensive publicly-funded childcare provision and emphasis on combining paid work with family responsibilities.[2] This model provides a useful additional dimension to the typology developed by Esping Andersen emphasizing the importance of domestic labour in determining women's relation to the labour market. The focus remains, however, on state provision that ignores the complexity of caring relationships. Women's lives tend to involve a complex interweaving of roles, which include both providing care and receiving support in their caring roles, through the market, through state provision and through the family and social community networks. These models, therefore, risk 'oversimplification masking both important commonalities and differences in women's experiences of citizenship' (Ackers 1998: 52). These informal arrangements are of particular importance for migrant women, both as providers and recipients of welfare.

The main comparative models tend to focus on childcare and therefore on a relatively limited period of women's lives (Ackers 1998: 52). Public intervention for the care of the elderly and disabled has been much more limited in most European states (Kofman and Sales 1996). The generosity of childcare facilities and benefits in Belgium and France for example, is not matched by support for residential care or domiciliary care for the elderly (Jamieson 1991), who are expected to be supported mainly by the family. In Italy, elderly people in need of care are dependent on the family, with virtually no public support, or the Church, which provides residential care for those who can afford it. Although the proportion of elderly will be the highest within the European Union by the next century, traditional family structures that provided care are breaking down, and this issue has not become part of public policy debates (Dell'Orto and Taccani 1992). In Britain, on the other hand, in spite of its limited provision of childcare, until recently elderly people had universal access to a range of medical and social services.

These differences reflect broader ideological differences in the relationship between the family and the state. The constitution of some European states (those categorized by Esping Andersen as 'conservative') includes an obligation on parents and children to care for each other. While family policy in France and Germany has been markedly different, in both there is a greater degree of familial solidarity than in the more atomized societies of either Britain or the social democratic regimes of Scandinavia.

Another danger with the concentration on state policies is that it ignores gendered struggles within the family and the 'informal' sphere of politics. The support for working mothers in official French policy for example, has co-existed with a strongly entrenched division of labour within the household. This disjunction emerges strongly in Ackers' research on intra-European migration: French women in her study, who had migrated to Britain, found greater equality in the domestic sphere in Britain, in spite of poorer public provision. This suggests that gender equality was not the main engine of French family policy (Ackers 1998: 325), whereas the British situation may reflect the relatively greater success of campaigns by the women's movement in challenging the domestic division of labour. Similarly, the Scandinavian model has also brought a strongly entrenched gendered division of labour in both public and private spheres (Siim 1993). Comparative analysis of gendered regimes therefore need to be broadened out to encompass an analysis of the relations between state, family and welfare institutions, as well as political movements (Kofman and Sales 1996).

Migration has been a major, though often largely unrecognized, element in sustaining the prevailing gender order. In the post-war welfare state, migration was important in enabling European women to remain as 'housewives' as both male and female migrant workers were recruited to fill labour shortages. As Williams notes in relation to Britain, many African-Caribbean women were forced economically into full time jobs while this activity was neither recognized, supported nor legitimated by existing welfare provisions (Williams 1995: 134). In Germany, female migration was relatively small: significant numbers, however, worked in the expanding industrial sectors whereas German women were encouraged to stay out of the labour market. The higher wages for males, however, made the notion of the 'male breadwinner' more of a reality than it was in Britain.

More recently, European women have entered the labour force in increasing numbers, dependence on migrant labour has shifted, and there are new demands for domestic and service labour for both childcare and care of the elderly. The reliance of conservative and liberal regimes on unpaid domestic labour has provided new spaces for migrant labour. Italy and Spain have seen major migrations of female service workers. The employment of household labour has allowed Italian women to avoid upsetting the gender balance within the home because working women do not have to make demands on their partners to increase their share of domestic tasks (Tacoli 1999: 117). Migrant labour is increasingly employed in this way in Britain (Anderson 1997b). In Germany, on the other hand, the female labour force has brought a polarization between full-time childless women workers and full-time mothers (Anderson and Phizacklea 1997). The proportion of working mothers remains smaller, with a correspondingly lower demand for migrant domestic workers. The prevalence of the dual-income family and publicly funded childcare in social democratic regimes has meant there has been less room for migrants either within the formal labour market or as domestic workers.

Esping Andersen's analysis of benefit regimes also has important implications for migrants' access to social rights. For example, social democratic regimes are most equalizing in relation to their own citizens, particularly in relation to gender. The principle of universalism, however, is based on an ideology of a broadly homogeneous society, which is challenged by immigration (Siim 1998). The notion of benefits based on citizenship can provide the basis for exclusion of non-citizens. Corporatist systems might be expected to provide more opportunities for migrants because they are characterized by earnings-related benefits, with entitlement dependent on work rather than citizenship (Faist 1995: 1798). Migrants, however, tend to have lower entitlement than citizens because they have spent less time in the formal labour force. The strict conditions of entitlement to benefit in liberal regimes tend to be most exclusionary to migrants. As Britain has moved increasingly towards a more 'targeted' benefit system, migrants have been major losers. The entitlement of those on work permits to the universal child benefit was removed in 1996, and recent legislation is removing all cash benefits from asylum seekers.

Access to benefits is also gendered with women's access often dependent on their marital status. The contrast between the direction of policy in relation to European citizens and non-citizens is stark. There have been moves to give European women entitlements in their own right, including through European Union legislation. Immigration rules on the other hand have tended to intensify the dependence of migrant women. The conditions of entry for family reunion and the rule of 'no recourse to public funds' prevent spouses gaining independent access to income through benefits in the early years of migration. In some states (e.g. Ireland and Germany) women and men entering in this way have no immediate right to enter the formal labour force, and they may therefore work in the informal sector in which they are not able to accrue benefits in their own right.

The extent to which migrant women can exercise autonomy depends therefore on a complex of factors, including the nature of the migratory and gendered regimes within the country of settlement, as well as their own characteristics and status.

Welfare restructuring

Although, as we have suggested, the welfare states that emerged in post-war Europe included a variety of distinct regimes, they shared a broad consensus around certain fundamental assumptions: that social provision should be a major and rising part of social expenditure, with a key role for the state in provision of both public services such as health and education, and of social insurance. They also shared at their foundation an adherence to a male breadwinner model, although distinctive gendered regimes emerged in subsequent decades.

These regimes were essentially national in character, and underpinned by national economic policies in which Keynesian policies of demand management to maintain high employment were prominent. The economic crises that developed in the 1970s, together with global restructuring of production, brought a challenge to the social consensus on which these welfare regimes were based. As international and regional economic integration has deepened, individual states have been less able to maintain independent policies.

All EU states embraced to varying degrees neo-liberal policies during the 1980s. Social policy is increasingly subordinated to the demands of maintaining competitiveness (Jessop 1993). This has meant the promotion of 'flexible labour markets' and an extension of the market into public services, either directly through sale of assets and contracting out of services to the private sector; or indirectly through the introduction of market criteria into public services ('internal' or 'quasi' markets). This strategy has been developed at EU level through the Single European Market and the Maastricht Agreement of 1993, which paved the way for monetary union. The convergence conditions for entry to the European Monetary Union required deflation for many economies, resulting in reduced and tighter social expenditure for example in Italy (Saraceno and Negri 1994).

The abandonment or retrenchment of the Keynesian Welfare State has exacerbated inequalities based on class, gender and ethnicity. Labour market deregulation has intensified the marginal position of women (Bennington and Taylor 1993: 124) and has underpinned an expansion of women's part-time employment in some parts of Europe, facilitated by the restructuring of production processes and the development of 'flexible' work practices. While a minority of women have benefited from the expansion of professional and managerial positions, others have been pushed into casualized employment with low pay and limited benefits. Migrants are disproportionately concentrated in the latter sectors, particularly personal services. Bruegel (1999) has shown that migrant men as well as women are over-represented in these traditionally female areas of work in London, reflecting inequalities within the male workforce.

Increased reliance on the private sector for welfare provision has exacerbated inequalities as access to services has become more dependent on ability to pay. This has also increased unpaid labour, predominantly of women, as services previously publicly provided are undertaken within the household and the community. This development has provided opportunities for the employment of migrant labour within the home.

Another aspect of the increased role of the market in welfare services has been the casualization of employment and increased use of temporary staff. In Britain, private agencies have been at the forefront in the recruitment of temporary staff in areas such as nursing, education and social work. A high proportion of these are migrants, many of whom have temporary residence. They thus play a vital role in maintaining services but, although they may earn relatively high wages, they are marginalized in terms of career structure and working conditions.

The imposition of financial targets in welfare services, combined with increasingly stringent application of immigration controls, has served to exclude migrants from access to services. The introduction of the 'internal market' into the British Health Service, for example, has meant that before giving treatment, hospitals demand proof that it will be paid for by the relevant health authority.

Non-citizens are often required to produce passports. Colleges of Further Education, which provide post-compulsory education, face stringent financial pressures and have become stricter in their pursuit of fee income. Students are subject to checks on their immigration status, and enrolment is conditional on the presentation of birth certificates, which refugees are unlikely to have. Service providers are thus drawn into scrutinizing immigration status (Owers 1994). By questioning the legitimacy of people of non-European origin, these developments have implications for all residents, regardless of their formal citizenship status (Sales and Gregory 1996).

These developments have been accompanied by shifts in official discourses of citizenship, from those based on rights, to those based on obligations (Lister 1997). Politicians have talked of an 'end to the something for nothing' culture, with so-called 'benefit scroungers' a particular target. This has been felt most sharply in relation to asylum seekers who have been represented by the media and politicians as 'bogus' and 'welfare tourists'. The French government attempted to remove benefits from undocumented migrants, but with the return of a socialist government this was not implemented.

As governments across Europe have introduced harsher policies towards asylum seekers, by reducing their benefits while at the same time denying them the opportunity for paid employment, many have been pushed into begging, prostitution, petty crime and marginal jobs such as cleaning car windscreens. Thus the reality of their lives reinforces these stereotypes.

EU social policy

As the completion of the Single European Market extended the free movement of capital, commodities and labour within the European Union, the European Commission has pressed for a wider development of social policy (the 'Social Dimension') in order to mitigate the worst ravages of competition unleashed by the Single Market, so-called 'Social Dumping'.[3] These developments have, however, remained limited and fragmented (Bailey 1992; Leibfried 1993). EU social policy has been confined mainly to attempts to define common goals rather than to create common institutions and strategies. The Social Charter of Workers Rights, for example, proposed certain minimum standards, many of which are existing practice in some member states. Implementation has involved a series of Directives that must be brought into domestic law by member states parliaments: a process that has been slow and conflictual.

The most vigorous element of EU social policy has been the development of equal opportunities policies (Hoskyns 1999). This has been confined largely to promoting equal treatment between men and women, a commitment to which is contained in Article 119 of the Treaty of Rome. A substantial body of policy initiatives have been developed in this area, which has had implications for working practices as well as for example pensions and other benefits. The sex discrimination legislation, however, is confined to the formal labour contract and depends on individual or groups of workers making complaints. Only those with secure, permanent jobs and the protection of a strong trade union may be in a position to insist on their rights (Sales and Gregory 1999). As employment protection legislation has been eroded, which has been particularly a feature of UK policy, more workers are in casualized employment without recourse to this form of legislation. Workers in 'informal' employment, such as home working, sweat shops and domestic service, are disproportionately women and migrants, particularly those with insecure residence status.

With European integration, the concept of European Union citizenship has developed to include social as well as political rights (Guild 1996). These rights, however, stem from the fundamental rationale of promoting labour mobility and are limited by the requirement that migrants should 'avoid becoming a burden on the social security system of the host Member State'.[4] Rights are therefore not universal but accrue to migrants according to their category (see Chapter 4). Family rights are therefore derived from the 'male breadwinner' and the rationale for their extension to family members 'rests on the notion that they directly or indirectly benefit the community workers and promote his [sic] mobility' (Ackers 1998: 314).

Ackers' (1998: 106) study of women migrants within the EU demonstrates the difficulties that these women face in gaining access to social rights in other member states. There has been considerable litigation over social rights in the community, with some movement beyond mobility and transference of benefits to claim competency over key areas of needs-based social provision. These include, for example, education and care of children with disabilities. This has not, however, brought any convergence at an institutional level.

Discrimination on grounds of nationality is illegal under community law. This protection is restricted to full citizens of member states who exercise their right to move within the Union and as Ackers' study shows, EU migrants have had difficulty in gaining access to equivalent social rights. No such protection is afforded to non-EU or third country migrants, while parallel provisions to the sex discrimination measures are not available for racial and minority ethnic groups (see Chapter 4). The European Parliament and Commission have produced a number of reports on racism that have recommended European legislation on the issue. Member states, however, have consistently opposed such moves. The Amsterdam Treaty of 1997 refers to opposition to racial discrimination in Article 6(a) (Hoskyns 1999). Any action under this heading would, however, require the unanimous agreement of all member states.

Migrants as providers of welfare

As we have argued above, migration has been an essential, although often largely invisible, element in the provision of welfare in Europe in both the formal and informal spheres. In the post-war period, migrant workers were important in the development of welfare regime. Colonial states in particular have long relied on immigrants, primarily from former colonies, to provide labour in health and education. The use of migrant labour in the formal welfare services has been most prominent in Britain, both in terms of the numbers involved, and the extent to which migrants have been embedded into the services providing for the general population. More recently, these movements have diversified both in terms of the countries of origin and destination, and the forms of work into which they have been recruited. Migrant women from outside the EU are increasingly concentrated in domestic labour, predominantly in 'informal' settings, while there have been moves to restrict conditions of entry and residence for non-EU migrants within the formal welfare services.

The promotion of free movement of labour within the European Union reflects the official policy of EU states of ending reliance on external migration. There remain, however, substantial barriers to mobility within the EU, based on language, culture and institutional differences. In spite of the moves towards mutual recognition of qualifications, national governments have retained their rights to demand specific qualifications. For example, the Irish government was allowed to retain the requirement for Irish language speakers in education, a move that effectively bars non-Irish from entering the profession (Ackers 1998). The organization of welfare systems, particularly education, remain distinct and there has been little progress towards convergence, making mobility difficult. A continuing barrier to mobility is family ties and the dependent status of people moving within the EU as families of labour migrants (see above).

Migrant labour has become increasingly important in other female-dominated professions, including teaching and social work. With the restructuring of welfare services, new private employment agencies have flourished, particularly to recruit staff for temporary posts. A major source of this new temporary labour is 'old Commonwealth' countries such as Australia, Canada, New Zealand and, more recently, South Africa. These groups are able to take advantage of special short-term work permits.

Many of the issues concerning the employment of migrant labour have been discussed in Chapters 3 and 5. In particular, it is worth noting that many ethnic minority women have found continued discrimination, as in the health service (Bhavnani 1997: 27), or occupied the lower rungs of these professions, for example, being predominantly State Enrolled Nurses rather than the higher status State Registered Nurses (Bhavnani 1997: 26). In some states, and especially for those without former colonial ties, formal discrimination prevents those without citizenship or national qualifications from occupying the secure and permanent posts, as we saw is the case in France. Within these professions, migrants tend to be most prominent in areas with casualized work practices, a pattern illustrated in the staffing of a social work team in inner London established to deal with support for asylum-seekers. Most of the team's fourteen members are women, only two are permanent, and only three are British born (one of whom is Black). The precarious employment position of most of its members mirrors both the team's marginalization within the Social Services department, where work with asylum seekers has low status, and of asylum seekers within the wider community.[5]

In Germany, which was the major receiver of migration during the early post-war period, migrants were recruited predominantly for the industrial labour force. These groups were not expected to settle, and were not encouraged to develop a sense of belonging to the local society through involvement in welfare services as either consumers or providers.

Many migrant women work in the informal sectors providing welfare. The development in Europe of 'global cities' (Sassen 1991)[6] has concentrated financial and producer services in a handful of centres that compete among themselves for skilled labour. These processes, however, also generate demand for low-level service sector activities, including welfare services in the public and private sectors (Kofman 1998). Childcare and care of the elderly has increased as women's labour force participation has increased. Demand is generated by national and international elites as well as the middle classes. This has occurred at a time when state provision is retrenching rather than expanding, leaving a large niche for the private sector. Privatization has taken a number of forms, including provision of formal marketed services, such as old people's homes; increased payment for state services such as home helps and nursing care; and increasingly the use of private domestic labour within the home. This latter sector is largely unregulated, generally involving no formal contract of employment.

Domestic work in private households is now the main area of employment for migrant women in Europe (Chapter 5). This growth has been important, particularly in southern Europe, but also in Britain and other northern European states. This form of work is most common for women whose residence status is insecure, either because they entered without documentation or because they have become 'overstayers'. The unregulated nature of the work combined with insecurity of legal status makes them particularly vulnerable to abuse.

Migrants as clients of welfare

In most European states, all residents are entitled to basic health care, and children are entitled to education, whereas access to other services depends on proof of entitlement. Social security benefits, however, are dependent on building up entitlement, and are therefore linked to employment as well as residence status. Where migrants work legally they acquire entitlements, as well as benefiting from national employment legislation on conditions of work. As we have suggested, however, a high proportion of migrants are outside the formal labour market, either because they have no entitlement to work, or through other forms of exclusion.

Access to welfare provision is dependent on citizenship status and on the nature of the migration and welfare regime that govern the formal rules of entitlement. These statuses are also gendered, with women often dependent on men for their status and access to rights (see Chapter 3). It is important, however, to distinguish between formal rights and the actual use that people are able to make of available services. Migrants may face barriers because of unfamiliarity with the language and with the institutional structures of welfare, and lack of knowledge of their entitlement. Although all migrants are likely to be familiar with schooling, for example, and to value educational opportunities, they may be less familiar with social work and, particularly those who have suffered under repressive regimes, may be suspicious of state officials. Ackers suggests that cultural preferences may also dictate use of services, for example, she found that European Union migrants in Scandinavia preferred to care for young children themselves rather than place them in state nurseries (Ackers 1998).

For many migrants, moving country means being removed from their own family and community networks. For Turkish-speaking women, for example, this becomes particularly important during pregnancy and childbirth when it is usual for the extended family, particularly mothers and mothers-in-law, to be heavily involved (Hoggart and Sales 1998). This can mean that they make more use of statutory services where they are available, and also depend on support from the voluntary sector and building up new community networks within the migration setting.

The willingness and ability of welfare providers to make their services appropriate to the needs of migrants depends on the broad state migration regime (see Chapter 3): in an exclusionary model, such as Germany, there is little attempt. The civic republican model typified by France precludes the acknowledgement of difference in provision. In multi-cultural models, such as Scandinavia, there is greater recognition of different needs. In all these models, however, the reality of services attempting to provide for new populations and to meet demands from communities that are beginning to organize on their own behalf, has led to recognition and some change in provision. This has been predominantly at local level rather than national strategy. Provision of special services, such as production of information about education and health in local languages, tends to be uneven. Furthermore, services aimed at particular groups tend to be seen as 'extras' rather than an integrated part of service, and are particularly vulnerable to funding cuts.[7]

In a number of European welfare systems, community 'mediators' have played a major role in facilitating access to mainstream services (see below). Another development has been alternative community-based services as a response to what are seen as inappropriate or discriminatory practices in mainstream services. Southall Black Sisters, for example, which is discussed in more detail in Chapter 7, provides support for Asian women facing domestic violence. They argue that welfare providers often have stereotyped notions of the communities and implicitly collude with pressures from 'community leaders'. They tend to be reluctant to intervene in family matters within migrant communities. Asian women who report marital violence, for example, are much more likely than White women to be told to resolve the matter within their own communities. As one of its full-time workers said, 'we do a lot of work social services should be doing' (*Independent* 10.12.1992). Although still based largely on voluntary labour, Southall Black Sisters now receives funding from the local council.

As we suggested in Chapter 4, current legislation has produced a complex hierarchy of migrants' rights to welfare according to their immigration and citizenship status. EU citizens have the highest level of rights, although these rights are tied to labour market status with the rights of 'dependants' derived from the worker. Labour migrants and those entering through family reunion from a third country have much lower levels of formal rights. The following section deals with refugees and asylum seekers, whose rights have been reduced dramatically by recent legislation. It should, however, be borne in mind that the ability of migrants to access appropriate services depends on a complex interaction between their formal rights and status; the place of their community within the local society (including the extent of racist practices and the community's own self-organization), and individuals' own capacities to negotiate their rights, which depends on such factors as class, education and language ability.

Refugees

Current debates around refugees and asylum seekers have tended to focus on the conditions of entry and for claiming status rather than on social support. The 1951 Geneva Convention, however, gives equal importance to the right to claim asylum and to the social rights of refugees within the country of asylum. These include residence rights, employment, social welfare, education and housing (European Consultation on Refugees and Exiles 1983). Although most European states carry out at least their minimum obligations to those to whom they grant convention status, the content and structures of their policies towards refugees differ considerably (Duke *et al.* 1999). Some, such as France and the Scandinavian countries, have permanent centralized settlement programmes, whereas others, such as Portugal, Greece and Ireland, provide more ad hoc support. This partly reflects the recency of arrival of asylum seekers in the latter countries.

Resettlement policy in Germany, which has received by far the largest number of refugees in Europe, is characterized by authoritarian treatment of asylum seekers – for whom living in reception centres is compulsory even if they have relatives in Germany – relatively ungenerous conditions, and limited support for integration. The Scandinavian countries have traditionally emphasized a more multicultural model of incorporation of migrants, including refugees, than either Germany or France (Soysal 1994). Britain has a long tradition of receiving asylum seekers, but has always refused to set up a permanent programme, preferring to see refugee flows as temporary. Current resettlement policy is based on equal access to general state provision and support for community self-help (Carey-Wood 1994).

The Danish Refugee Council conducted a comparative study of the legal and social rights of refugees, asylum seekers and those with humanitarian status in sixteen Western European countries (Liebaut and Hughes 1997). This shows that most Convention refugees have the same formal rights as nationals although their ability to gain access to these rights is severely restricted.

The experiences of refugees mean they have distinctive needs that necessitate specific policies in the short run if resettlement is to be successful. In a study for the British Home Office, Carey-Wood *et al.* (1995) found that two-thirds of their sample experienced stress, anxiety and depression, while physical health problems affected sixteen per cent. Many also suffer physical disabilities as a result of their experiences (Refugee Council, n.d.). Sexual abuse of women is common (Forbes Martin 1992; Crawley 1997). The effects of war and persecution are compounded by adverse experiences in exile, such as social and cultural isolation, unemployment, language difficulties and concern about friends and relatives who remain in their home countries. Stress is aggravated by anxiety about legal status and delays in processing applications, the threat of deportation and by separation from families who have no right to join asylum seekers or people without full refugee status.

The Home Office research also showed, however, that refugees bring important skills and experience that can be used for the benefit not only of their own communities but the wider society. In their sample, most came from urban areas with good educational backgrounds (one-third with a degree or professional qualification) and 66 per cent had been employed in their home country (Carey Wood *et al.* 1995).

The restructuring of welfare services, the introduction of market conditions, and the requirement to meet externally imposed targets have made it difficult to sustain programmes aimed at meeting specific needs. Others have found it difficult to gain access to mainstream services. Refugees in Britain, for example, report being unable to register with a doctor, because their particular needs make them too 'expensive'.[8]

Unemployment of refugees is high throughout Europe (Liebaut and Hughes 1997). Many have no opportunity to prepare themselves for flight and may seek asylum in countries with which they have no former connection and little knowledge of the language, culture or job market. Since welfare benefits in Europe are increasingly based on contributions, they are unlikely to gain anything but the bare minimum. This may affect access to health care, where provision is partially tied to contributions, as for example in Germany. Portugal discriminates against refugees and other migrants by limiting municipal housing to households containing at least one Portuguese citizen (Liebaut and Hughes 1997: 194), but shortage of public housing in other European states means that refugees are often housed in inadequate and overcrowded conditions.

One theme that has emerged from recent research on refugee resettlement is that women seem to find it easier than men to adapt to changed status (Kay 1989; Buijs 1993; Summerfield 1993; Refugee Council 1996). It is often men who lose most status as a result of flight. Unable to work and to fulfil their traditional role of 'breadwinner' they may also have lost a public political role as well.

In contrast, many women refugees experience new opportunities, often for the first time acquiring independent income through benefits or employment, and taking on new roles, both paid and unpaid, within the community. These patterns were evident in a small-scale study based on interviews with Somali refugee women in London (Sales and Gregory 1998).

Asylum seekers

A greater disparity exists between states in provision for asylum seekers (see Table 6.1). Fairly generous benefits were available in some states whereas in others, which rely heavily on reception centres, help is largely confined to pocket money and benefits in kind. Conditions in German reception centres have been a cause for concern to NGOs (Liebaut and Hughes 1997: 93). In Greece

Table 6.1 Income of asylum seekers

Adult monthly allowance (US$)		
Austria	36.5	pocket money (payable to those under 'federal care': approximately 30% of asylum seekers)
Belgium	639	
Denmark	174	(plus board and lodging)
Finland	384	(plus accommodation)
France	247	(plus one-off payment of 380 – no allowance for children)
Germany	26	(pocket money)
Greece	none	
Ireland	617	(includes rent allowance)
Italy	480	(payable for 45 days)
Luxembourg	343	
Netherlands	76	(pocket money plus clothing)
Norway	139	(pocket money)
Portugal	none	(for 96% under accelerated procedure)
	178	(for those in normal determination procedure)
Spain	271	(6 months) or $50 pocket money if in reception centre
Sweden	315	(105 if meals provided)
UK	173	(plus housing benefit to port applicants)
	zero	(to country applicants and refusals – food vouchers provided by local authorities)

Source: Liebaut and Hughes 1997

and Portugal asylum seekers receive minimal state help, and rely on charity for basic needs.

There is increasing differentiation between groups of asylum seekers in relation to income and access to accommodation. In most states, asylum seekers are not allowed to work, although in some they may apply for a work permit after a certain length of time (three months in Finland and Germany, six in the United Kingdom). Belgium, Spain and Sweden have some flexibility. Many asylum seekers work illegally, particularly in Greece, Italy and Portugal where limited funds are available, and in Britain where welfare payments have been withdrawn. Recent changes in asylum laws across the EU have reduced access to welfare for refugees and tightened conditions for claiming benefits. A system of national preference in relation to welfare has become more acceptable, for example by removing the obligation on local authorities to provide public housing to asylum seekers.

In Britain, cash benefits were withdrawn in 1997 from in-country applicants and those appealing against refusal. Cash benefits have been removed from all asylum seekers and replaced with vouchers to be exchanged in designated supermarkets in the 1999 Asylum and Immigration Bill. There is to be no choice in accommodation with the possibility of dispersal throughout the country. Opposition to the proposed legislation in parliament centred on its impact on women as mothers (Refugee Council 1999: 2) and some minor concessions were won. These concessions did not, however, confront the punitive ideology embodied in the legislation, or its broader implications for women. The proposals isolate refugees from society, making them likely targets for xenophobia and racist attacks. Dispersal would cut women off from those communities that have been vital to their ability to find a sense of belonging in Britain and increase their dependence on the immediate family.

Migrants as 'mediators' within and between welfare services

The developments outlined above suggest that there is a growing gap between the needs of migrant groups for welfare provision and the services they are actually able to enjoy. For those with secure residence this gap between their formal entitlement and their ability to access it may be because of language and cultural differences. For others, such as asylum seekers, their formal entitlement is extremely limited, while their needs may be very acute. The restructuring of welfare services has exacerbated both of these problems by tying access to services more closely to ability to pay and to residence status, while making it more difficult to maintain non-statutory services such as those aimed specifically at migrant or refugee groups.

These developments have led to an increase in the provision by migrant groups of welfare for their own communities. These range from family networks that support relatives when they arrive in a new country, for example with finding accommodation; to broader community networks that help members find employment and housing; through to formal organizations that provide a range of services to the community. The emphasis of community organizations varies according to the relations of the community to the host society and their reasons for migration. Joly (1996), for example, distinguishes between refugee groups according to whether they are political with a 'project' in their home country; and those who were not personally engaged in the conflict. The focus of community groups mainly made up of the former (which would include, for example, Kurdish communities) tend to be on the country of origin. The groups' activities tend to be dominated by the politics of the homeland. Although for the latter (which would include, for example Somalis) a major part of their activities involve retaining cultural traditions, they also provide advice and information to their communities and act as a bridge to the wider society.

One study of Somali women in London found that community groups play an important role for most women (Sales and Gregory 1998). Those with better language and other skills are able to support other members of the community who rely heavily on the groups for help in interpreting, negotiating with officials, and pursuing their claims for asylum. Men's response to this success is often ambivalent and there was considerable opposition to a separate women's group being set up.

As migrant communities become more settled, members of these communities are increasingly used as 'mediators' between the welfare services and the community. In the Somali case, the involvement in the community had helped give some women professional and more formal status. Several women had taken courses to enable them to work in health promotion within the community. One, a former gynaecologist, who was unable to work in this country because she did not have a British-recognized qualification, has worked with social services in promoting awareness of the health risks of female genital mutilation. The work of these groups has also promoted awareness of the need for Somali speakers within local schools and social services, and led to some appointments within these mainstream services.

Lutz (1993) describes the role of the Turkish women social workers and teachers in the Netherlands and Germany, the overwhelming majority of whom are involved in 'ethnic activity'. In London, Turkish-speaking communities are more embedded in mainstream welfare provision. Cypriots formed part of colonial migration in the 1950s and there are many first and second generation teachers in schools. The expansion of Turkish speaking populations in the 1980s and 1990s (the latter mainly Kurdish refugees) however, has brought a need for services to help this group access services. A Turkish- and Kurdish-speaking health advocacy service has been established in Hackney in inner London. The advocates are not merely interpreters, but are involved in providing information to patients, and even taking case histories and making home visits.[9] These organizations may replace the kin support networks that existed in Turkey, for example during childbirth. There is a danger, however, that some women become over dependent on the advocates. Many lead isolated lives and do not learn English even after many years in London, so that their interaction with the welfare services is always through someone else.[10]

In a number of European countries (Belgium, France, Germany, Netherlands) a system of mediators has emerged in recent years (Hassan 1999). In Belgium, unlike other countries, it has become a collective project enabling migrant women to participate as citizens in the life of their locality and town. In France, a system of mediators has been established for over fifteen years. There are now some 600 throughout the country. While their activities were recognized by the minister of Social Affairs and Integration in 1993, their activities have not been put on a permanent or professional footing (Delacroix 1997). Their activities include a range of activities, including advice, advocacy with local services and informing professionals about the needs and culture of migrant groups. Delacroix makes a distinction between *femmes relais* who are broadly concerned with relaying information and with assimilating migrants into the mainstream; and *médiatrices* who would play a more critical role in relation to existing services.

In all these examples, women represent the overwhelming majority of mediators. It may be that this kind of community development work is thought to be a safe place for women, an extension of domestic roles and not real politics, which is a male preserve (see Chapter 7). The involvement of women in this kind of work can, however, have a profound impact on gender relations (Delacroix 1997; Sales and Gregory 1998). The association of women with advocacy, however, means that men have less access to services so their needs are not met.

The job of 'mediator' may also be to represent the community to the outside world. These women are expected, by the welfare services, to act as experts on all aspects of their community. Lutz argues that their position is vulnerable because, as members and 'representatives' of their community, they may find it difficult to establish boundaries. They are viewed not only as professionals, but 'as one of the community', opening up their private lives and their 'respectability' to the scrutiny of traditional informal community leaders (Lutz 1993: 491). These anxieties are mirrored in the Somali community: Mariam, who took a leading role in establishing the group discussed above, told us:

> The men say to me, 'We like what you are doing for the community, but keep away from our wives. We don't want them to become independent like you.'[11]

A tension raised in all these groups is about the loyalties of advocates or mediators and whom they represent. Most of these projects have arisen out of voluntary social and political activity within the community, and the groups have struggled to get their needs recognized. The process of becoming part of the mainstream service represents an acknowledgement of their professionalism. It also removes control from the community. This is a tension common within the voluntary sector as services become established and formalized. It becomes particularly acute for some communities where there are profound problems of social exclusion and isolation from mainstream society. In the Turkish-speaking communities this is compounded by community divisions. The politicization of the Kurdish community has led to demands from the (male-dominated) community groups that Kurdish advocates are provided for them, although advocates claim that women are happy with Turkish or Cypriot advocates. On the other hand, the more conservative nature of the Kurdish community means that Kurdish women have not been encouraged to become advocates themselves.

Conclusion

Our discussion has emphasized the importance of migrants as providers of welfare both to their own communities and to the wider communities in which they settle. Much of this work is invisible because it takes place within private homes, or as unpaid voluntary labour within the family and community. While self-provision has always been a part of the migrant experience, the current trend towards excluding certain categories of migrant from benefits and welfare services is likely to make this a more prominent and longer lasting feature of the migration experience. Welfare provision remains a largely female activity and has ambivalent implications for women: on the one hand it places burdens on them, but, on the other, involvement in community activities provides opportunities for developing independence and the possibility of transforming gender relations.

The gap between needs and provision is most acute for recent arrivals, particularly refugees, and recent legislation means that this will grow. Research has suggested the importance of providing support in the short term to allow refugees to find a place in their country of settlement. Current policy is tending towards the creation of permanent social exclusion rather than allowing European societies to gain the benefits of the skills and experience of its new residents.

Notes

1 As examples of strong breadwinner states Lewis selects Ireland and Britain. In Ireland, the state and the Church together ensured that women's primary role was within the family as mothers, carers and dependants, a role enshrined in the 1937 Constitution. Britain has historically followed a strong breadwinner model. In Britain, the Beveridge Report, which laid the basis of the welfare state, saw the concept of full employment applying only to men, with women dependent on the male wage. Germany also represents a strong breadwinner state. The welfare system encourages strongly polarized male breadwinner and housewife roles through the fiscal system and a low level of childcare provision. It was only in 1977 that the constitutional clause requiring husbands' permission for wives to work was annulled in Germany (Ostner 1993: 98).

2 France has one of the highest levels in Europe of women in full-time employment, especially of mothers with children under ten years. The

weak male-breadwinner model applies to Sweden, as well as to Denmark and Finland. Women in Sweden now have one of the highest labour force participation rates and by far the highest hourly rates of OECD states (90 per cent of the male rate). The model has not, however, overcome gender divisions, but entrenched them in new forms. Entitlements, such as parental leave, continue to be largely taken by women, thus consolidating gender segregation in both private and public spheres.

3 'Social dumping' refers to the potential for the erosion of national provision as a result of the increased competition unleashed by the Single Market and the drive to cut costs. This is particularly problematic in view of the wide regional disparities within the EU – increased with recent additions to membership – and differences in social provision.

4 Council Directive 90/365, quoted in Ackers (1998: 314).

5 Information from research project on *Refugees and Social Services in London*. Funded by Middlesex University.

6 Sassen's study included London as well as New York and Tokyo. Other European centres that could be described as 'global cities' include Frankfurt, Milan and Paris.

7 For example, cuts to the budget of the local Health Authority have led to staff reductions and restructuring of the Turkish- and Kurdish-speaking Advocacy Service, which provides support within the Health Service in Hackney, London.

8 Refugee worker, speaking at a conference on *Refugees and health* organized by Hackney Refugee Training Consortium, 1996.

9 One advocate complained that 'we are being asked to do the job of health visitor'. Interview with advocate, from research project *Turkish speaking mothers in Hackney: an evaluation of needs and use of health provision and a trial of a volunteer visiting scheme for first time mothers*, funded by the Inner City Research and Development Programme of the National Health Service.

10 From interviews with advocates, see previous note.

11 Somali woman, quoted in Sales and Gregory (1998).

Chapter 7

Migrant women and politics

Political citizenship generally remains the last right that migrants gain in the country of settlement. Non-citizens acquire a range of social rights through employment, extended residence and through collective organization. But access to the formal political process remains firmly associated with citizenship status. For some communities, particularly refugees, their political activities are further limited by their immigration status[1] whereas fear of state repression from the state they have left may also inhibit political activity.[2] Migrants have therefore been seen, by academics and politicians, as 'objects of political discourse, rather than as participating subjects' (Hargreaves and Wihtol de Wenden 1993: 1), a view even more firmly entrenched for migrant women.

Such views, however, are based on narrow definitions of politics. Political activity is not confined to the electoral process. Migrants have been drawn into myriad political activities in the country of settlement, often of necessity in order to defend their own rights and those of their family and community. As the social and civil rights of migrants have been eroded in the ways described in previous chapters, this has brought new forms of engagement, and migrant women frequently take the lead in this form of activity.

The scope for migrant women's involvement in political life varies according to the political structures and opportunities in the country of settlement; their length and security of residence; their position within their own communities, and the links of that community with homeland politics. Insecurities of residence and employment limit political activity among newer migrant groups, and in southern European countries, which have only recently become countries of immigration, migrants have had less opportunity to build political organizations (Danese 1998a). In

Britain and France, where there are long-established communities with citizenship rights there are more long-standing associations and migrant women, particularly second generation, have started to enter the formal political sphere.

For some, who migrated for broadly political reasons, political activity in the receiving country may be a continuation of their activities in their homeland, albeit in different forms and under different sets of constraints. For others, migration may open up new opportunities for wider involvement within the community and the broader society. Migration frequently brings with it shifts in gender relations. Family structures built on a sharp separation of roles may not be sustainable within the new setting. On the other hand, the loss of status that frequently accompanies migration, particularly for men, can bring attempts within the family and community to reinforce more conservative values. Much of the political activity in which migrant women have engaged stems from the so-called private sphere, for example campaigns against domestic violence, and for the rights of women who are made dependent on men by immigration law. These campaigns have often been born out of their own experience and begun within their own communities but they have built broader alliances to fight for change.

In this chapter we aim to highlight the wide range of political activities in which migrant women engage, and the ways in which they have attempted to challenge and renegotiate existing power relations in the home, the community and society. Although many of these activities begin at the local level, they have sometimes involved networking at national, European and global levels. We begin by reviewing the scope of political activity and feminist challenges to conventional notions of the political. We then highlight some of the problems that have beset feminist engagement with migrant politics. The following sections discuss issues concerning migrant women in political parties, in campaigns for migrant rights, in community activity and in political activity connected with their homeland. As we discuss in this chapter, migrant women engage in a wide range of political activity, both to help in adapting to the conditions of the receiving country, but also to reconstitute these conditions for the migrant family and community. Migrant women have also networked successfully to increase their public profile in Europe. However, most academic work in this field has been based on country case-studies or on specific community organizations with no comprehensive or integrative studies being undertaken so far. In this chapter we aim to give a flavour of some of the issues raised using examples drawn from a variety of European states. We also call for more research in this area to bring together the ways in which migrant women's agency has both resisted and reconstituted gendered and racist societies in Europe and in home countries.

Gender and political activity

Conventional definitions of politics locate it firmly within the public sphere. This includes electoral politics – which is dominated by professional politicians – but also participation in political parties and trade unions. Throughout Europe these activities continue to be dominated by men. Women's political citizenship is limited by both caring responsibilities (Lister 1997) and by ideologies that exclude them from the public sphere or confine them to a supportive rule. Although, for example, the number of women members of parliament has increased, in no state does it reflect their proportion of the population. Many migrant women come from states where women are firmly excluded from politics through state laws or religious prohibitions. Some migrants, especially those from non-democratic states, may also have been involved in clandestine activities. These activities tend to be male-dominated and place a premium on community loyalty, making it dangerous to raise alternative agendas such as feminist demands (Sales 1997: 126). Women therefore tend to be excluded or play a supportive role.

Feminist political movements have arisen as a response to women's resistance to existing political organization, resisting closures around the political and delimitation of the political to formal institutions (Kofman and Peake 1990). They have contested the distinction between the public and the private spheres of social life, which has been central to liberal political theory. Their work has analysed power relations in both the public sphere (of work, the state and formal politics) and the private sphere (of the family and household) and the ways in which these interrelate to reinforce gender subordination. The public-private distinction is ideological rather than a description of two discrete categories. Craske (1993: 133) argues that it is not useful to think of public and private as binary categories but as a continuum 'which would allow us to use the concepts in a mutable and unfixed way'. Women as well as men occupy both spheres. What is now referred to in Europe as the 'traditional' family was based on the exclusion of women from the public sphere of work, and involved their economic dependence on the male breadwinner. This pattern has only ever existed in a minority of privileged households and was built on the labour of working class and non-European women. In contemporary Europe, migrant women have rarely been able to afford to remain within the private world although their access to the public sphere may be constrained. The growth of homeworking demonstrates the fluidity of the distinction between public and private.

State policy is crucial in maintaining and transforming the boundaries of the public and private (Waylen 1998) and represents a contradictory arena for feminist struggle. The slogan of second wave feminism 'the personal is political' widened the definition of the political, forcing onto the political agenda issues that had been defined as 'private' such as rape and domestic violence. Feminists have fought to secure legislation on issues such as domestic violence, which had been seen as outside the remit of legislation and problems to be resolved within the home. Although these campaigns have been initiated outside the formal political process, in states where women's formal representation has increased it has been easiest to bring these issues on to the public agenda, albeit in circumscribed ways (Bystydzienski 1992). On the other hand, they have also pressed for autonomy from the state in relation to sexuality and the control of women's fertility.

Migration law (which stems from the public domain) has influenced the private space in which migrants establish and maintain households, for example, through rules on family reunion. Metaphors are often deployed that characterize the state as protecting the home (the nation) from outsiders (migration), with the territorial boundaries of the state enclosing the private space of the nation (Bhattacharya 1997). In claiming to maintain the integrity of the national home, states can violate the home of those deemed 'outsiders'.

Migrant women conceive of the term home in at least three contexts: as constructed through close kin relations; as the wider kin group including the larger migrant community with which they may identify; and thirdly as the country of origin (Bhattacharya 1997). They may engage politically at all these levels, and the boundaries between these three spheres become blurred through this activity. They may be forced to fight to maintain their family home through struggles with immigration authorities but also to engage in struggles within the home to maintain their own autonomy. This activity also involves the wider migrant community, where they may find support but also opposition if they are seen as breaching community norms. Through their responsibility for the socialization of the next generation, women often inspire their children to fight against the discrimination of which they have been victims (Siddiqui 1999), but also to retain an identity with the home country. In her study of the Bangladeshi community in London, Summerfield (1993) found that the children of migrants dominate Sylheti expatriate politics. In this time of a resurgence in racism and xenophobia, women are often propelled into the front line as symbols and bearers of ethnic values and identities and reproducers of the group (Yuval-Davis and Anthias 1989). The affirmation of ethnic identity often focuses on traditional practices, including the most patriarchal aspects, and women's conformity to these values (Kofman and Sales 1992).

The continuity in exile of women's role as primary carers for the family, often without the support of an extended family, constrains their activity, but it also provides opportunities for engagement with the wider community. This activity may begin as an extension of service roles, and be regarded as 'moral' rather than 'political'. Blumberg and West (1990) differentiate between organizations on the basis of the different social roles that they emphasize: those linked to women's role as economic providers, their nurturing role, those linked to national and ethnic issues, and those that aim to extend their rights as women. However, these roles are interconnected and women's participation in one activity often provides the basis for their involvement in another, which may include organizing for formal political representation. This distinction may therefore be unhelpful. Women's participation in community politics may not be overtly gendered, but can lead to shifts in gender relations.

Feminism and anti-racism

The relationship between feminism and the politics of migration and race has been fraught with tensions. In the resurgence of 'second wave feminism' in the 1970s, gender was seen as the overriding social division, with sisterhood between women seen as being more powerful than divisions between them. The feminist movement was never homogeneous, and many recognized the importance of other divisions including class and race. The main preoccupations were, nevertheless with issues that often appeared of marginal importance to migrant women and there was little engagement with specific issues confronting migrant women.

This lack of engagement stemmed not merely from ignorance or lack of willingness to take on these issues, but from the theoretical understanding of women's oppression. The major theoretical development of second wave feminism was its analysis of the nuclear family as a site of women's oppression. Feminists exposed the inequalities within the family, the exploitation of women's unpaid domestic labour, their economic dependence on the male 'breadwinner wage' and the prevalence of domestic violence.

During the 1980s, a vigorous critique of 'White feminism' was launched, arguing that it is Eurocentric, and the emphasis on the family as the prime site of oppression did not reflect the experience of Black and migrant women (Amos and Parmar 1984). For women facing racism in their daily lives, the family and community is also a refuge and source of support. This contradictory relation to the family is not of course confined to ethnic minority women, but the tensions and conflicts of loyalties may be more sharply felt in the face of racism. For many migrants, the male breadwinner wage was unattainable because of racism in the labour market. Furthermore, for many migrant women whose families are divided by racist immigration, the right to a family life may be their main priority. For these women, the most important rift may lie between Whiteness and Blackness rather than along the gender divide.

At the same time, feminists have struggled to have gender acknowledged within anti-racist theory and practice. Crenshaw has argued that Black women have been excluded both from feminist theory and from anti-racist policy discourse because 'both are predicated on a discrete set of experiences that often does not accurately reflect the interaction of race and gender' (1998: 315). Thus the specific experience of Black women is theoretically erased (Collins 1990). Arguing against the tendency to counterpose different forms of oppression, Sen asserts 'the importance of gender as a crucial parameter in social and economic analysis is complementary to, rather than competitive with, the variables of class, ownership, occupations, incomes and family status' (Sen 1990: 123). What is required is not merely to extend the analysis of subordination by sex to include the experiences of those at the periphery, but to restructure feminist theory and practice in the light of such experiences. In the words of Carby, 'feminism has to be transformed if it is to address us' (1982: 232).

Many migrant women have therefore been reluctant to identify themselves with a feminist movement that is seen as insensitive to their own experience. As Chatterjee (1995) noted, many women in the Bengali Women's Support Group in Sheffield did not want to be associated 'too closely with Western, and perhaps abrasive, notions of feminism.' They did not want to make 'artificial choices between the individual and the group, between femininity and feminism'.

The portrayal of feminism as alien to migrant women can, however, serve to sustain power relations within these communities. In the face of racism in the 'host' society, there has been a reassertion of community norms often based on the more conservative elements in the culture. Religious fundamentalism has deepened tensions between demands for women's autonomy and certain definitions of 'community traditions', which have often 'been focused through forms of religious belonging' (*Feminist Review* 1993: 1). These processes have tended increasingly to conflate religion with ethnicity, with Asian populations identified as 'Muslim' or 'Hindu', rather than by nationality, or the more political term 'Black'. Versions of fundamentalism have developed in all major religions, but it has as common themes: both adherence to fixed interpretations of written texts, and an assertion of patriarchal values (Saghal and Yuval Davis 1992). These values have led in many cases to increased control over ethnic minority women by 'community leaders', as '[communal] boundaries often use differences in the way women are socially constructed as markers ... for example expectations about honour and purity' (Anthias and Yuval Davis 1992: 113–4). This has brought intensified 'policing' of women's behaviour and more explicit mechanisms for excluding women from political activities.

The legitimization of conservative practices is often abetted by 'multicultural' policies promoted by local authorities that tend to be based on static and stereotyped views of immigrant family structures and reinforce restrictive notions of women's role. Some on the Left in Europe have sometimes given uncritical acceptance to claims by community leaders to be defending their 'traditional culture'. This is partly a response to the criticisms from Black feminists of the Eurocentricity of feminist theory. In the name of 'equal opportunities' feminists have sometimes colluded in rendering invisible the struggles of women.

The divisions between feminists were well illustrated in the 'headscarf' affair, which became a cause célèbre in France during the late 1980s. Three Muslim girls were forbidden to wear headscarves to school, since this conflicted with the secularism of the school system. The issue divided Left and Right, including feminists and the anti-racist movement in France. While some argued for a compromise, which would allow for cultural expression, others took a more secular line. Spensky (1990) argued that the ban on headscarves provided a space for women to dispense with the symbols of men's control over women. Within the Muslim population itself, attitudes were profoundly divided: of a group of Muslims interviewed for an opinion poll at the time, 30 per cent were in favour of allowing the wearing of headscarves in state schools, but more than 45 per cent were not (Hargreaves 1991: 7). The vice president of SOS Racisme, Hayette Boudjema, declared that the headscarf was a sign of oppression and constraint exercised upon Muslim women (Hargreaves and Stenhouse 1991: 30).

The difficulties involved in finding a space for Black women's concerns has led some to set up their own organizations. In the Netherlands, this led to the establishment of *Flamboyant*, a national centre for ethnic minority women, subsidized by the city of Amsterdam (Essed 1996), which was later replaced by another organization, *Zami*. Black women, tired of being caught between the ethnic minority policy and women's emancipation policies demanded their own policy to fit their own requirements. Successful lobbying, especially by the first Black woman on the National Women's Emancipation Council, Yasemin Tumer, urged the council to reflect on the specific problems faced by Black women. This has resulted in one seat on the council being reserved for an ethnic minority representative.

Black women are, of course, heterogeneous, divided by class, sexual orientation, nationality and religion, among others. Therefore, Black feminism 'reflects differing priorities and differences of emphasis. These differences are themselves reflective of the divisions among the various constituencies of Black women' (Charting the Journey Editorial Group 1987: 6). The heterosexism of many migrant women's organizations, for example, has excluded the concerns of homosexual migrant women confronting both heterosexist migration legislation and homophobic societies (Zehra 1987).

Attempts to transcend these political choices based on single axes are being explored through experiments in 'transversal' politics. This is based on notions of 'rootings' – an awareness of women's own positionality and politics – and 'shiftings' – a commitment to dialogue, to exchanging information and understanding with those in different situations and with different identities. Transversalism implies a willingness to address difference and to negotiate across these differences, as opposed to universalism, which assumes unified positionings and goals. Italian feminists in Women's Centres in Bologna and Torino have engaged with this form of activity (Yuval-Davis 1998). Zami in the Netherlands aims to facilitate co-operation between women with different migrant status including ethnic minority citizens and refugee women. A successful coalition between Caribbean, Turkish, Moroccan, Moluccan and Indonesian women in the Netherlands has been set up in an attempt to confront racism within Europe (Zamikrant 1992).

The possibility for transversal politics is, however, limited by irreconcilable differences that may exist between women because of their diverse positionings and politics (Yuval-Davis 1998). The inadequate emphasis on the need for structural change and the insistence on the diversity of women's perspectives make it difficult for this politics to confront seriously the major political issues facing migrant women. In the face of growing divergence between migrant groups in terms of economic and citizenship status, the divergent political demands of different groups places strain on the success of the transversal approach. Nevertheless, these examples point to the possibilities of developing alliances on specific and short-term goals.

Electoral politics

The most distinctive element in political citizenship is the right to vote and stand for election and thus to exercise power within the state at national or local level. In most EU states, these rights are based on citizenship, although these vary considerably between member states (see Chapter 4). Even where migrants (or second generation migrants) have these rights, their participation in the formal politics of the receiving country tends to be low, especially for women. This, however, varies according to their own country of origin and their reasons for migration, as well as the political structures and rules of political citizenship of the country of settlement.

A study of political participation of migrant women in Norway conducted in 1991–2 looked at women from Pakistan, India, Chile and Vietnam (Gill, n. d.) and pointed to marked differences in the participation of these groups. It found that 7.7 per cent had participated in political meetings, 5.8 per cent in political strikes, 9.4 per cent were members of political parties and 1.9 per cent had contested elections. However, in the less formal political arena the figures for participation increased with 21.2 per cent participating in 'signature' campaigns, 21.2 per cent in local community work and 28.8 per cent holding membership of voluntary organizations. Political participation is particularly limited for the first few years after entry. Vietnamese women, who were mainly refugees and the most recent migrants, were most likely to consider voting unimportant. Pakistani women, who were mainly migrant workers, were more likely to have a political understanding of employment but were largely absent from most formal political arenas. Chilean women, many of whom had fled Chile when the political rights of its citizens were restricted during Pinochet's dictatorship, had the highest participation in local elections, precisely because of their political activities and beliefs.

Members of migrant communities are under-represented in elected offices, and those who have stood have been overwhelmingly male. In Britain, there are now a handful within the parliament, of whom two are women. Geddes (1993) in a study of British local elections found that Asian men were the largest group of ethnic minority councillors. Asian women were almost non-existent except in London where they are still heavily outnumbered by men. A more even balance exists within the Afro-Caribbean community, which however, is overall less well represented. He explains the lack of involvement by ethnic minorities on the basis of the cost of political activity in terms of foregone income; alienation from the mainstream political system; and for women by 'cultural constraints, relating to religious belief' (Geddes 1993: 49).

While patriarchal control over women's political activity has limited their participation, this has not been the only cause. Migrant men and women may join the rank-and-file of political parties, but it is often harder for them to reach positions of responsibility. Women may be involved in local politics as councillors, but are less likely to receive party support to stand at the more significant national elections. Kauppi (1999) found that French women were more likely to be selected as candidates for European Parliamentary elections and that they often used success at the European level to enter mainstream French political systems. Procedures for selection of candidates often operate in discriminatory ways, especially at the national level. Women find it easier to be selected in multiparty systems, which uses proportional representation rather than first past the post; multi-member constituencies, rather than single member constituencies; and devolved power with the option of participating and influencing the political process at sub-national levels (Norris 1993). However, it is not clear whether these factors also improve migrant women's chances of obtaining a party ticket.

Movements demanding the use of quota systems to increase participation of women have met with different degrees of success. The 300 plus movement, which demands parliamentary representation in proportion to the gender break-down of the population in the UK and the Parity movement in France have not addressed the issue of migrant women per se. French liberal feminists, who have argued for the significance of gender disparities in national power structures, have often discounted other axes of difference, notably those around ethnicity and 'race' (Mossuz-Lavau 1996). Often, Black women have found the issue of their representation being treated as a subset of representation of Black people rather than by the feminist movements.

Migrant women elected to office face intense conflicts of loyalty. With so few elected, they raise high expectations among the communities, which may not be deliverable. Most are elected as members of parties, but the party programmes may come into conflict with their own views and those of the community. Where they regard themselves as representative of the community, they tend to be marginalized within the party. Although Black candidates are generally seen as a liability in national elections, in some areas with high migrant populations this is not the case, as they are seen as necessary to bring out the vote. Central party offices may impose 'acceptable' Black women candidates in areas with high migrant populations, without consulting local party activists (Ali 1999). Such women, even if elected, do not have contacts with the grassroots and may see their role as being part of the mainstream. The British Labour Party has moved away from its traditional voters, distancing itself from 'traditional' Black working class men, who do not match New Labour's 'modern' image. Significantly, it is women from these communities who may well become the acceptable face of 'modern Labour' politics (Ali 1999).

In many parts of Europe the local state has been a crucial area for political participation of ethnic minorities and the development of policies on integration. In Germany and Belgium local advisory councils on 'ethnic minority issues' have been in existence for two decades and are consulted by local elected bodies, although their influence is limited (Essed 1996). In France, the state maintains a strongly secularist position, with citizenship based on adherence to a common French culture (Anthias and Yuval Davis 1992). Republican orthodoxy refuses any formal recognition of ethnic differentiation (Poinsot 1993) but, at local level, multicultural initiatives have been developed since the 1970s, involving provision of specific services, and the involvement of community groups in a consultative capacity (Hargreaves and Wihtol de Wenden 1993; Schain 1993). At the same time, openly exclusionist policies were carried out in other local areas, and these practices have increasingly been forced, through the initiative of the Right, into the arena of national politics.

At local level in Britain where competition for seats is less intense, there has been a tendency for clientist politics to develop. Many Labour-run councils created special Race Equality units whose agenda tends to conflict, and be seen in competition with those of the Women's units set up at the same time, giving little space to Black and migrant women.

Studies of voting behaviour have shown that minority ethnic communities tend to support parties of the Left (Geddes 1993; Schain 1993). Migrant populations (including Irish and Commonwealth citizens, as well as second generation) represent some of the most loyal voters for the Labour party in Britain. This pattern is also seen elsewhere in Europe. However, many factors influence voting patterns and social mobility tends to weaken this attachment. Asian Women Conservatives held their first conference in London in 1996. The chair, describing the participation of Asians in entrepreneurship and their belief in the family and tradition declared that 'Asian values are Conservative values'. Those of Indian origin are most likely of any ethnic minority group to vote Conservative. The Conservative Party has been uneasy about making direct linkages of minority identities with their party politics. The Labour Party, on the other hand, has been more accommodating although the Black Section is not formally recognized.

Where migrants have the vote, their participation in elections varies with ethnic groups in complex ways. In the Netherlands, the turn-out of Turkish and Moroccan women is less than that of men, but in Sweden the participation of Turkish women has increased and is equal to that of men (Rath 1990). Organizations such as Operation Black Vote have lobbied to encourage Black people's participation in national and European elections, making links with organizations in countries such as Norway and Germany. Whether they specifically target women is, however, not clear. Similarly, SSU Botvida, a social democratic movement in Botkyrka, Sweden, attempts to encourage young migrant women to engage in political activities as part of its integration project in Stockholm (Gomes and Norlander 1998). The two organizations, which were set up to encourage political participation by men and women of North African background (France Plus) and to fight racism (SOS Racisme), have pursued an integrationist stance and republican values (Poinsot 1993).

Women's organizations have often 'challenged the idea that women's interests are best served by participation in the conventional politics of party organization, election procedures and government by elected representatives of the people' (Siddiqui 1999).

Struggles in the workplace

As we discussed in Chapter 5, migrant women's participation in the workforce is very varied both in its extent and nature. African-Caribbean women in Britain, for example, are more economically active within the formal sector than either African-Caribbean men or White British women and are, therefore, heavily represented in the membership of trade unions. For some groups, legal and structural barriers to the labour market may force them into informal sectors such as homeworking, domestic work and the sex industry. These sectors are notoriously isolated and difficult for conventional trade union organization, but women have found new forms of workplace activism.

The nature of trade unionism in Europe has undergone major transformations over the past two decades as economic restructuring has brought the rise of service industries and the decline of manufacturing. Their total membership and influence have declined as the old bastions of traditional unionism in manufacturing and mining have been decimated, but they have also been forced to change their priorities to reflect their changed membership and their new circumstances. Trade unions have traditionally been dominated by white working class men and they have often supported or colluded with exclusionary practices against both women and ethnic minorities (Walby 1990; Cockburn 1992). Phizacklea and Miles (1987) argue that the British Trade Union Movement shifted from overt to covert racism through the 1980s and institutionalized racist practices in their own political structures, excluding Asian and African-Caribbean men and women from elected offices within the movement. Black women in Britain in the 1980s, for example, were twice as likely as White women to be in trade unions, but half as likely to be officials of these unions (CRE 1992). In Sweden, participation by migrant women is generally high. In Belgium, Austria and Poland, participation is also high but extremely variable by sector.

Black workers have formed their own movements with organizations, both to press trade unions to address issues of race, and to mobilize workers within their own ethnic groups to join and support the wider trade union movement. The Indian Workers' Association, established in 1938, has discouraged separatism. The role of women in such organizations often remains limited. In Sweden, migrants have formed their own labour union, although the extent and form of women's participation in the union is not clear. This pressure, together with the changing membership and the adoption of an equal opportunities agenda within the mainstream, has forced changes in trade unions. They have become an important political tool for constructing and enforcing equality legislation (Singh 1998).

Migrant women often participate in the least secure forms of work, and their participation in labour unions is therefore limited. Some of the most important struggles of Black women have been to gain recognition of their trade union from employers. In 1993, women from Gujarat waged a long (but ultimately unsuccessful) struggle for union recognition at Burnsall's factory in Birmingham. Their leader, Darshan Kaur, was awarded a civil liberties award (*Independent* 10.12.1993). One of the most crucial British labour disputes of the 1970s, at Grunwicks in North London, was also waged by a largely female Asian workforce. It too was a struggle for union recognition, and it gained mass support from the Left and rank-and-file trade unionists.

Many migrant women are prevented from entering the formal labour market. Asylum seekers are not allowed to work in the first

months of their stay in Europe and some European states ban
women entering through family reunion from employment. Many
are forced into casualized illicit employment. The scope for
organization is minimal because they are vulnerable to deportation if found to be working illegally. For others, language barriers
and racism, together with patriarchal control over their movements, prevent them from working outside their home.
Homeworking may provide the only means of entry into the labour
market. Their atomized status has made it difficult for homeworkers
to organize themselves, but some successful campaigns have been
established, such as the Leicester Outworkers Campaign and the
West Yorkshire Homeworking Group, which have documented the
extent of homeworking, provided information on wages and
working conditions in a number of languages and have supported
individual women's claims to payment (Tate 1993). Homeworking
groups have actively collaborated with unions representing casualized workers from other parts of the world, particularly the Self-
Employed Women's Association (SEWA) in India, but also parallel
organizations in Europe. The Women's Union in the Netherlands,
which represents both wives of industrial workers and women
employed in industry, has set up Homework Support Centres to
help women in this sector and has campaigned to keep their
concerns at the forefront of trade union negotiations. The
Homeworkers' Campaign gained a major victory when the
International Labour Organization agreed to recognize them as
workers with the same rights as other workers in relation to
standards of pay and conditions, and to organize as workers
(Rowbotham 1998).

While many women employed in homeworking have rights of
residence, large numbers of those involved in domestic work and
the sex industry have no legal residential status in Europe. A concession introduced by Margaret Thatcher's government allowed
foreign employers and expatriates to bring in their domestic workers
with them, but tied those workers to that employer so that they had
no immigration or employment status in their own right (see
Chapter 5). The Commission for Filipino Migrant workers was set
up to support Filipino migrants in the UK, many of whom were
domestic workers (Anderson 1993). The Commission increasingly
gave support to workers of other nationalities. It became clear that
the immigration law was at the root of the problem. Alliances were
forged with other groups, including trade unions, lawyers and other

immigrant groups, to form *Kalayaan*. After ten years campaigning, on 23 July 1998, the UK government agreed to regularize the position of migrant domestic workers[3].

In Italy, almost half of all migrants are women, who are often unaccompanied, and enter low-wage service sector occupations such as domestic work. For live-in domestic workers, the workplace is foreclosed as a site of political activity. Hence, domestic workers regularly meet in public places and 'friendship groups' have become an important site of social support from which political activity has emerged (Campani 1997). Informal groups thus provide the space for some women's politicization. However, trade unions have had a particularly strong influence over African and North African groups, such as the Senegalese in Italy.

Campaigning for migrant rights

As the rights of large groups of migrants, particularly asylum seekers, have been eroded, the focus of political activity is increasingly on securing the most basic means of survival for community members. In the context of the tightening of the conditions under which migrants are able to enter and remain in Britain, campaigns for the rights of women migrants have sought to end their dependence on men and to secure autonomous status. These campaigns have often been based around individual cases, for example of women facing deportation, but have often broadened out into more general campaigns, involving coalitions of migrant women, women's groups and voluntary organizations working for migrant rights. Some European countries provide subsidies through local government to fund women's community groups whereas others are entirely voluntary or benefit from charitable donations.

The Immigrant Woman's Collective founded in France in 1982 involved more than twenty organizations of migrant women from different racial and ethnic groups. It formed in response to a French government immigration review in 1981, which found that 80 per cent of migrant women were 'illegal' (Haif 1986). Women divorcees, heads of household and those separated from their husbands did not have legal rights of residence. Furthermore, some of those with rights to stay had no rights to employment. Hence, a number of homeworkers and domestic workers found that they were legal residents but illegal workers. The Collective pressed for legislative changes such as recognition of family reunification without impositions (such as that of residence), rights to autonomous residence and employment status, and for recognition as political refugees in their own right. They also pressed for protection of rights for those whose status changed because of divorce, separation or widowhood, or through economic problems (Haif 1986). Although similar problems exist across Europe, most campaigns have been organized at national rather than European levels. In France, *Rajfire* (*reseau pour l'autonomie des femmes immigrées et réfugiées*) was formed in 1998 from a number of groups several years ago and it campaigns for women to be given autonomous status independent of their relationship to a male migrant. In Germany, *Paragraph 19* is campaigning to reduce the years of dependency, which is currently three years for Turkish women and four years for all other migrant women. Similar issues are addressed by RIFFI, a migrant women's association based in Sweden. Migrant women, especially from Africa, have been extremely prominent in the Sans Papiers movement in France, which put an enormous amount of pressure in 1996 on the French government to grant an amnesty to the undocumented, many of whom had become so because of the harsh measures introduced by Pasqua in 1993/4 (see Chapter 3). The Sans Papiers made connections with other social movements and gained a great deal of press and public sympathy (Costa-Lascoux 1999).

The withdrawal of the 'primary purpose' rule by the Labour Government in the UK in 1997 followed years of campaigning by a number of groups including those representing migrant women and voluntary organizations with broader membership. But the ending of the ruling has not been welcomed by all women potentially affected. With the establishment of a second generation community in Britain, British-born women were used to bring in men, especially from Pakistan. Bands of young men have set themselves up as 'bounty hunters' to locate and 'return' girls who flee from such marriages. Such practices have been widely condoned within the community. The primary purpose rule provided one possibility of escape from these marriages because women were able to claim to immigration authorities that their husbands were using marriage for immigration. Southall Black Sisters (SBS) found themselves facing this conflict when women seeking refuge with them urged them to utilize racist migration laws to deport violent husbands (Griffin 1995; Patel 1999). This condemnation of the government in the name of women's rights for its withdrawal of a racist rule illustrates the complexity of the struggles that migrant women's organizations have to face (Patel 1999). Women's rights are indeed precarious if they depend for their protection on a rule that treats their own nationals as objects of suspicion. A more positive response has been the campaign within the community to make forced marriages illegal and to get sexual relations within forced marriages recognized as rape. The condemnation of these marriages by the Muslim Parliament on 12 July 1999 was hailed as a major victory.

In spite of the abolition of the primary purpose rule, the problem of families divided by immigration law remains. Zuber and Khatija Latif fought a long campaign to prevent their separation, which won all-party support on the local council.[4] Khatija (a British citizen) was held captive by her family for several months and subject to mental and physical abuse in an attempt to force her to marry a 'suitable' husband. Although she escaped and married Zuber, he remained under threat of deportation for many years. His leave to remain ran out while she was imprisoned, and the marriage for which Khatija suffered was treated as 'suspicious'. Zuber was finally given leave to stay in November 1999 after twelve years in Britain.

Like many anti-deportation campaigns, theirs was called the Latif 'family campaign', stressing the right to family life that immigration law threatens. This has proved useful in building support from the widest possible constituency, but campaigners have had to tread a careful path between defending this right to family life and supporting other aspects of the 'family'. Southall Black Sisters has been at the forefront of campaigning against domestic violence within Asian families and has braved the community's hostility for this work. The organization has, however, sometimes made alliances with conservative groupings in order to defend women's rights. In the fight for justice for Zoora Shah, a Pakistani Muslim who killed her husband after years of abuse, SBS secured support from religious organizations whom they felt were more likely to be listened to by politicians. The organization has also worked closely with traditional non-feminist women's groups such as the Women's Institute and the Townswomen's Guild on the issue of domestic violence.

Another area of campaigning has been for the recognition of women as refugees in their own right. Current conventions emphasize political persecution within the public sphere, thus men are more likely to be seen as political refugees. Feminists have pointed out the need to recognize gendered harm and gendered persecution as valid reasons for seeking asylum. In Britain, the Refugee Women's Legal Group (RWLG), which brings together refugee women, lawyers and other activists, has been at the forefront of this campaign. It has worked with many organizations to produce Gender Guidelines for the Determination of Asylum Claims in the UK. RWLG is also campaigning to extend its influence at the European level through the European Council on Refugees and Exiles.

In contrast to the highly localized concerns of most migrant groups, some have had a national brief. In Britain, the Organization of Women of African and Asian descent (OWAAD) was initially effective in bringing together local groups, but lack of resources was an important factor in its demise. The National Association of Women of Afrikan Descent (NAWAD) was established in 1989, but was unable to expand beyond its membership of Caribbean women based in the south-east and is now also defunct. The Black Women for Wages for Housework campaign nationally for recognition of Black women's unwaged work and improved rights to benefits (Sudbury 1998). *Black Women Against Rape* now campaigns for rights to asylum for women who have been sexually abused. *Les Nanas Beurs* was established in 1985 to support migrant women from North Africa. The group has aimed to address the practical difficulties that women face as they tread the difficult path between patriarchal oppression and the 'burden of their origins' (Benani 1995: 79) on the one side, and being held up as models of successful integration on the other. It provided legal and practical support to women in crisis as a result of the immigration laws. The organization helped a number of women who had been kidnapped by male relatives and taken to North Africa to be married so that they were either refused re-entry to France or were forced to enter 'illegally'. It has also advised women who fled North Africa, because they were refused abortion as unmarried mothers.

Solidarity groups, mainly of European women, may play an important role in supporting migrant organizations. These relationships may be sensitive, and there is a danger that solidarity groups may 'allow overbearing "maternalism" to set the tone' (Castro 1986). While solidarity groups aim 'to guarantee the autonomy of migrant women's organizations without interfering with their specific demands' (Castro 1986) this aim is difficult to achieve in practice. In Italy, groups such as FILEF (Federation of Emigrant Workers of Communist Origin) and the Fernando Santi Institute, which had campaigned for the rights of Italy emigrants are now addressing issues of migrant rights.

Many women's forums have actively networked with one another and with other feminist and anti-racist organizations. The MiRA centre in Norway has links with over 500 migrant organizations in Norway and also represents migrants' views at the Nordic Women's Forum (Salimi 1995). SBS has been working closely with the Women's Institute, the Townswomen's Guild and with Justice for Women on the issue of domestic violence. The NGO Working Group on Migrant and Refugee Women organized a panel at Nairobi to focus attention on the ways in which migrant women had mobilized themselves: members of various community groups such as the Immigrant Collective in France attended the meeting. This facilitated the building of larger international coalitions and networks – vertical and horizontal – with other women's organizations. Organizations, such as TIYE International in the Netherlands, have also highlighted the connections between women in the North and the South, focusing on issues of development in the South (Essed 1996). They operate from an integrationist perspective, campaigning to provide migrant women with equal access to employment, appropriate working conditions and control over economic resources.

Community political activity

Community groups play an important role for many migrant women. They draw on a sense of belonging both to the locality within which they are currently resident and to the ethnic, national or regional grouping in the place of origin. However, communities both cohere and fracture along lines of gender, ethnic group, class and other axes. They serve both to create a sense of inclusion and of exclusion because community political activity involves a privileging of ethnic belongingness. Community activism may involve mobilizing around issues of gender within the community; across these gender divisions around policies in the home country; or around polices and legislation in the country of settlement. They may thus seek to influence policy at local, national and international level. Women's participation in community politics may arise from the obstacles they face in entering the formal political arena. Local political associations may provide them with the only forum for lobbying for change.

Moser (1993) differentiates between organizations dealing with practical gender needs and those fighting for strategic gender needs. The former, she argues, are ameliorative but do not question the basis of inequality, whereas the latter challenge unequal power structures and therefore involve moves towards larger structural shifts in women's experiences. A number of migrant women's organizations have adopted a welfarist approach, providing services aimed primarily at meeting women's practical gender needs without necessarily questioning the broader structures that impact on women's lives. In practice, however, the distinction is not that clear-cut. Craske (1993) argues that welfare issues, such as fertility and childcare, are not merely practical day-to-day problems but are of strategic significance for women. Participation in community political activities may also be the first step towards a broader political involvement, which can lead women to enter a more formal arena. Women and men may use their experience within organizations to become mediators between the group and the local state, through political structures or within welfare services. The women who are able to take on this role often represent the elite because of their social or economic capital.

Although women's participation in community networks may arise out of concerns for the community, this activity inevitably brings them into contact with the wider social network in which the group exists. The activity may extend both to other areas within the country of residence and to the country of origin. *La Baraka, Salon de Provence* was started in 1980 by an Algerian woman who had joined her husband through family reunion (Delacroix 1997). The small town where she lived was built at the end of the 1960s to house people repatriated from North Africa and miners from the North who were seeking to move into in other sectors. Social and political tensions were high, partly because of its changing and mixed population and unemployment (30 per cent) and there was a high vote for the National Front. The Association was set up with the aim of getting individuals off welfare assistance. It also promoted communication with local institutions and between residents with different cultures and religions. The group often took a critical attitude towards social policy, and this brought it into conflict with local state institutions. Its activities have extended beyond France to Algeria, where it has attempted to improve conditions for abandoned children and orphans in Constantine. It has taken risks and has stayed independent and critical of political parties. It is seen by the local state as being too informal and spontaneous, and thus not easily controlled by the authorities.

Community activity may face migrant women with conflicting loyalties between their rights as women and those of ethnic identity, particularly in the context of the growing racism across Europe. Women who participate in Maghrebi associations in France, for instance, are more likely than men to press for secularism, for sexual equality and rights to birth control (Wihtol de Wenden 1994). This may well bring them into conflict with men, whereas they may work with Maghrebi men to press for rights within French society.

The conflict between ethnic and feminine identities has been felt acutely in struggles over domestic violence and women's sexuality. Another issue, which has posed these issues particularly starkly, is female circumcision. For Somali women within a hostile and racist society, belongingness and economic security may depend on conformity to community norms that may restrict women's behaviour. The pressures on women to have their daughters circumcised may become overwhelming (D-Ashur 1992). This issue is likely to remain a major source of division within the community. Although many women with young daughters brought up in Britain have resolved not to have them circumcised it is still common for daughters to be sent to Africa to be circumcised because the practice is illegal in Britain. Uncertainty about how long they will remain in Britain has implications for the continuation of this practice. Many Somalis fear that if their daughters are not circumcised, they would be ostracized from the community and this would be more intense in Somalia itself (Sales and Gregory 1998).

Women have sometimes set up their own community organizations because they feel excluded from male-dominated associations. A group of Somali women in London began meeting in each other's homes until given permission to use local authority premises. The men who used the same premises tried at first to prevent the women having access, but the group continues to thrive, offering a range of advice and support to women. Men's response to this success is often ambivalent. As we saw in chapter seven in relation to the Somali community, men may be willing to support women's work for the community, but also fear the impact of these activities in providing a means of escape from patriarchal control. By bringing them into contact with wider organizations, networks and ideas, these activities can be a means for women to start to question aspects of community norms and to gain some measure of autonomy.

Women involved in these activities are under scrutiny not for their politics or their activities for the group, but as women. Criticism of women's sexual behaviour can be used by men as a means of maintaining control over women's political activities (Roy 1995).

Although groups are divided along ethnic lines, women have tended to be more open to working with women from other groups. Women are often amongst the first to cross ethnic lines and involve themselves in cross-ethnic group activities. Essed argues that their relative exclusion from ethnic mobilization means that they have fewer differences with women from other ethnic groups and suffer less from the divisive policies of national governments. Furthermore, a similar pattern of exclusion by male ethnic group members provides a common platform for women and a basis for forming coalitions (Essed 1996).

Sales and Gregory (1998) found that Somali women collaborated in community and education projects and friendships span the two main ethnic groups. Those with better language and other skills are able to use these to support other members of the community. Those who speak little English rely heavily on the groups for help in interpreting, negotiating with officials, and pursuing their claims with the Home Office. Similarly, the Turkish Women's Group in Botkyrka, Sweden, which organized itself in order to provide better activities for young women who faced limits to their mobility, also admits Chileans, Syrians, Iranians, Rumanians and Bosnian women of many religious denominations (Gomes and Norlander 1998).

In countries with relatively heterogeneous migrant populations, such as Spain and Italy, community groups have found it difficult to overcome their differences and have found themselves competing against each other for small amounts of funding. The issue of representation has also been contentious. A Maghrebi organization in Rome claimed to represent the interests of all Maghrebi migrants, which was challenged by other organizations representing Maghrebi migrants (Danese 1998b)

Politics and the country of origin

The role played by first and second generation migrants in the politics of their country of origin is often disproportionate to their

numbers. As generally relatively better-resourced members of the
nation they have been able to sponsor political activism in their
home countries. This kind of activity tends to be dominated by
men, reflecting the male domination of politics both at home and
within Europe. Women have, however, become active both through
mainstream political activity and in work specifically aimed at
supporting women. For some, particularly those who went into
exile for political reasons, this reflects a continuation of previous
concerns and involvement, whether this involved specifically
gendered concerns or affiliation to broader political and social
movements. For others, including second generation migrants, this
may develop out of their involvement in the country of immigration. Southall Black Sisters, for example takes part in the *Alliance
Against Communalism and for Democracy in South Asia*. Women's activity
is often very practical. For instance, *Les Nanas Buers* gives support
to Algerian women who been politically persecuted because they
refused to wear the veil.

Migrant women have both participated in broader political
campaigns in the country of origin and also set up their own
organizations. The *Mouvement des Femmes Algériennes pour la Démocratie*
(MFAD) was established in Paris in 1990 in response to the
worsening situation of women in Algeria following the local elections. MFAD is a network of women that seeks to advance democracy
in both Algeria and France, working with French and international
NGOs to facilitate communication with Algerian women. The
organization involves 'Algerian women, of immigrant origin or
descendants of immigrants' and challenges 'the rise of intolerance
and archaic attitudes which threaten the rights of all Algerians' and
'the intolerance, racism and discrimination we face in France'. It
campaigns for the 'separation of political power and religion,
respect for private and public freedoms; the equality of rights
between women and men' in Algeria and for civil and social rights
for Algerian women in France.

When demonstrations by women take place in Algeria, MFAD
tries to create parallel demonstrations in France. It also organizes
in partnership with other North African women's organizations
such as *Nanas Beurs* and *Pluri-Elles*. MFAD undertakes social as well
as political activity in relation to Algeria, for example, it supports
women's groups, sending items such as office equipment. As part
of its work to promote citizenship, it has participated in the creation of a Centre for Associations (a resource, documentation and

training centre) in the suburbs of Algiers. The Centre was launched following a telethon in Algeria in 1992. A group of several NGOs, *Collectif Solidarité Algérie*, presented the plan to the EC and obtained finances to set up the centre. In France, the MFAD also does work in neighbourhoods, especially in areas of high immigrant population in inner Paris.

Men tend to retain a disproportionately greater interest in the politics of the home country and often seek to maintain patriarchal control over political activity. Women have tended to be less involved in campaigns for dual citizenship, which would allow migrants to retain voting rights in their home country. They are less likely to want to return to their country of origin than men: 51 per cent of migrants applying for naturalization in France are women although they make up only 40 per cent of the general population (Costa-Lascoux 1995). Their political involvement in the politics of the host country reflects this. Women who participate in Maghrebian associations in France are more likely than men to press for integration into French society (Wihtol de Wenden 1994) and this may well influence their attitude to and participation in politics in the Maghreb.

Political affiliations with parties in the home country tend to be reflected in migrant organizations in Europe. Major schisms within the Indian Worker's Association (UK) have reflected the allegiance of some sections with political parties in India. The Turkish- and Kurdish-speaking communities in Europe are riven with conflict reflecting political struggles in Turkey. Women refugees have sometimes found themselves marginalized in the exile community, with men seen as the main political activist, even if the women themselves were politically involved (Lopez Zarzosa 1998), and this has sometimes redirected their activity towards the country of settlement. As we suggested above, women's groups tend to be more open to making alliances across ethnic lines.

Pan-European organization

The state is neither monolithic nor unchanging, and opportunities for political change present themselves both through shifts within the state and through shifts in the relationship between states. The shifting nature of inter-state relations within the EU has provided a whole arena for political activity for migrant women. European integration policy on migration has both curtailed migrant rights and provided the impetus for resistance by migrant groups. As migration policy is increasingly formulated at European union level, migrant groups have operated at European level to contest its exclusionary implications. At the same time, the European Commission and Parliament have provided some space and resources for those campaigning for migrant rights, although member states have challenged and curtailed the role of the Commission in migration policy (see Chapter 4). European structures, such as the Parliament and the European Court of Justice, have also provided forums for challenging and sometimes overturning exclusionary national legislation (Geddes 1998).

Migrants' formal representation within the European Union has been limited, but in 1991 the EU established the Migrants Forum to operate as the official channel of communication between migrants groups and European institutions (Danese 1998a). The Forum has campaigned for migrant rights at the European level, including the right to free movement within the EU for third country nationals. Very few women's organizations are represented through the Forum and still fewer women are sent as representatives of mixed groups (Hoskyns 1996).

The European Women's Lobby was established in 1990 to represent women's interests in the Commission and Parliament. Each member state has four national delegates but the basis on which they are chosen is not specified and only in the Netherlands has a seat been specifically targeted to represent ethnic minority interests. The European Women's Lobby has by and large been resistant to issues of racism but it has funded individual projects. In order to facilitate access to mainstream women's lobby groups, a European Black Women's Network was launched in 1993. It acts as a pressure group independent of political parties and attempts to incorporate and address problems raised by all Black women, regardless of nationality.

While migrant groups have maintained their independence from political parties, some parties have given them support. The Green Party organized the first conference on immigrant women from the Third World, which laid the basis for the establishment of the Black Women's Network. Mrs Tidja Tazdait, a second-generation North African from Lyon was elected to the European Parliament in 1984 as a Green Party candidate.

The extent to which migrant women have utilized European political space to represent their interests depends on the national context within which they operate, their own migration history, the kinds of associations they form in their country of settlement, the know-how and resources they are able to share and the cultures in their country of origin (Danese 1998a). The national and subnational levels provide the most significant forums for lobbying the EU (Geddes 1998). The Filipino Women's Commission, based in Rome, has had some access to EU funds and has been one of the most successful of migrant women's groups operating at the EU level. The Council of Europe has also funded a project, Young Women from Minorities, to bring together work undertaken for and by ethnic minority women in Europe (Uma 1999). Many of these initiatives do not challenge the structural inequalities that shape migrant women's lives and remain confined to a narrow welfarist agenda. Some groups, such as *La Voix des Femmes* in Brussels, have been able to adopt a more overtly political approach as they have become more established (Hoskyns 1996).

The European Union has provided a unique opportunity for women's organizations, although these opportunities have not so far been sufficiently exploited, either by migrant women or women's groups more generally. A number of Pan-European organizations of migrant women have emerged outside EU structures. These often use the country of origin as the basis for entry and participation. One example is the *Turkish Women Migrants of Europe*. Sub-Saharan women have also been particularly active in organizing at the European level (Costa-Lascoux 1995). Another successful organization is *Babaylan*, The Network of Philippine Women in Europe, named after a priestess who held a high position in pre-Spanish Philippine society. The First Conference of Philippine Women in Europe in September 1992 brought together 68 women from organizations across Europe to discuss the problems of class, race and gender inequalities both in the workplace and in the home. The organization became registered under Dutch Law as a Europe-wide Federation. It aims to empower women through campaigning on issues affecting Filipino women in Europe and in the Philippines and through training, education and sharing information. It provides a network to connect Filipino women in Europe with women of other nationalities, both in the Philippines and in Europe (Carlos Valencia 1996). Groups campaigning for the rights of bi-national families (Austria, France, Germany, Italy, the Netherlands and Switzerland) have exchanged information and held conferences. Often it has been citizen women married to migrant men who have initiated these groups (see Chapter 3).[5]

European-level representation of migrant interests has frequently been facilitated through labour unions, which have tended to marginalize women's involvement. The Church, particularly the Catholic Church, has also played a major role in this area. For many migrants, including Filipinos and Indian nurses, the church facilitates the migration process. The Church has used this role as an agent of migration to help migrants to adapt, but also controlled the ways in which these women socialize and interact in the host country (Escriva 1997; Danese 1998b).

Conclusion

The activities described in this chapter illustrate the wealth of political activity in which migrant women engage. Far from being passive victims of patriarchal social systems and racist immigration policy, migrant women have challenged the constraints on their political activities and engaged in and reworked the definition of the political.

Many face legal exclusion from the formal political process, while the demands of maintaining a day-to-day existence for themselves and their families can also inhibit political involvement. These demands, however, force them to devote their energies towards establishing themselves in the country of settlement and thus to involvement in society and in building support networks within and beyond their communities. These activities can seem less significant than the major struggles that have propelled them to migrate. But they can provide the confidence and independence to allow them to become political actors in their own right, whether in the politics of the homeland or in that of the country of settlement.

Political citizenship is thus complex and multidimensional. Constraints on participation in the formal political process have not prevented women from participating in other aspects of political citizenship through struggles to extend their rights and those of others. The success of some of these campaigns demonstrates the possibilities of action by those legally on the margins of society. But they also demonstrate the continuing relevance of formal citizenship status.

The campaigns in which migrant women have participated illustrate the continuing importance of struggles for women's basic rights. They also offer a crucial area for feminist engagement and for building effective political alliances at national and European level. Given women's, particularly migrant women's, limited access to policy-making bodies, women have used other forums and other forms of representation to present their interests. Some people argue that these new forms of associations and networking provide better means of accommodating the new pluralism and multiplicity of identities among migrants in Western society. However, at least some of these forums reinstate gendered and racist hierarchies. Besides, these networks can only be one strategy within the multipronged approach necessary to improve public provision and representation of migrant women in Europe.

Notes

1 The standard letter granting refugee status or Exceptional Leave to Remain in the UK includes the following sentence: 'You should, however, fully understand that if you take part in activities involving the support or encouragement of violence or conspiracy to cause violence the (Home Secretary) may curtail your stay or deport you' (Refugee Council, undated).
2 In the case of a Kurdish community, the Turkish state has made attempts to prevent exiles organizing politically.
3 Research conducted by Annie Phizacklea and Brigid Anderson as part of the project on Regularizarion of Undocumented Workers and their Children in the UK (ESRC Transnational Programme).
4 Information supplied by Zuber and Khatija Latif.
5 Information on the activities of bi-national groups has been generously provided by Betty de Hart, a member of the Dutch organization Lawine.

Chapter 8

Conclusion

Our main aim in this book has been to present a more accurate account of past and contemporary migration in Europe, through bringing women in from the margins and making them central to our analysis. A gendered analysis, however, involves not merely rendering women 'visible', but a transformation in the way in which we conceptualize migration theory. The motives underlying migration, and the changing structures of demand for migrant labour, can only be understood by using a framework that takes account of developments in both the public and private spheres of social life. Such an analysis also dissolves the rigid distinctions between analysis of employment, welfare and politics.

In seeking to raise the importance of female migration on the academic and political agendas, we are conscious that we are to some extent swimming against the tide of contemporary developments in feminist theory and practice. The current preoccupation with cultural phenomena and with identity, while potentially enriching our understanding of migrant experience, has also tended to overshadow concern with issues of basic rights and to discourage rather than galvanize collective political response. Much of the contemporary debate on 'race' also takes place in isolation from discussion of the process of migration, and in particular neglects the issues arising from insecurity of legal status that we have highlighted in this book. Thus, in emphasizing the diversity of migrant experience, we are concerned with the legal and political conditions that structure migrants' opportunities as well as with the process by which individuals negotiate and challenge these structures.

State policies on migration throughout Europe have become more repressive, not least in areas such as the conditions of family reunion which are of particular concern to women. Official and popular discourses have attempted to construct a national and European identity based on myths of origin that exclude the past and contemporary contribution of non-Europeans. Migration in this view is seen as a new phenomenon that is disruptive of existing social structures rather than part of a continuing process of economic and cultural development. Even multicultural discourses, while attempting a more positive view of migrants, tend to counterpose new 'ethnic minorities' to a pre-existing homogeneous society.

The history of Europe, however, has been one of massive movements of people as well as goods and finance. The contribution of colonies to the economy of Europe (particularly Britain and France) is well known, but less acknowledged has been the substantial immigration from the colonies during the colonial period, and even less visible the contribution of women. During the post-war period Europe gained substantial benefits from immigration as it was able to drawn on labour whose reproduction costs had been incurred elsewhere. The contribution of migrants has been much wider than the economic sphere, encompassing the language, cultural and political life in Europe.

While European states have since the 1970s continued, refuse to varying degrees, to portray themselves as societies of immigration, migrants play a major role in sustaining economic and social structures, a contribution in which women are increasingly prominent. The tone of contemporary debate on immigration has, however, been relentlessly negative. Current policy initiatives are led by demands to control the movement of asylum seekers. The attempt to create a distinction between 'genuine refugees' and 'economic migrants' denies the economic and social contribution of both groups to European economic and social life.

It has also provided the ideological context for attacks on the human rights of migrants. European harmonization is producing ever more sophisticated mechanisms for the surveillance and control of immigrants. These measures affect not only those deemed outside the law, they create a climate of xenophobia that undermines the rights and security in society as a whole. An understanding of these developments is vital to feminist and progressive movements if they are to be able to rebuild movements for social justice based on equality and freedom.

In this concluding chapter, we firstly summarize some of the key themes that we have developed in the rest of the book. We then discuss briefly future research agendas in the context of likely developments in relation to migration flows and policy. The final section discusses strategies and priorities for campaigning around the rights of migrant women.

The importance of gender

The overriding theme of this book has been the need to make gender a key dimension in our understanding of contemporary migration. We have argued that the feminization of migration, though increasingly acknowledged in academic circles, has so far had little impact on mainstream theory and remains largely invisible in policy discussion. The integration of this gender dimension, however, forces us to challenge the way we think about migration. We argued in Chapter 2 that the forces that precipitate migration can only be understood if we recognize the links between the private and public spheres, and the ways in which economic change impacts differentially on men and women. Similarly, in examining the economic contribution of migrant women in Europe, we have adopted a wider definition of work and welfare that encompasses both paid and unpaid work, and paid labour in both formal and informal settings. The definition of political also becomes widened as campaigns around what have often been considered 'private' concerns force a broader conception of politics. Our understanding of the scope of political activity is extended to embrace a range of community activities, which may have the effect of transforming gender relations in complex and unexpected ways.

The insertion of migrant women into the economies of western Europe has often tended to reinforce traditional gender roles, both in professional occupations such as nursing and in 'unskilled' caring work. As European women have been drawn into the paid labour force, while publicly provided care is withdrawn or underdeveloped, migrant women have often filled the gap in the sphere of reproduction. The fact that male migrants have formed a significant minority in these traditionally feminized occupations is indicative of their low and precarious status within Europe. Migrant women have also been prominent in the caring professions, particularly those traditionally seen as 'women's work'. Shortages in these areas have become chronic because they are generally accorded relatively low status and are poorly paid, although they require a long period of training and dependence on migrant labour is likely to be intensify. We have, however, argued in Chapter 5 that we need to look beyond these traditional sectors of migrant labour and to acknowledge the contribution of migrants in a diversity of occupational groups. Here again the gender dimension is crucial: it is often women who have been most successful in seizing opportunities, both among groups struggling to make a new life in the period immediately following migration, and among more settled and second generation migrants.

The complexity of migration strategies challenges the simplicities of migration theories that base themselves primarily on individual motivation or on broad structural determinants. The inclusion of the dimension of the household into migration theory has broadened our understanding of the migration process, but the household has to be seen not as a homogenous decision-making unit but as a complex social structure, embodying both conflict and inequality as well as mutual support and shared resources. The incentive for migration for many women may include the possibility of escape from the household as well as the means to provide income for themselves and their families. Migration theory is needed that can link individual motivations to broader structural features, and that takes account of intervening institutions such as family, kinship and community networks, as well as formal agencies. This understanding of migration also suggests the need for the sort of in-depth qualitative studies that feminists have pioneered, which can illuminate the motivations and strategies that are hidden within statistics. These studies, however, need to be placed in the context of broader structured developments that require more refined and gender sensitive statistics on migratory movements.

Although women are increasingly the main actors in migration, their status is often restricted by legal structures that view women primarily as dependants. We have argued in Chapter 4 that gender is a crucial dimension of migrant rights. As state polices create an increasingly diverse hierarchy of rights according to formal legal status, length of residence and the category under which people entered Europe, gender is a crucial element in that hierarchy. As western European women have achieved – albeit unevenly – greater legal and economic equality with men, immigration policy continues to restrict the autonomy of migrant women. Equal opportunities between men and women, which has been one of the cornerstones of EU social policy, has not been extended to migrants.

At the same time, gendered ideologies and practices also restrict women's independence. These patriarchal structures operate both at the level of the state and in the broader society (for example in relation to employment opportunities) as well as at the level of 'traditional practices' within the household. In Chapter 7 we challenged the counterposition between women's rights and the rights of migrants or of ethnic minorities. The campaigns around the specific rights of migrant women confront both state racism and sexism, and also the attempts by conservative elements within migrant communities to dictate particular forms of behaviour. These campaigns offer potentially fruitful areas of co-operation between feminists and migrant women.

The importance of citizenship status

Current policies are producing increasing diversity of rights for migrants, based on their legal status, length of residence and the status under which they entered Europe, and their own gender, class and ethnic background. Migrants have been incorporated into aspects of social citizenship within the country of settlement in a variety of ways. This blurring of the boundaries between formal citizenship and the rights traditionally associated with citizenship has, as we have seen, led some commentators to suggest that formal citizenship status is becoming less relevant in an age of migration and 'post-national citizenship'. The extent and nature of this incorporation depends on the particular state welfare regime, migratory regime and tradition of conferring citizenship, as well as on the status and characteristics of the individual migrant. In spite of the powerful forces favouring inclusion, however, formal citizenship status remains of crucial importance. As legally permanent residents have gained some of the social rights associated with citizenship, increasing numbers of new labour migrants and asylum seekers are being denied these rights.

The notion of 'post-national citizenship' has had little reality in the formal political arena. The right to vote and to stand for elections remains firmly related to formal citizenship status in most EU states. Although denied access to the formal political process, migrants have been able to exercise some political rights in other arenas, for example through membership of trade unions and through campaigning and community organizations. It is in the informal sphere of community activity that much of migrant women's activity is concentrated.

It is perhaps in the arena of civil rights that formal citizenship retains most importance, although it is the least studied within academic literature. Non-citizens enjoy certain civil rights (e.g. access to legal process), but even these tend to be conditional rather than absolute. The recent increase in detention and deportation of asylum seekers demonstrates starkly the importance of the nationality of one's passport. Furthermore, freedom of movement is sharply curtailed: for some this means regular reporting to the immigration authorities and restrictions on travel abroad. For domestic workers this can mean being tied to a particular employer.

European integration and the development of European Union Citizenship has paradoxically increased the importance of national membership. The rights of EU citizens have been extended through the Social Charter of 1989 and the opening up of employment and welfare and some voting rights in other European Union states through the Maastricht Treaty. 'Post-national citizenship' has therefore increasing validity for EU citizens, but it can be obtained only through citizenship of a member state. These processes have therefore increased the gap between the rights of citizens and non-citizens.

In an era when citizenship rights in Europe have been under threat from neo-liberalism and the rhetoric of 'responsible citizenship' it would be unwise to take for granted rights that have been won only after decades of campaigning. Citizenship and 'social inclusion' is becoming increasing conditional on paid employment, while punitive policies are imposed on those who do not conform. The scenario suggested in the concept of 'post-national citizenship' appears even more Utopian in the context of the threats to basic rights contained in much current migration policy.

Future research agendas

In this book we have attempted to draw out some important themes in contemporary migration in Europe and to integrate a gender dimension into our analysis of a range of issues – including employment, welfare and politics – which existing literature tends to treat as discrete issues. We have started to develop a framework for analysis of these issues within which our future research can develop. We have become acutely aware of the unevenness and inadequacy of existing knowledge of the experiences of migrants within contemporary Europe. Research is more advanced in older countries of migration such as Britain or in France, from which we have drawn much of our material, but remains at a much more preliminary stage in newer countries of immigration such as Italy and Spain. These limitations have impeded our own ability to develop a gender analysis. We are conscious that in much of the book, our focus has had to be primarily on women rather than on gender relations.

Research on migration in Europe takes place within very different institutional contexts, traditions of migration and citizenship, and political and policy debates. These shape the kinds of questions asked as well as the extent of the research. Gender issues have tended to be marginalized in research in all European states, but there has been more scope for its inclusion in states with strong traditions of feminist inquiry and practice. The multicultural models of incorporation, which recognize and to some extent legitimize difference, also offer more scope for incorporating a gender analysis.

One of our major preoccupations has been with the diversity of migrant experiences. We have suggested that there is a deepening hierarchy of migrant rights, ranging from those with citizenship status to those who entered 'illegally', or who have become 'illegal'. Formal legal status is, however, cross-cut by gender, class, length of residence, the extent of community organization and a host of other factors that affect migrants' insertion into the country of settlement so that formal and substantive rights do not coincide in an obvious way. Little is known of the extent to which migrants have been able to access basic rights in many European states, and the strategies they have used to overcome exclusion from these rights. Understanding of these issues needs to be taken forward through in-depth studies in individual states, using both qualitative analyses as well as more sensitive quantitative data.

We have argued that motives for migration to Europe are complex and cannot be understood purely as a response to economic motives in the case of labour migrants, or as the desire for family reunion in the case of dependants. For women in particular, migration may offer opportunities for greater personal autonomy and escape from intolerable pressures to conform to conventional roles. The ostensible reason for immigration, as defined by the status on entry, may hide other motives and takes no account of the changes in migrants' lives after entry. Thus treating those who enter through family reunion merely as dependants renders invisible their independent contribution. Women joining husbands may also do so partly to escape the extended family and may use this means of entry to gain access to the labour market and thus achieve economic autonomy. Refugees may enter in order to escape persecution, but are often able to make a significant economic contribution in their country of settlement, particularly if positive policies towards education, retraining and employment are available.

Research is needed to evaluate the economic contribution of migrants and the extent to which the economies of Europe depend on it. The work of many migrants is largely invisible because they work within the 'informal' sector, where their contribution is unrecorded. We acknowledge, however, that this raises highly sensitive issues, because highlighting the work of those with insecure status could have the perverse consequence of creating negative publicity and precipitating repressive policy developments. Of equal importance, however, is to acknowledge the contribution of migrants in providing the skilled labour on which European society depends.

In researching this book, we have been confronted with a number of discrete literatures that shed light on aspects of the migratory experience, but which do not appear to be engaged in mutual dialogue. Our major preoccupation has of course been with the largely separate development of the literature on gender from mainstream migration literature, and the need for developments in social theory to be incorporated into theorizing on migration. But within the migration literature a number of dichotomies continue to exist. One key area is the distinction between analyses of the conditions that precipitate migratory movements and the debate around the conditions under which migrants are able to settle. Studies aiming to link these could draw on a strong tradition of studies on internal and international migration from within the field of development studies. The literature on internal EU migration is relatively underdeveloped, and this aspect of migration has been largely ignored in most current literature on contemporary European migration. Comparisons between intra- and extra- European immigration could shed interesting light on the relationship between formal rights and the substantive rights migrants are actually able to access. Another distinct set of literature has developed around refugee studies, which has developed specific concepts and preoccupations to a large extent in isolation from the broader literature on migration.

Progress towards developing these analyses would be greatly enhanced if more gender-sensitive data were available to allow more detailed analysis of migratory flows. Much official data are based on very broad categories, which are often not broken down by sex. European states are developing more sophisticated techniques for monitoring the movement of immigrants. As repression of asylum seekers and undocumented migrants continues, the gaps in knowledge are likely to increase as more people seek to evade monitoring.

European Union migration policy is becoming more closely harmonized in relation to the conditions of entry and residence of new migrants, but individual states have also introduced their own legislation that has taken forward this agenda in different ways. Legislation in Italy in 1998, for example, included some measures to facilitate the integration of legal residents, while greatly strengthening measures against undocumented migrants. The British Asylum and Immigration Act 1999 was almost wholly repressive in tone and content, and contained no measures to promote the settlement of legally resident migrants. European states have increased the number of detention centres for immigrants, while immigration controls are increasingly taking place before entry through consulates, and through forcing airlines and other carriers to scrutinize potential passengers. There is a need to follow closely the development of legislation and policy in each state. The atmosphere in which these debates are conducted means that much legislation gets little scrutiny.

Much of the policy is contained in semi-formal rules and regulations that do not appear in the legislation itself. In the case of the British Asylum and Immigration Act 1999, for example, amendments were introduced at the last minute to introduce curfews on the movements of asylum seekers, while much of the detail of the implementation of the new social support system will be contained in rules that do not have to go before parliament. Organizations such as Statewatch and other voluntary groups through Europe are essential to monitor these changes. It is important that they incorporate the gender dimension into their own scrutiny of the legislation and policy process.

Campaigning priorities

As we described in Chapter 7, there have been a host of activities by migrant groups in defence of migrant rights, which have sometimes been linked to wider agendas for social change, including broadly feminist campaigns. These campaigns have, however, often revolved around the immediate need to defend particular individuals from deportation or other forms of persecution and have closed down when the immediate issue has been resolved. Although similar concerns exist across Europe, they have remained predominantly nationally based. The extent to which they have involved a broader constituency has also varied: some have built broad alliances sometimes involving groups not normally associated with radical politics. There has been, however, limited success in linking demands for migrants' rights to more general social and political movements, or the specific needs of migrant women to a more general feminist agenda. This partly reflects the weakness of the left and the decline of activism, as well as the fragmentation of the feminist movement and the dominance of more individualist preoccupations. There are, however, a number of campaigns to which we have referred in previous chapters that could unite a broad radical and human rights constituency and could lead to constructive engagement between migrant women and feminists. These campaigns challenge not only the racist foundations of immigration law, but pose a wider definition of politics, which gives prominence to the personal.

The campaign in support of gender guidelines for the process of asylum application has gained some broad support in Britain and needs to be extended throughout Europe. This demand challenges conventional constructions of politics by raising the importance of informal resistance and placing on the agenda the importance of sexual persecution. Another key campaign has been for the legal and economic autonomy of women migrants. The period of probation for spouses, the 'one-year rule' in Britain, entrenches dependence, and in many states this is reinforced by prohibition on the right to work. These campaigns challenge the notion of women as primarily dependants. They have sometimes been linked to campaigns against the deportation of women who have fled violent marriages, which have placed the issue of domestic violence on the political agenda both within migrant communities and within the wider society and have succeeded in breaking down potent taboos.

All European states prevent asylum seekers from seeking employment in the first months after entry while at the same time access to cash benefits is often limited. Current legislation is making it more difficult to gain settlement within Europe as the trauma of flight and movement is compounded by social exclusion and isolation in exile, and asylum seekers are increasingly becoming targets for xenophobia. Campaigns have developed across Europe against deportations and detention and, following the Tampere Summit in October 1999, there have been attempts to develop an EU-wide network to coordinate these activities.

Restrictions on family reunion have been the source of much trauma for migrants and refugees. The conditions placed on the entry of family members make it difficult for many migrants. Current EU legislation gives more rights to EU citizens based in another member state than those living in their own home country because the former are allowed to bring in a spouse and dependent children as of right, whereas in some states this is conditional for the latter. Concern within the EU at the rights that this legislation provides has led to new moves to scrutinize marriages. As well as the problems of gaining access for those spouses and children, the definition of the family is often narrow, and prevents networks of family to help with caring. This means that it is immigration law that decides who is included in the family, rather than the individuals concerned.

The campaigns around these issues have been fragmented and often short lived, and localized. There is a need to develop European-wide networks of resistance as European mechanisms of exclusion are developed. The Internet has facilitated networking and information sharing between groups. Restrictions of language and differences of political culture mean, however, that the campaigns are always likely to be predominantly nationally based.

The racist right has made considerable gains across Europe, both in electoral terms and through increased membership and activity. This growth has been uneven within and between states. More worrying has been the adoption by mainstream politicians, including those of left and social democratic traditions, of much of the agenda and rhetoric of these groups. Official debate is carried on in almost entirely negative terms, with the assumption – explicit or implicit – that majority opinion in Europe is hostile to immigration. In failing to challenge these preoccupations, they of course reinforce these tendencies.

In spite of the overwhelmingly hostile political and media discourse, we remain unconvinced that these views do in fact represent majority opinion. When confronted with the realities of migrant experiences, Europeans have often responded positively to the presence of immigrants. There are a host of ways in which Europeans have given support and solidarity to refugees and migrants. A recent report in the Italian newspaper *La Repubblica* described the amazement of local officials as a whole village in southern Italy turned out to rescue and welcome a group of refugees who had been thrown into the sea by smugglers. Members of such disparate groups as Church congregations, trade unions, voluntary organizations and campaigning groups regularly engage in activities in support of asylum seekers.

'Cultural centres' have sprung up across Italy that campaign around migrants rights, while in France the 'Sans Papiers' movement unites migrants groups with wide sections of French society. Perhaps as significant as the campaigns themselves is the fact that most people in European cities spend their lives in an increasingly multicultural environment. The denial of migrants' contribution is contradicted by day-to-day experience of seeing migrants as colleagues, neighbours, customers and friends. But the most crucial element in defending migrants' rights is the energy and resilience of the migrants themselves.

We believe, therefore, that campaigns in support of migrant rights are not only necessary, but can unite people from a wide cross-section of views and backgrounds and thus have an impact on the policy agenda. Migrant women will continue to be at the forefront of this activity and it is crucial that their specific concerns are made central to these campaigns.

Bibliography

Abadan-Unat, N. (1980) 'International labour migration and its effect upon women's occupational and family roles: a Turkish view', in UNESCO (ed.) *Women on the Move. Contemporary Changes in Family and Society*, Paris: UNESCO, 133–58.

Ackers, L. (1996) 'Citizenship, gender and dependence in the European Union: women and internal migration', *Social Politics* 3(2/3): 316–330.

— (1998) *Shifting Spaces. Women, citizenship and migration within the European Union*, Bristol: Polity Press.

Adjin-Tettey, E. (1997) *Defining a particular social group based on gender,* York University, Canada: Refuge.

Adler, N.(1994) 'Competitive frontiers: women managing across borders', *Journal of Management Development* 13(2): 24–41.

Ali, Y. (1999) 'The Invisible Woman: Some thoughts on the political construction of South Asian Women in Britain', paper presented at Theoretical Considerations on Gender and the South Asian Diaspora, Leicester.

Alund, A. (1991) 'The power of definitions: immigrant women and problem ideologies', in A. Alund and C. U. Schierup (eds) *Paradoxes of Multiculturalism: essays on Swedish Society*, Aldershot: Avebury.

— (1998) 'Swedish multi-cultural society', *Soundings* 9: 176–80.

Alund, A. and Schierup, C. U. (1993) 'The thorny road to Europe: Swedish immigrant policy in transition', in J. Wrench and J. Solomos (eds) *Racism and Migration in Western Europe*. Oxford: Berg, 99–128.

Amos, V. and Parmar, P. (1984) 'Challenging Imperialist Feminism' *Feminist Review* 17: 3–20.

Andall, J. (1996) 'Catholic and State constructions of Domestic Workers', paper presented to the ERCOMER conference, Utrecht, Netherlands.

Anderson, B. (1997a) *Labour Exchange: Patterns of Migration in Asia*, London: Catholic Institute of International Relations.

— (1997b) 'Servants and slaves: Europe's domestic workers', *Race and Class* 39(1): 37–49.

— (2000) *Doing the Dirty Work*, London: Zed Press.

Anderson, B. and Phizacklea, A. (1997) *Migrant Domestic Workers: A European*

Perspective. Brussels: European Commission, Equal Opportunities Unit. (The full version is published as B. Anderson, Zed Press, 2000).

Ansay, T. (1991) 'The new UN Convention in the light of German and Turkish Experience', *International Migration Review* 25: 831–47.

Anselin A. (1990) *L'immigration antillaise en France. La troisième île*, Paris: Karthala.

Anthias, F. (1993) 'Gendered Ethnicities in the British Labour Market' in H. Rudolph and M. Morokvasic (eds) *Bridging States and Markets*, Berlin: Sigma.

Anthias, F. (1997) 'Diasporas: Beyond ethnicity?', *Sociology* 32(3): 557–80.

Anthias, F. and Yuval Davis, N. (1992) *Racialized Boundaries*, London: Routledge.

Aukerman, M. (1995) 'Discrimination in Germany: a call for minority rights', *Netherlands Quarterly of Human Rights* 13(3): 237–57.

Autant, C. (1995) 'La tradition au service des transitions. Le mariage des jeunes Turcs dans l'immigration', *Migrants-Formation* 101: 168–79.

Bailey, J. (ed.) (1992) *Social Europe*, Harlow: Longman.

Barbi, A. and Miklavi-Brezigar, I. (1999) Domestic work abroad: a necessity and an opportunity for rural women from the Goriöka borderland region of Slovenia, in J. Momsen (ed.) *Gender, Migration and Domestic Service*, London: Routledge.

Barker, M. (1981) *The New Racism*, Brighton: Junction.

Baubock, R. (1991) 'Migration and citizenship', *New Community* 18(1): 27–48.

— (1993) 'Entitlement and regulation. Immigration control in welfare states', in H. Rudolph and M. Morokvasic (eds) *Bridging States and Markets*, Berlin: Sigma, 19–47.

— (1994a) *Transnational Citizenship: Membership and Rights in International Migration*, Aldershot: Edward Elgar.

— (ed.) (1994b) *From Aliens to Citizen*, Aldershot: Avebury.

Beaverstock, J. (1996) 'Lending jobs to global cities: skilled international labour migration, investment banking and the City of London', *Urban Studies* 33: 1377–94.

BELC (1976) 'Les Femmes Immigrées et la Formation', *Migrants-Formation* 14-15

Ben Jouadi, K. (1997) 'Le MFAD, un mouvement qui lutte tous azimuts pour la démocratie', *Regards. Femmes d'Ici et d'Ailleurs* 80: 18–23.

Benani, S. (1995) *Les Nanas Beurs, Immigrant Women and Integration*, Strasbourg Council of Europe, 79–86.

Bennington, J. and Taylor, M. (1993) 'Changes and challenges facing the UK welfare state in the Europe of the 1990s', *Policy and Politics* 21(2), 288–307.

Bentchicou, N. (ed.) (1997) *Les Femmes de l'Immigration au quotidien*, Paris: L'Harmattan.

Bevelander, P. (1999) 'The employment integration of immigrants in Sweden', *Journal of Ethnic and Migration Studies* 25(3): 445–68.

Bhabha, J. (1996) 'Embodied rights: gender persecution, state sovereignty, and refugees', *Public Culture* 9: 3–32.

Bhabha, J. and Shutter, S. (1994) *Women's Movement. Women Under Immigration, Nationality and Refugee Law*, Stoke-on-Trent: Trentham Books.

Bhachu, P. (1993) 'Identities constructed and reconstructed: representations of Asian women in Britain', in G. Bjuis (ed.) *Migrant Women*, Oxford: Berg, 99–118.

Bhattacharya, A. (1997) 'The public/private mirage: mapping homes and undomesticating violence work in the South Asian Immigrant community', in J. Alexander and C. Mohanty (eds) *Feminist Genealogies, Colonial Legacies, Democratic Futures*, London: Routledge, 308–29.

Bhavnani, R. (1997) *Black and minority ethnic women in the labour market in London: first major London review*, London: Fair Play.

Bimbi, F. (1993) 'Gender, "gift relationship" and welfare state cultures in Italy', in J. Lewis (ed.) *Women and Social Policies in Europe. Work, Family and the State*, Aldershot: Edward Elgar.

Birnbaum, B. *et al.* (1981) *The Clothing Industry in Tower Hamlets*, London: Tower Hamlets Council.

Bjeren, G. (1997) 'Gender and reproduction', in T. Hammar, G. Brochmann, K. Tamas and T. Faist (eds) *International Migration, Immobility and Development. Multidisciplinary Perspectives*, Oxford: Berg, 219–46.

Bloch, A. and Levy, C. (eds) (1999) *Refugees, Citizenship and Social Policy in Britain and Europe*, London: Macmillan.

Blumberg, R. L. and West, G. (1990) *Women and Social Protest*, New York: Oxford University Press.

Bohning, W. (1984) *Studies of International Migration*, London: Macmillan.

Bonacich, E. (1973) 'A Theory of Middleman Minorities', *American Sociological Review* 38: 538–94.

Bonacich, E. and Modell, J. (1980) *The Economic Basis of Ethnic Solidarity*, Berkeley: University of California Press.

Bonney, N. and Love, J. (1990) Gender and migration: geographical mobility and the wife's sacrifice, *Sociological Review* 39: 335–48.

Bonoli, R. (ed.) (1991) *L'Emigrazione al femminile: Atti del convegno*, Bologna, Regione Emilia-Roagna: Consulta Regionale per l'Emigrazione e l'Immigrazione.

Booth, H. (1985) *Migration Processes in Britain and West Germany*, Aldershot: Avebury.

Boulahbel-Villac, Y. (1994) 'La famille intermédiaire: comportements familiaux dans et pour l'immigration', in N. Bensalah (ed.) *Familles turques et magrébines aujourd'hui: évolution dans les espaces d'origine et d'immigration*, Paris: Maisonneuve et Larose p. 33

Bourne, J. (1980) Race and Class.

Bovenkerk, F. Gras, M. and Ramsoedh, D. n. d. *Discrimination against Migrant Workers and Ethnic Minorities in Access to Employment in the Netherlands*, Geneva: ILO.

Boyd, M. (1989) 'Family and personal networks in international migration: recent developments and new agendas', *International Migration Review* 23: 638–70.

— (1997) 'Migration policy, female dependency, and family membership: Canada and Germany', in P. Evans and G. Werkele (eds) *Women and the Canadian Welfare State*, Toronto: University of Toronto Press, 142–69.

Boyle, P. and Halfacree, K. (eds) (1999) *Migration and Gender in the Developed World*, London: Routledge.

Brah, A. (1993a) Difference, diversity, differentiation: processes of racialisation and gender, in J. Wrench and J. Solomos (eds) *Racism and Migration in Western Europe*, Oxford: Berg, 195–214.

— (1993b) 'Re-framing Europe: En-gendered racisms, ethnicities and nationalisms in Contemporary Western Europe', *Feminist Review* 45: 9–29.

— (1996) *Cartographies of Diaspora*, London: Routledge.

Brinker-Gabler, G. and Smith, S. (eds) (1997) *Writing New Identities: Gender, Nation and Immigration in Contemporary Europe*, Minneapolis: University of Minnesota Press.

Brown, C. (1984) *Black and White Britain: The Third PSI Survey*, London: Heinemann.

Bruegel, I. (1996) 'The trailing wife: a declining breed? Careers, geographical mobility and household conflict in Britain 1970–1989', in R. Crompton, D. Gallie and K. Purcell (eds) *Changing Forms of Employment: Organisations, Skills and Gender*, London: Routledge, 235–58.

— (1999) 'Globalization, feminization and pay inequalities in London and the U.K.', in J. Gregory, R. Sales and A. Hegewisch (eds) *Women, Work and Equality: the Challenge of Equal Pay*, London: Macmillan.

Buijs, G. (ed.) (1993) *Migrant Women: Crossing Boundaries and changing identities*, London: Berg.

Bundesanstalt für Arbeit (1980) *Sonderdruck Sozialversicherungspflichtig Beschäftigte Arbeitnehmer, Ende Juni, 1979*, Nürnberg: Germany.

Bystydzienski, J. (1992) 'Influence of Women's Culture in Public Politics in Norway' in J. Bystydzienski (ed) *Women Transforming Politics: Worldwide strategies for empowerment*, Bloomington: Indiana University Press, 11–23.

Caglar, A. (1995) 'German Turks in Berlin: social exclusion and strategies for social mobility', *New Community* 21(3): 309–24.

Campani, G. (1993a) 'Immigration and racism in southern Europe: the Italian case', *Ethnic and Racial Studies* 16(3):507–35.

— (1993b) 'La condition des femmes immigrées', in ADRI *L'Intégration des minorités immigrées en Europe*, Centre National de la Fonction Publique, 81–101.

— (1993c) 'Labour Markets and Family Networks: Filipina Women in Italy' in M. Morokvasic and H. Rudolf (eds) *Bridging States and Markets*, Berlin: Sigma.

— (1995) 'Ethnic networks and associations, Italian mobilisation and immigration issues in Italy', *Ethnic and Racial Studies,* 143–7.

— (1997) ' "Women and social exclusion: the case of migrant women" inclusion and exclusion: international migrants and refugees in Europe and North America', Paper presented at the International Sociological Association, New York.

Campani, G., Carchedi, F. and Piccolini, A. (1997) 'Le trafic des femmes immigrées à des fins d'exploitation sexuelle en Italie,' *Migrations Société* 52: 105–14.

Camus-Jacques, G. (1989) 'Refugee women: the forgotten majority', in G. Loescher and L. Monahan (eds) *Refugees and International Relations*, Oxford: OUP, 141–58.

Carby, H. (1982) 'White woman listen! Black feminism and the boundaries of sisterhood', in Centre for Contemporary Cultural Studies *The Empire Strikes Back: Race and Racism in 70s Britain*, London: Hutchinson, 212–35.

Carey-Wood, J. (1994) Meeting Refugees' Needs in Britain: The role of refugee specific initiatives, Unpublished report to the Home Office.

Carey-Wood, J., Duke, K., Karn, V. and Marshall, T. (1995) *The Settlement of Refugees in Britain*, London: HMSO.

Carlos Valencia, D. (1996) 'Babaylan: A successful European network of Migrant Associations Migrant Women in Action: First European Conference on and with migrant women', proceedings of the Athens Conference, *The Forum Series*, 3: 46–50.

Carver, T (1998) 'Sexual citizenship. gendered and de-gendered narratives', in T. Carver and V. Motter (eds) *Politics of Sexuality. Identity, Gender and Citizenship*, London: Routledge, 13–23.

Castells, M. (1975) 'Immigrant workers and class struggles in advanced capitalism: the Western European experience', *Politics and Society* 5(1): 33–66.

Castles, S. (1999) 'International migration and the global agenda', *International Migration* 3(1): 5–20

Castles, S. and Kosack, G. (1973/1985) *Immigrant Workers and Class Structure in Western Europe*, Ist/2nd edn, Oxford: OUP.

Castles, S. and Miller, M. (1998) *The Age of Migration*, 2nd edn, London: Macmillan.

Castro, G. (1986) 'Migrant Women: Issues in Organization and Solidarity' in *Migrant Women Claim their Rights Nairobi and After: A selection of documents for study and action*, Migration Secretariat, World Council of Churches.

CCCS (1982) *The Empire Strikes Back: Race and Racism in 70s Britain*, London Hutchinson.

Ceasarani, D. and Fullbrook, M. *Citizenship, Nationality and Migration in Europe* London: Routledge.

CERC (1999) *Immigration, emploi et chomage: un état des lieux empirique et théorique*, Les dossiers de CERC, no. 3.

Chamberlain, M. (1994) Family and identity: barbadian migrants to Britain, in R. Benmayor and A. Skotnes (eds) *Migration and Identity*, vol. 3, OUP, Oxford.

Chamberlayne, P. (1992) 'Income maintenance and institutional forms: a comparison of France, West Germany, Italy and Britain 1945–90', *Policy and Politics* 20(4): 299–318.

Charbit, Y. and Bertrand, C. (1985) *Enfants, Familles, Migrations*, INED Cahier no. 110. Paris: Presses Universitaires de France.

Charting the Journey Editorial Group (1987) *Charting the Journey: Writings by Black and Third World Women*, London: Sheba Feminist Publishers.

Chatterjee, D. (1995) 'Harnessing Shakti: the work of Bengali Support Group', in G. Griffin (ed.) *Feminist Activism in the 1990s*, London and Bristol: Taylor and Francis.

Chell, V. (1997) 'Gender selective migrations: Somalian and Filipina women in Rome', in R. King and R. Black (eds) *Southern Europe and the New Immigrations*, 75–92.

Cissé, M. (1997) *The Sans-Papiers. The New Movement of Asylum Seekers and Immigrants Without Papers in France – a Woman Draws the First Lessons*, London: Crossroads.

Citizens Advice Bureau (1996) *A Right to Family Life: CAB Clients' Experience of Immigration and Asylum*, London: CAB.

Cochrane, A. and Clarke, J. (1993) (eds) *Comparing Welfare States. Britain in International Context*, London: Sage.

Cockburn, C. (1991) *In the Way of Women: men's resistance to sex equality*, London: Macmillan.

Cohen, R. (ed.) (1995) *The Cambridge Survey of World Migration*, Cambridge: Cambridge University Press.

Cohen, R. (1997) *Global Diasporas. An Introduction*. London: University College Press.

Cohen-Emerique, M., Munoz, M. C. and Dirgon, P. (1998) *Le Regroupement Familial. Epouaser au Pays. L'accueil des Familles Rejoignantes*, Paris: Service Social d'Aide aux Emigrants.

Collins, P. (1990) *Black Feminist Thought: Knowledge, Consciousness and the Politics of Empowerment*, Boston: Unwin Hyman.

Collinson, S. (1993) *Europe and International Migration*, London: Pinter.

Colwill, J. (1994) 'Beveridge, women and the welfare state', *Critical Social Policy* 41, 53–77.

Coordination Européenne pour le droit des étrangers à vivre en famille (1998) *L'Impact de l'immigration dans l'Italie des années 90*, Brussels.

Condon, S. and Ogden, P. (1991) 'Emigration from the French Caribbean: the origins of an organized migration', *International Journal of Urban and Regional Research* 15(4): 505–23.

Costa-Lascoux, J. (1989) *De l'immigré au citoyen*, Paris: La Docuementation Française.

—— (1995) *Immigrant Women: Out of the Shadows and on to the Stage*, Immigrant Women and Integration, Council of Europe.

—— (1999)'L'illusion de la maitrise, la politique migratoire en trompe l'oeil', in E. Balibar *et al.* (eds) *Sans-papiers: l'archaisme fatal*, Paris: La Déouverte, 35–62.

Cox, R. (1999) 'The role of ethnicity in shaping the domestic employment sector in Britain', in J. Momsen (ed) *Gender, Migration and Domestic Service*, London: Routledge.

Crawley, H. (1997) *Women as Asylum Seekers. A Legal Handbook*, London: Immigration Law Practitioners Association.

Crenshaw, K. (1998) 'Demarginalizing the intersection of race and sex: A Black feminist critique of antidiscrimination doctrine, feminist theory and antiracist politics', in A. Phillips (ed) *Feminism and Politics* Oxford: Oxford University Press, 314–43.

Cross, M. (1998) Editorial *Journal of Ethnic and Migration Studies*, 24(2), 245–48.

Curtis, L. (1984) *Nothing But the Same Old Story* London: Information on Ireland.

D-Ashur, S. (1992) *Silent Tears*, London Black Women's Health Project.

Danese, G. (1998a) 'Transnational collective action in Europe: the case of migrants in Italy and Spain', *Journal of Ethnic and Migration Studies* 24(4): 715–34.

— (1998b) 'Enjeux et limites du mouvement associatif immigré en Italie: quel avenir pour la participation?', *Migrations Société* 55: 67–74.

Davis, A. (1982) *Women, Race and Class*, London: Women's Press.

de Hart, B. (1999) ' "It just went according to the rules with us" Binational families, marriage, migration and shifting identities' *Euroconference on Migrant Families and Human Capital Formation in Europe*, Leiden.

Delacourt, J. (1975) *The Housing of Migrant Workers: A Case of Social Improvidence*, Brussels: European Commission.

Delacroix, C. (1997) 'Mediatrices Socio-culturelles, citoyennes innovantes' in N. Bentchicou (ed.) *Les Femmes de l'immigration au Quotidien*, Paris: L'Harmattan.

Dell'Orto, F. and Taccani, P. (1992) 'Family carers and dependent elderly people in Italy', in J. Twigg (ed.) *Informal Care in Europe*, York: SPRU, University of York.

Del Re, A. (1993) 'Vers l'Europe: politiques sociales, femmes et état en Italie entre production and reproduction', in A. Gautier and J. Heinen (eds) *Le Sexe des Politiques Sociales*, Paris: Côté-Femmes.

Department of Employment (1976) *The Role of Immigrants in the Labour Market*, London: Unit for Manpower Services, Department of Employment.

Diken, B. (1998) *Strangers, Ambivalence and Social Theory*, Aldershot: Ashgate.

Doezema, J. (1998) 'Forced to Choose: Beyond the Voluntary v. Forced Prostitution Dichotomy' in K. Kempadoo and J. Doezema (eds) *Global Sex Workers*, London: Routledge, 29–34.

Duke, K., Sales, R. and Gregory, J. (1999) 'Refugee settlement in Europe', in A. Bloch and C. Levy (eds) *Refugees, Citizenship and Social Policy in Europe*, London: Macmillan.

Dumon, R. (1976) 'Family Migration and family reunion', *International Migration* XIV, 1(2): 53–83.

Einhorn, B. (1993) *Cinderella Goes to Market*, London: Verso.

Enloe, C. (1989) *Beaches, Bananas and Bases*. Pandora.

Escrivá, A. (1997) 'Control, composition and character of new migration to south-west Europe: the case of Peruvian women in Barcelona', *New Community* 27(1): 43–58.

Esping Andersen, G. (1990) *Three Worlds of Welfare Capitalism*, Cambridge: Polity.

Essed, P. (1996) *Diversity: Gender, Color and Culture*, MA: University of Massachusetts Press.

European Commission (1996) *Equal Opportunities for Women and Men in the European Union*, Brussels: European Commission, Employment and Social Affairs.

European Consultation on Refugees and Exiles (1983) *Asylum in Europe: A Handbook for Agencies Assisting Refugees*, 3rd edn, Rotterdam: European Consultation on Refugees and Exiles.

European Women's Lobby (1995) *Confronting the Fortress. Black and Migrant Women in the European Union*, Luxembourg: European Parliament.

Eurostat (1994) *Migration Statistics. International Migration in the European Union and EFTA*, 1993. Luxembourg: European Commission.

Eurostat (1997) *Statistics in Focus: Population and Social Conditions*, Brussels: European Commission.

Evans, M. (1997) *Introducing Feminist Thought Contemporary*, Cambridge: Polity Press.

Faist, T. (1995) 'Boundaries of welfare states: immigrants and social rights on the national and supranational level' in R. Miles and D. Thranhardt (eds) *Migration and European Integration: The Dynamics of Inclusion and Exclusion*, London: Pinter.

Farine, P. (1998) 'Allemagne vers un réforme du code de la nationalité', *MigrationsSociété* 10(60): 127–8.

— (1999) 'Au fil des jours', *Migrations Société* 62: 143–6.

Fekete, L. (1997) 'Blackening the economy: the path to convergence'. *Race and Class* 39(1): 1–17.

Feldman-Bianco, B. (1992) 'Multiple layers of time and space: the construction of class, ethnicity and nationalism', in N. Schiller *et al.* (eds) *Among Portuguese Immigrants. New York Academy of Sciences*, no. 645

Feminist Review (1993) 'Thinking Through Ethnicities', no. 45.

Findlay, A. (1995) 'Skilled transients: the invisible phenomenon?' in R. Cohen (ed.) *The Cambridge Survey of World Migration*, Cambridge: Cambridge University Press, 515–22.

Findlay, A. and Gould, W. (1989) Skilled international migration: a research agenda, area 21: 3–11.

Findlay, A. and Li, F. (1998) A migration channels approach to the study of professionals moving to and from Hong Kong, *International Migration Review* 32: 682–703.

Forbes Martin, S. (1992) *Refugee Women*, London: Zed Books.

Friese, M. (1995) 'East European women as domestics in Western Europe

– new social inequality and division of labour among women', *Journal of Area Studies* 6: 194–202.

Gabaccia, D. (ed.) (1992) *Seeking Common Ground: Multidisciplinary Studies of Immigrant Women in the United States,* Connecticut: Greenwood.

Gabaccia, D. (1995) *From the Other Side: Women, Gender and Immigrant Life in the US 1820–1990,* Indiana University Press.

Gaffikin, F. and Nickson, A. n. d. *Jobs Crisis and the Multi-nationals: The Case of the West Midlands,* Birmingham: Trade Union Resource Centre.

Gamman, L., Hall, C., Lewis, G., Phoenix, A., Whitehead, A. and Young, L. (1993) *Editorial in Special Issue: Thinking Through Ethnicities,* 45, 1–3.

Gaspard, F.(1992a) 'La société française confrontée à la polygamie: quelques éléments de réflexion', *Revue française des Affaires Sociales* 46, Hors série, 181–96.

— (1992b) 'Assimilation, insertion, intégration: les mots pour devenir français', *Hommes et Migrations* 1154: 14–23.

— (1994) *Obstacles in Society to Equality of Opportunity for Immigrant Women. The situation in France, Belgium, Italy and Spain,* joint specialist group on migration, cultural diversity and the equality of women and men, Strasbourg: Council of Europe.

Geddes, A. (1993) Asians and Afro-Caribbean representation in elected local government in England and Wales, *New Community,* 20(1), 43–58.

Geddes, A. (1998) 'The representation of "migrants' interest" in the European Union, *Journal of Ethnic and Migration Studies,* 24(4), 695–713.

Ghai, Y. (1997) Migrant workers, markets and the law, in W. Gungwu (ed) *Global History and Migrations,* Oxford: Westview.

Gill, V. n. d. *Citizenship in Practice: A Comparative Study of Political Participation by Immigrant Women in Norway, A Pre-Study,* Norway: University of Bergen.

Glick Schiller, N., Basch, L. and Blanc-Szanton, C. (eds) (1992) 'Towards a transnational perspective on migration. race, class, ethnicity and nationalism reconsidered', *Annals of the New York Academy of Sciences,* no. 645, July.

Goldberg A., Mourinho, D. and Kulke, U. (1995) 'Labour market discrimination against foreign workers in Germany', *International Migration Papers* 7, Geneva: International Labour Organization.

Goldberg, D. (1993) *Racist Culture: Philosophy and the Politics of Meaning,* Oxford: Blackwell.

Golub, A., Morokvasic, M., and Quiminal, C. (1997) 'Evolution de la production des connaissances sur les femmes immigrées en France et en Europe', *Migrations Société* 52: 19–36.

Gomes, N and Norlander, L. (1998) *Tjejer I Botkyrka,* Tumba: Mangkulturellt centrum.

Goodman, C. (1987) 'A day in the life of a single Spanish woman in West Germany', in H. C. and J. M. Buechler (eds) *Migrants in Europe,* Connecticut: Greenwood Press, 207–20.

Goss, J. and Lindquist, B. (1995) 'Conceptualizing international labor migration: a structuration perspective', *International Migration Review*, 29(2): 317–51.

Gould, W. (1988) 'Skilled international migration', *Geoforum* 19: 381–6

Graham, M. and Soninen, M. (1998) 'A model for immigrants? The Swedish corporate model and the prevention of ethnic discrimination', *Journal of Ethnic and Migration Studies*, 24(3): 523–39.

Granotier, B. (1979) *Les travailleurs immigrés en France*, Paris: PUF.

Grasmuck, S. and Pessar, P. (1991) *Between Two Islands: Dominican International Migration*, Berkeley: University of California Press.

Gray, B. (1996) 'The home of our mothers and our birthright for ages?: Nation, diaspora and Irish women', in M. Maynard and J. Purvis (eds) *New Frontiers in Women's Studies*, London: Taylor and Francis.

— (1997) 'Unmasking Irishness: Irish women, the Irish nation and the Irish diaspora', in J. MacLaughlin (ed) *Social Location and Dislocation and Irish Identities* Cork: Cork University Press, 209–35.

Gregson, N. and Lowe, M. (1994) *Servicing the Middle Classes: Class, Gender and Waged Domestic Labour in Contemporary Britain*, London: Routledge.

Griffin, G. (1995) 'The struggles continue – an interview with Hannana Siddiqui of Southall Black Sisters' in *Feminist Activism in the 1990s*, London and Bristol: Taylor and Francis, 79–89.

Groenendijk, K. and Hampsink, R (1995) *Temporary Employment of Migrants in Europe*, Nijmegan: Reeks Recht and Samenleving.

Guardian (1997) 'Bonn cracks down on foreigners', 16 January.

Guardian (1997) 'Field day for illegal hunters', 25th April: 10.

Guardian (1999) Abused wives can quit marriage and stay in UK, 17 June.

Guild, E. (1996) 'The legal framework of citizenship of the European Union', in D. Ceasarani and M. Fullbrook (eds) *Citizenship, Nationality and Migration in Europe*, London: Routledge.

Guillaumin, C. (1972) *L'idéologie raciste*, Paris: Mouton.

— (1995) *Racism, Sexism, Power and Ideology*, London: Routledge.

Guiraudon, V. (1998) 'Third country nationals and European law: obstacles to rights expansion', *Journal of Ethnic and Migration Studies* 24(4): 657–74.

Haif, A. (1986) 'Immigrant Women in France', in *Migrant Women Claim their Rights Nairobi and After: A Selection of Documents for Study and Action*, Migration Secretariat, World Council of Churches.

Halfacree, K. and Boyle, P. (eds) (1999) *Gender and Migration in Developed Countries*, London: Routledge.

Hall, S. (1992) 'Europe's other self', *The Runnymede Bulletin*, February: 2–3.

Hammar, T. (1990) *Democracy and the Nation-State*, Aldershot: Avebury.

Hansen, R. (1998) 'A European citizenship or a Europe of citizens? Third country nationals in the EU', *Journal of Ethnic and Migration Studies* 24(4): 751–68.

Hantrais, L. and Mangen, S. (eds) (1994) *The Policy Making Process and the Social Actors*, Loughborough: Cross-National Research Papers, 3(1).

Hardill, I. and MacDonald, S. 'Choosing to relocate: and examination of the impact of expatriate work on dual career households', *Women Studies International Forum* 21: 21–9.

Harding, S. (ed.) (1987) *Feminism and Methodology*, Milton Keynes: Open University Press.

Hargreaves, A. (1991) 'Islam in France: Introduction', *Modern and Contemporary France* 45, 3–7.

Hargreaves, A. and Stenhouse, T. (1991) 'Islamic beliefs among youths of North African origin in France', *Modern and Contemporary France* 45: 27–35.

Hargreaves, A. and Wihtol de Wenden, C. (1993) 'Guest editors introduction', *New Community*, 20: 1.

Haskey, J. (1997) 'The ethnic minority and overseas-born population of Great Britain', *Population Trends*, 88: 13–30.

Haut Conseil à l'Intégration (1998) *Lutte contre la Discrimination*, Paris: La Documentation Française.

Heitlinger, A. (1999) *Emigré Feminism. Transnational Perspectives*, Toronto: Toronto University Press.

Hickman, M. (1998) 'Reconstructing deconstructing 'race': British political discourses about the Irish in Britain', *Racial and Ethnic Studies* 21(2): 288–307.

Hickman, M.J. and Walter, B. (1997) *Discrimination and the Irish community in Britain*, London: CRE.

Hoggart, L. and Sales, R. (1998) 'Researching the maternal needs of Turkish speaking mothers in Hackney', paper presented to annual conference of *Social Policy Association*. Lincoln, July.

Hollifield, J. (1992) *Immigrants, Markets and States*, Cambridge: Harvard University Press.

Home Office (1997) *Control of Immigration Statistics United Kingdom 1996*, London: HMSO.

Hommes et Migrations (1999) special issue Connaître et Combattre les discriminations, no. 1217.

Hondagneu-Sotelo, P. (1994) *Gendered Transitions: Mexican Experiences of Immigration*, Berkeley; University of California Press.

hooks, b. (1983) *Ain't I a woman*, London: Pluto.

Hoskyns, C. (1996) *Integrating Gender: women, law and policy in the European Union*, London: Verso.

— (1999) 'Then and Now – Equal Pay in European Union Politics', in J. Gregory, R. Sales and A. Hegewisch (eds) *Women, Work and Equality: the Challenge of Equal Pay in a Deregulated Market*, London: Macmillan.

Hoskyns, C. and Orsini-Jones, M. (1994) *Immigrant Women in Italy*, Coventry: Coventry University.

Houston, M. R., Kramer, G. and Barrett, J. M. (1984) 'Female predominance of immigration to the United States since 1930: A first look', *International Migration Review* 18(4): 908–63.

Humbeck, E. (1996) 'The politics of cultural identity: Thai women in Germany,' in M. D. Garcia Ramon and J. Monk (eds) *Women of the European Union. The Politics of Work and Daily Life*, London: Routledge, 186–201.

Hugo, G. (1994) *The Economic Implications of Emigration from Australia*, Canberra: Commonwealth of Australia.

Hune, S. (1991) 'Migrant women in the context of the international convention on the protection of the rights of all migrant workers and members of their families', *International Migration Review* 25(4): 800–17.

Indra, D. (ed.) (1999) *Engendering Forced Migration. Theory and Practice*, Oxford: Berghahn.

Institute for Race Relations (IRR) (1996) European Race Audit, 17 January and 18 March. London.

International Organization for Migration (1995) *Trafficking and prostitution: the growing exploitation of migrant women*, Geneva: IOM.

Iredale, R. (1997) *Skills Transfer. International Migration and Accreditation Issues*, Wollongong: University of Wollongong Press.

— (1999) 'The need to import skilled personnel: factors favouring and hindering its international mobility', *International Migration* 37(1): 89–124.

Iris di Rimini, X. (1995) *Immigrati: Pericolo o Risorsa?*, Rimini: Istituto Ricerche Sociali.

Jamieson, A. (1991) 'Community care for older people: policies in Britain, West Germany and Denmark', in G. Room (ed) *Towards a European Welfare State?*, Bristol: SAUS.

Jeffers, S. (1991) 'Black Sections in the Labour Party: The end of ethnicity and "Godfather politics"', in P. Werbner and M. Anwar (eds) *Black and Ethnic Leaderships: the Cultural Dimension of Political Action*, London: Routledge, 63–83.

Jessop, B. (1993) 'Towards a Schumpeterian welfare state? Preliminary remarks on post-Fordist political economy', *Studies in Political Economy* 40.

Joint Council for the Welfare of Immigrants (1994a) *The Right to Family Life for Immigrants in Europe*, London: JCWI.

— (1994b) 'Family reunion policies in six European countries', *Eurobriefing*, 1.

— (1997) *Immigration, Nationality and Refugee Law Handbook. A User's Guide*, London: JCWI.

Joly, D. (1996) *Haven or Hell? Asylum Policies and Refugees in Europe*, London: MacMillan.

Joppke, C. (1995) 'Multiculturalism and Immigration: a comparison of the United States, Germany and Britain', *European University Working Paper* SPS no. 95/1, 1995.

— (1997) *Challenges to the Nation-State*, Oxford: OUP.

Kabeer, N. (1994) 'The structure of "revealed" preference: Race, community and female labour supply in the London clothing industry', *Development and Change*, 25: 307–31.

Kauppi, N. (1999) 'Power or subjection: French women politicians in the European parliament', *European Journal of Women's Studies*, 6(3): 329–40.

Kay, D. (1989) 'The politics of gender in exile: Chileans in Glasgow' in D. Joly and R. Cohen (eds) *Reluctant Hosts: Europe and its Refugees* Aldershot Avebury.

Kelly, K. and Nic Giolle, T. (1990) *Emigration Matters for Women*, Dublin: Attica Press.

Kempadoo, K. (1998) 'The migrant tightrope: Experiences from the Caribbean', in K. Kempadoo and J. Doezema (eds) *Global Sex Workers*, London and New York: Routledge, 124–39.

Khan, V. (1977) 'The Pakistanis: Mirpuri villagers at home and in Bradford', in J.L. Watson (ed.) *Between Two Cultures*, Oxford: Blackwell.

King, R. (ed.) (1993) *A New Geography of Migration in Europe*, London: Belhaven.

King, R. Connell, J. and White, P. (eds) (1995) *Writing Across Worlds*, London: Routledge.

Kloosterman, R., van der Leun, J. and Rath, J. (1998) 'Across the border: Immigrants' economic opportunities, social capital and informal business activities', *Journal of Ethnic and Migration Studies* 24(2): 249–68.

Klug, F. (1989) in ' "Oh to be in England"; the British case', N. Yuval-Davis and F. Anthias (eds) *Woman–Nation–State*, London: Macmillan, 16–35.

Kofman, E. (1993) 'National identity and sexual and cultural differences in France', in M. Kelly and R. Bock (eds) *France: Nation and Regions*. Southampton: University of Southampton Press, 102–11.

—— (1995) 'Citizenship for some but not for others: spaces of citizenship in contemporary Europe', *Political Geography* 14(2): 121–37.

—— (1997) 'In search of the missing female subject: comments on French immigration research', in M. Cross and S. Perry (eds) *Population and Social Policy in France*, London: Pinter, 78–91.

—— (1998) 'Whose city? Gender, class and immigration,' in R. Fincher and J. Jacobs (eds) *Cities of Difference*. New York: Guilford, 279–300.

—— (1999) 'Birds of passage a decade later: gender and immigration in the European Union', *International Migration Review* 33: 269–99.

—— (2000) 'The invisibility of skilled female migrants and gender relations in studies of skilled migration in Europe', *International Journal of Population Geography* 6(1): 1–15.

Kofman, E. and Peake, L. (1990) 'Into the 1990s: a gendered agenda for political geography' *Political Geography Quarterly* 9(4): 313–36.

Kofman, E. and Sales, R. (1992) 'Towards fortress Europe?', *Women's Studies International Forum*, 15(1): 29–39.

—— (1996) 'Gender and the geography of welfare in Europe', in J. Monk and D. Garcia Ramon (eds) *Women of the European Union: Employment and the Politics of Daily Life*, London: Routledge, 31–60.

—— (1997) 'Gender differences and family reunion in the European Union: implications for refugees', *Refuge* 16(4): 26–31.

—— (1998) 'Migrant women and exclusion in Europe', *Journal of European Women's Studies* 5(3/4): 381–98.

Kolinsky, E. (1996) 'Non-German minorities in contemporary German society', in D. Horrocks and E. Kolinsky (eds) *Turkish Culture in German Society Today*, Oxford: Berghahn, 71–112.

Koser, K. and Lutz, H. (eds) (1998) *The New Migrations in Europe: Social Constructions and Social Realities*, London: Macmillan.

Koslowski, R. (1998) 'European migration regimes: emerging, enlarging and deteriorating', *Journal of Ethnic and Migration Studies*, 24(40): 735–50.

Kuijsten, X. (1994) International migration in Europe: patterns and implications for receiving countries', in M. Macura and D. Coleman (eds) *International Migration: Regional Processes and Responses*, UN Population Fund Studies no. 7, New York and Geneva: UN.

Kuttner, S. (1997) 'Gender-related persecution as a basis for refugee status: the emergence of an international norm', *Refuge* 16(4): 17–21.

Lahav, G. (1996) 'International vs. national constraints in family reunification migrant policy: a regional view from Europe,' (unpublished paper) San Diego: International Studies Association Conference.

Langan, M. and Ostner, I. (1991) 'Gender and welfare', in G. Room (ed) *Towards a European Welfare State?*, Bristol: School of Advanced Urban Studies.

Leandro, E. (ed) (1997) *Les Familles Portugaises et la Société Française. Interaction France–Portugal*, Paris: Editions W.

Lebon, A. (1995) Migrations et Nationalités en France en 1994, Paris: La Documentation Française.

Lebon, A. (1997) Immigration et présence étrángère en France 1995/ 1996, Paris: La Documentation Française.

Lee, S. (1996) 'Issues in research on women, international migration and labor', *Asian and Pacific Migration Journal* 5(1):5–26.

Lega Italo-Filippina Filippini Emigrati (LIFE) (1991) *Filipino Migrant Women in Domestic Work in Italy*, Geneva: International Labour Organization.

Leibfried, S. (1991) 'Towards a European welfare state? – on integrating poverty regimes in the EC', in G. Room (ed) *European Developments in Social Policy*, Bristol: Bristol University Press.

—— (1993) 'Conceptualising European Social Policy; the EC as Social Actor', in L. Hantrais and S. Mangen (eds) *The Policy Making Process and the Social Actors*, Loughborough: Cross-National Research Papers, vol. 3, no. 1, August.

Leidholdt, D. (1996) 'Sexual trafficking of women in Europe: A human rights crisis for the European Union', in R. Elman (ed.) *Sexual Politics and the European Union*, Oxford: Bergahn, 83–96.

Leonetti, I. and Levi, F. (1979) *Femmes et Immigrées*, Paris: La Documentation Français.

Lévi, F.(1975) 'L'évolution de femmes portugaises immigrées à Paris et dans la banlieue parisienne', *l'Année Sociologique* 26: 153–77.

Lewis, J. (1992) 'Gender and the development of welfare regimes', *Journal of European Social Policy* 2(3): 159–73.

—— (ed) (1993) *Women and Social Policies in Europe. Work, Family and the State* Aldershot: Edward Elgar.

Lichter, D. (1983) 'Socioeconomic returns to migration among married women', *Social Forces* 62: 487–503.

Liebaut, F. and Hughes, J. (1997) *Legal and Social Conditions for Asylum*

Seekers and Refugees in Western European Countries, Copenhagen: Danish Refugee Council.

Lim, L. and Oishi, N. (1996) 'International labour migration of Asian women: distinctive characteristics and policy concerns', *Asian and Pacific Migration Journal*, 5 (1): 85–116.

Lister, R. (1992). ' Citizenship engendered', *Critical Social Policy* 32: 65–71.

— (1997) *Citizenship. Gender Perspectives*, London: Macmillan.

Lloyd, C. (1997) 'Struggling for rights: African women and the 'sans papiers movement in France', *Refuge* 16(4): 31–4.

— (1998) 'Rendez-vous manqués: feminisms and antiracisms in France: a critique', *Modern and Contemporary France* 4(1).

Lochak, D. (1993) 'Discrimination against foreigners under French law', in D. Horowitz and G. Noiriel (eds) *Immigrants in Two Democracies: French and American Experience*, New York: University of New York Press.

Lopez Zarzosa, H. (1998) 'Internal exile, exile and return: a gendered view', *Journal of Refugee Studies* 11(2): 189–98.

Lovenduski, J. and Norris, P. (1993) *Gender and Party Politics*, London: Sage.

Lutz, H. (1993) 'In between or bridging cultural gaps? Migrant women from Turkey as mediators', *New Community* 19(3): 485–94.

— (1994) *Obstacles to Equal Opportunities in Society by Immigrant Women, with Particular Reference to the Netherlands, the United Kingdom, Germany and the Nordic countries*, Strasbourg: joint specialist group on migration, cultural diversity and equality of women and men, Council of Europe.

— (1997) 'The limits of European-ness: immigrant women in Fortress Europe', *Feminist Review* 57: 93–111.

MacDonald, J. and MacDonald, L. (1972) *The Invisible Immigrants*, London: Runnymede Trust.

Machado, F. and Perista, H. (1997) 'Femmes immigrées au Portugal, identités et differences', *Migrations Société* 52: 91–104.

Macklin, A. (1994) 'On the outside looking in: Foreign domestic workers in Canada', in W. Giles and S. Arat-Koc (eds) *Maid in the Market*, Halifax, Canada: Fernwood Publishing.

MacLaughlin, J. (ed) (1997) *Social Location and Dislocation and Irish Identities*, Cork: Cork University Press.

Mahé, A. (1992) 'Les femmes dans les associations musulmanes', *Migrations Etudes* 38: 1–4.

Malik, K. (1996) *The Meaning of Race*, Basingstoke: Macmillan.

Marie, C.-V. (1996) 'Femmes, antillaises Outre-Mer', *Espace, Populations, Sociétés* 2-3: 521–8.

Mars, G. and Ward, R. (1984) 'Ethnic business development in Britain' in R. Ward and R. Jenkins (eds) *Ethnic Communities in Business*, Cambridge: Cambridge University Press.

Marshall, T. H. (1950) *Citizenship and Social Class*, Cambridge: Cambridge University Press.

Martin, J. (1991) 'Multiculturalism and feminism', in G. Bottomley, M. de Lepervanche and J. Martin (eds) *Intersexions*, Sydney: Allen and Unwin.

Martin, X. and Widgren, X. (1996)

Massey, D. et. al. (1993) 'Theories of International Migration: A review and appraisal', *Population and Development Review,* 19(3):432–66.

Maynard, M. (1996) 'Challenging the boundaries: towards an anti-racist women's studies' In M. Maynard and J. Purvis (eds) *New Frontiers in Women's Studies,* London: Taylor and Francis.

Maynard, M. and Purvis, J. (eds) (1998) *The New Migration in Europe: Social Constructions and Social Realities,* London: Macmillan.

Mehrlander, A. (1994) La politique allemande en matière de migration: stade actuel du débat', in B. Falga, and C. Leggwire (eds) *Au Miroir de l'autre. De l'immigration a l'intégration en France et en Allemagne,* Editions du Cerf: Paris, pp. 235–52

Meillassoux, C. (1981) *Maidens, Meals and Money,* Cambridge: Cambridge University Press.

Migration News Sheet (1996) June, no.159/96, Brussels: Migration Policy Group.

— (1997a) January, no.166/97, Brussels: Migration Policy Group.

— (1997b) March, no.168/97, Brussels: Migration Policy Group.

Miles, R. (1987) 'Recent Marxist theories of the Nationalism and the issue of Racism', *Journal of Sociology* XXXVIII(1):24–34.

— (1989) *Racism,* London: Routledge.

— (1993) *Racism After 'Race Relations',* London: Routledge.

Miles, R. and Thranhardt, D. (eds) (1995) *Migration and European Integration,* London: Pinter.

Miller Matthei, L. (1996) 'Gender and international labor migration: a networks approach', *Social Justice* 23(3): 38–53.

Mitchell, K. (1997) 'Different diasporas and the hype of hybridity', *Environment and Planning D: Society and Space,* 15, 533–53.

Modood, T. (1998) 'Ethnic diversity and racial disadvantage in employment', in T. Blackstone, B. Parekh and P. Saunders (eds) *Race Relations in Britain. A Developing Agenda,* London: Routledge, 53–73.

Modood, T. and Berthoud, R. (1997) *Ethnic Minorities in Britain: Diversity and Disadvantage.* London: Policy Studies Institute.

Morawska, E. and Spohn, W. (1997) 'Moving European in the globalizing world: Contemporary migrations in a historical-comparative perspective (1955–1994 v. 1870–1914)', in W. Gungwu (ed) *Global History and Migrations,* Oxford: Westview, 23–62.

Morokvasic, M. (1975) 'L'immigration féminine en France: l'état de la question', *L'Année Sociologique* 26: 563–75.

— (1980) 'Migrant women in Europe: a comparative perspective', in *Women on the Move. Contemporary Changes in Family and Society,* Paris: UNESCO, 111–31.

— (1983) 'Women in Migration' in A. Phizacklea, (ed), *One Way Ticket,* London: Routledge.

— (1984) 'Birds of passage are also women', *International Migration Review,* 18(4): 886–907.

— (1987) 'Immigrants in the Parisian Garment Industry', *Work, Employment and Society* 1(4): 441–62.

— (1991a) 'Fortress Europe and migrant women', *Feminist Review* 39: 69–84.

— (1991b) 'Roads to independence: self-employed immigrants and minority women in five European states', *International Migration* 29: 407–20.

— (1993) 'In and out of the labour market', *New Community* 19(3), 459–83.

— (1997) 'Entre Est et Ouest, des migrations pendulaires', in M. Morokvasic and H. Rudolph (eds) *Migrants. Les Nouvelles Mobilités en Europe*, Paris: L'Harmattan, 119–58.

Morokvasic, M. and de Tinguy, A. (1993) 'Between East and West: a new migratory space', in H. Rudolph and M. Morokvasic (eds) *Bridging States and Markets. International Migration in the Early 1990s*, Berlin: Sigma, 245–63.

Morokvasic, M. and Rudolph, H. (eds) (1997) *Migrants. Les Nouvelles Mobilités en Europe*, Paris: L'Harmattan.

Moser, C.O.N. (1993) *Gender Planning and Development: Theory, Practice and Training*, London: Routledge.

Mossuz-Lavau, X. (1996) 'De l'éligibilité des femmes: la France lanterne rouge de l'Europe', *Après Demain*, 380–1, 9–11.

Munz, R. and Ulrich, R. (1998) 'Germany and its immigrants: a socio-demographic analysis', *Journal of Ethnic and Migration Studies* 24(1): 25–56.

Murray, A. (1998) 'Debt-bondage and trafficking: Don't believe the hype', in K. Kempadoo and J. Doezema (eds) *Global Sex Workers*, London and New York: Routledge, 51–65.

Najaf, B. (1996) 'Das Rudgeberert im Auslandergesete. In beitrage zur feministischen theorie und praxis', *Entfremdung Migration und Dominanz Gesellschaft* 42(19).

Naples, N.(1998) *Women's Community Activism in Community Activism and Feminist Politics: Organizing across Race, Class and Gender*, London: Routledge, 327–50.

Neveu, C. (1994) 'Is "black" an exportable category to mainland Europe? Race and citizenship in a European context', in J. Rex and B. Drury (eds) *Ethnic Mobilisation in Multicultural Societies*, Avebury.

Newham Asian Women's Project Annual Report 1991–1992, London.

Nikolinakos, M. (1975) *Draft of a General Theory of Migration in Late Capitalism'*, Proceedings of the International Conference on Migrant Workers, ICSS, Berlin.

Norris, P. (1993) 'Conclusion' in J. Lovenduski and P. Norris (eds) *Gender and Party Politics*, Sage, London.

Office of National Statistics (1997) *International Passenger Survey*, London: HMSO.

Oommen, T. (1989) 'India: 'brain drain' or the migration of talent', *International Migration Review*, 27: 411–26.

Organization for Economic Cooperation and Development (OECD), (1998).

Osaki, K. (1997) 'When refugees are women: emergence of the issue on the international agenda', *Refuge* 16(4): 9–16.

Ostner, I. (1993) 'Slow motion: women, work and the family in Germany', in J. Lewis (ed) *Women and Social policies in Europe. Work, Family and the State*, Aldershot: Edward Elgar.

O'Sullivan, P. (ed) (1995) *Irish Women and Irish Migration*, Leicester: University Press.

Owers, A. (1994) 'The Age of Internal Controls?', in S. Spencer, (ed) *Strangers and Citizens: A Positive Approach to Migrants and Refugees*, London: Rivers Oram Press, 264–81.

Patel, P. (1999) 'Difficult alliances: treading the minefield of identity and solidarity politics', *Soundings*, 115–26.

Pateman, C. (1988) *The Sexual Contract*, Cambridge: Polity.

— (1989). 'The patriarchal welfare state', in C. Pateman (ed) *Disorder of Women* Oxford: Polity, 179–209.

Patterson, S. (1969) *Immigration and Race Relations in Britain 1960–1967*, Oxford: Institute of Race Relations/Oxford University Press.

Penninx, R. (1996) 'Immigration, minorities policy and multiculturalism in Dutch society since 1960', in R. Baubock and A. Zolberg (eds), *The Challenge of Diversity: integration and pluralism in societies of immigration*, Aldershot: Avebury, 187–206.

Pesman, R. (1996) *Duty Free*, Melbourne: Oxford University Press.

Petras, E. (1981) 'The global labour market in the modern world economy', in M. Knitz, C. Keely and S. Thomasi (eds), *Global Trends in Migration*, New York: Center for Migration Studies, 44–64.

Phillips, A. (1991a) *Engendering Democracy*, Cambridge: Polity.

— (1991b). 'Citizenship and feminist theory', in G. Andrews (ed) *Citizenship*,

Phillips, A. and Taylor, B. (1980) 'Sex and Skill' *Feminist Review*, 6: 56–79.

Phizacklea, A. (1982) 'Migrant women and wage labour: The case of West Indian women in Britain', in J. West (ed.) *Work, Women and the Labour Market*, London: Routledge.

— (ed) (1983a) *One Way Ticket: Migration and Female Labour*, London: Routledge.

— (1983b) 'In the front line', in A. Phizacklea (ed) *One Way Ticket: Migration and Female Labour*, London: Routledge and Kegan Paul.

— (1987) 'Minority women and economic restructuring: The case of Britain and the Federal Republic of Germany', *Work, Employment and Society*, 1(3): 309–25.

— (1990) *Unpacking the Fashion Industry*, London: Routledge.

— (1996) 'Women, migration and the state', in S. Rai and G. Lievesley (eds) *Women and the State. International Perspectives*, London: Taylor and Francis, 163–73.

— (1998) 'Migration and globalization: A feminist perspective', in K. Koser and H. Lutz (eds) *The New Migration in Europe*, London: Macmillan, 21–38.

Phizacklea, A. and Miles, R. (1980) *Labour and Racism*, London: Routledge.

— (1987) 'The British trade union movement and racism', in G. Lee and R. Loveridge (eds) *The Manufacture of Disadvantage*, Milton Keynes: Open University Press.

Phizacklea, A. and Ram, M. (1996) 'Being your own boss: Ethnic minority entrepreneurs in comparative perspective', *Work, Employment and Society*, 10(2): 319–39.

Phizacklea, A. and Wolkowitz, C. (1995) *Homeworking Women*, London: Sage.

Phoenix, A. (1997) 'Representing new identities: "Whiteness" as contested identity in young people's accounts', in K. Koser and H. Lutz (eds) *The New Migration in Europe*, Basingstoke: Macmillan, 109–23.

Pieterse, J. (1991) 'Fictions of Europe, *Race and Class* 32: 2

Piper, N. (1998) *Racism, Nationalism and Citizenship. Ethnic Minorities in Britain and Germany*, Ashgate:

Pinto Coelho, D. (1997) 'Un ailleurs au quotidien', in B. Varine (ed) *Les Familles Portugaises et la Société Française*, Paris: Editions W.

Poinsot, M. (1993) 'Competition for political legitimacy at local and national levels among young North Africans in France' *New Community*, 20 (1).

Poiret, C. (1996) *Familles africaines en France*, Paris: L'Harmattan.

Portes, A. (1997) 'Immigration theory for a new century: some problems and opportunities', *International Migration Review* 31: 799–827.

Psimmenos, I. (1996) 'The making of perphractic spaces: the case of Albanian undocumented immigrants in Athens City', ERCOMER Conference 1996, Utrecht, The Netherlands.

Quack, S. (1997) 'L'intégration professionnelle des femmes aussiedler en Allemagne', in M. Morokvasic and H. Rudolph (eds) *Migrants. Les Nouvelles Mobilités en Europe*, Paris: L'Harmattan, 241–65.

Quiminal, C. (1997) 'Un réseau d'associations de femmes africaines', *Hommes et Migrations*, 1208.

Raghuram, P. and Hardill, I. (1998) 'Negotiating a business, case study of an Asian woman in the Midlands', *Women's Studies International Forum*, 21(5), 475–83.

Rajfire (Reseau pour l'autonomie des femmes immigrées et réfugiés) (2000) Brochure no. 2, 36 pp.

Randall, V. (1998) 'Gender and power: women engage the state', in V. Randall and G. Waylen (eds) *Gender Politics and the State*, London: Routledge, 185–205.

Rath, J. (1990) 'Voting rights', in Z. Layton-Henry (ed) *Political Rights of Migrant Workers in Western Europe*, London: Sage.

Rea, A. (1995) 'Social citizenship and ethnic minorities in the European Union', in M. Martinello (ed) *Migration, Citizenship and Ethno-National Identities in the European Union*, Aldershot: Avebury, 170–98.

Refugee Council (Undated) *Refugee and Training: A Positive Policy for the 1990s*, London: Refugee Council.

— (1996) *Women Refugees*, London: Refugee Council.
— (1999) 'In Exile', *Refugee Council Magazine*, April.
Reitz, J., Frick, J,. Calabrese, T. and Wagner, G. (1999) 'The institutional framework of ethnic employment disadvantage: a comparison of Germany and Canada', *Journal of Ethnic and Migration Studies*, 25(3): 397–443.
Retzilaff O'Carroll, U. (ed) (1996) *Femmes Migrantes, Femmes Actives*, Cahiers du Forum des Migrants, no.3.
Rex, J. (1970) *Race Relations in Sociological Theory*, London: Weidenfeld and Nicolson.
— (1973) *Race, Colonialism and the City*, London: Routledge.
Rezai, C. and Wihtol de Wenden, C. (1998) *Le Regroupment Familial. Séparation Familiale et Insertion des Réfugiés*, Paris: Service Social d'Aide aux Emigrants.
Ribeiro, I. (1997) 'Les concierges portugaises en Ile de France', in B. Varine (ed.) *Les Familles Portugaises et la Société Française*, Paris: Editions W, 197–206.
Robinson, V. (1996) 'Redefining the front line: the geography of asylum seeking in the New Europe', in P. Rees, A. Convey and M. Kupiszewski (eds) *Population Migration in the European Union*, Chichester: John Wiley.
Rowbotham, S. (1998) 'Weapons of the weak: Homeworkers' networking in Europe', *European Journal of Women's Studies* 5(3–4): 453–64.
Roy, A. (1995) 'Asian women's activism in Northamptonshire', in G. Griffin (ed) *Feminist Activism in the 1990s*, London and Bristol: Taylor and Francis.
Rude-Antoine, E. (1997) *Des vies et des Familles. Les Immigrés, la loi et la Coutume*, Paris: Editions Odile Jacob.
Rudolph, H. (1996) 'The new *gastarbeiter* system in Germany', *New Community*, 22(2): 287–300.
Rudolph, H. and Hillmann, F. (1998) 'How Turkish is the donar kebab? Turks in Berlin's food sector', *Scottish Geographical Magazine* 114(3): 138–47.
Sahgal, G. and Yuval-Davis, N. (1992) *Refusing Holy Orders. Women and Fundamentalism in Britain*, London: Virago.
Sainsbury, D. (1996) *Gender Equality and Welfare States*, Cambridge: Cambridge University Press.
Saint-Blancat, C. (1998) 'Les marocaines en Vénétie', *Migrations Sociétés* 55:107–15.
Sales, R. (1997) *Women Divided: Gender, Religion and Politics in Northern Ireland*, London: Routledge.
Sales, R. and Gregory, J. (1996) 'Employment, citizenship and European integration: The implications for ethnic minority women', *Social Politics* 3(2.3):331–50.
— (1998) 'Refugee women in London: the experience of Somali women', *Refuge* 17(1):16–20.
— (1999) 'Immigration, ethnicity and exclusion: implications of European integration', in J. Gregory, R. Sales and A. Hegewisch (eds) *Women, Work*

and Equality: The Challenge to Equal Pay in a Deregulated Market, London: Macmillan.

Salimi, F. (1995) 'Self organisation of immigrant and refugee women in Norway: The MiRA centre, Oslo, Norway', in J. Costa-Lascoux, (ed) *Immigrant Women: Out of the Shadows and on to the Stage*, Immigrant Women and Integration, Council of Europe.

Salt, J. (1988) 'Highly skilled international migrants, careers and internal labour markets', *Geoforum* 19: 87–99.

— (1992) 'Migration processes among the highly skilled in Europe', *International Migration Review* 26: 484–505.

Salt, J. and Ford, R. (1995) 'Skilled international migration in Europe: The shape of things to come?', in R. King (ed) *Mass Migration in Europe. The Legacy and the Future*, Chichester: John Wiley, 293–309.

Salt, J. and Singleton, A (1995) 'The international migration of expertise: The case of the United Kingdom', *Studi Emigrazione* 117: 12–30.

Salt, J., Singleton, A. and Hogarth, J. (1994) *Europe's International Migrants*. London: HMSO.

Samers, M. (1998) 'Immigration, "ethnic minorities" and "social exclusion" in the European Union: a critical perspective', *Geoforum* 29(2): 123–44.

Saraceno, C. and Negri, N. (1994) 'The changing Italian welfare state', *Journal of European Social Policy* 4(1): 19–34.

Sassen, S. (1991) *The Global City: New York, London, Tokyo*, Princeton: Princeton University Press.

— (1996a) *Losing Control? Sovereignty in an Age of Globalization*, New York: Columbia University Press.

— (1996b) Beyond sovereignty: immigration policy making today, *Social Justice* 23(3): 9–20.

Schmidt, S. (1999) 'Immigration policy and new ethnic minorities in contemporary Germany', in K. Cordell (ed) *Ethnicity and Demcratisation in the New Europe,* London: Routledge, 91–105.

Sen, I. (1990) *A Space within the Struggle: Women's Participation in People's Movements*, New Delhi: Kalfor women.

Seyhan, A. (1997) 'Scheherazade's daughters: the thousand and one tales of Turkish-German women writers', in G. Brinkler-Gabler and S. Smith (eds) *Writing New Identities: Gender, Nation and Immigration in Contemporary Europe.* Minneapolis: University of Minnesota Press, 230–48.

Siddiqui, F. (1999) *Political Women: Country Experiences in Identity and Gender Debate*, New Delhi: Kanishka Publishers.

Siim, B. (1993) 'The gendered Scandinavian welfare states: the interplay between women's roles as mothers, workers and citizens in Denmark', in J. Lewis (ed) *Women and Social policies in Europe. Work, Family and the State*, Aldershot: Edward Elgar.

— (1998) 'Vocabularies of citizenship and gender: Denmark', *Critical Social Policy* (special issue on citizenship) no. 56.

Simon, J. and Brettell, C. (eds) (1986) *International Migration: The Female Experience*, New Jersey: Rowman and Allenheld.

Singer-Kerel, J. (1980) 'Foreign labour and the economic crisis: the case of France', paper delivered to the ESF Conference, Akademic Klausenhof, 4123 Hammiinkeln-uber-wessel, 10–12 December.

Singh, R. (1998) *Gender Autonomy in Western Europe: An Imprecise Revolution*, Basingstoke: Macmillan.

Skrobanek, S., Boonpakdi, N. and Janthakeero, C. (1997) *The Traffic in Women: Human Realities of the International Sex Trade*, London: Zed Books.

Smith, D. (1977), *Racial Disadvantage in Britain*, Harmondsworth: Penguin.

Sohn, A.M. (1992) 'Entre deux guerres. Les roles féminins en France et en Angleterre', in G. Duby and M. Perrot (eds) *Historie des Femmes en Occident*, Paris: Plon.

SOPEMI (1990) *Trends in International Migration* Paris: OECD.

— (1995) *Trends in International Migration* Paris: OECD.

— (1998) *Trends in International Migration* Paris: OECD.

Southall Black Sisters (1997) 'The one year immigration rule. A stark choice: domestic violence or deportation?', *National Women's Network Newsletter* July/August, 1.

Soysal, Y. (1994) *Limits of Citizenship: Migrants and Postnational Membership in Europe*. Chicago: University of Chicago Press.

— (1996) 'Changing citizenship in Europe: remarks on postnational membership and the national state', in D. Ceasarani and M. Fulbrook (eds) *Citizenship, Nationality and Migration in Europe*, London: Routledge.

Spensky, M. (1990) 'Identities multiples: l'affaire du foulard', *Modern and Contemporary France*. 42, 48

Stalker, P. (1994) *The Work of Strangers: a survey of International Labour Migration*, Geneva: ILO.

Stanley, L. and Wise, S. (1993) *Breaking Out Again: Feminist Ontology and Epistemology*, London: Routledge.

Stark, O. (1984) 'Migration decision-making: a review article, *Journal of Development Economics* 14: 251–9.

Stasilius, D. (1997) 'International migration, rights and the decline of 'actually existing liberal democracy'', *New Community* 23(2): 197–214.

Stolcke, V. (1995) 'Talking culture: New boundaries, new rhetorics of exclusion in Europe', *Current Anthropology*, 16(1):1–23.

Sudbury, K. (1998) *Other Kinds of Dreams. Black Women's Organisations and the Politics of Transformation*, London: Routledge.

Summerfield, H. (1993) 'Patterns of adaptation; Somali and Bangladeshi women in Britain' in G. Buijs, (ed.) *Migrant Women: Crossing Boundaries and Changing Identities*, Oxford: Berg.

Sutton, C. (1992) 'Some thoughts on gendering and internationalizing our thinking about transnational migrations', in N. Glick, L. Schiller, L. Basch and C. Blanc-Szanton (eds). *Towards a Transnational Perspectives on Migration. Race, Class, Ethnicity and Nationalism Reconsidered*, Annals of the New York Academy of Science, no. 645, 241–50.

Taboada-Léonetti, I. and Lévi, F. (1978) 'Femmes et Immigrées. L'insertion des femmes immigrantes en France', *Migrations et Société 4*, Paris: La Documentation Française,

Tacoli, C. (1999) 'Just like one of the family' in J. Gregory, R. Sales, and A. Hegewisch, (eds) *Women, Work and Equality: the Challenge of Equal Pay in a Deregulated Market* London: Macmillan.

Tapinos, G. (1992) 'Immigration féminine et statut des femmes étrangères en France', *Revue Française des Affaires Sociales*, 46 hors série, 29–60.

Taravella, L. (1984) *Les Femmes Migrantes: Bibliographie Analytique Internationale (1965–1983)*, Paris: l'Harmattan.

Tarr, C. (1999) 'Ethnicity and identity in the *cinéma de banlieue*', in P. Powrie (ed) *French Cinema in the 1990s. Continuity and Difference*, Oxford: OUP, 172–84

Tate, J. (1993) 'Homework in West Yorkshire', in S. Rowbotham and S. Mitter (eds) *Dignity and Daily Bread: New forms of Economic Organising Among Poor Women in the Third World and the First*, London: Routledge, 193–217.

Thadani, V. and Todaro, M. (1984) 'Female migration: A conceptual framework', in J. Fawcett, S. Khoo and P. Smith, (eds) *Women in the Cities of Asia*, Boulder: Westview Press.

Todaro, M. (1969) 'A model of labour migration and urban unemployment in less developed countries', *American Economic Review* 59: 138–48.

— (1976) *Internal Migration in Developing Countries*, Geneva: ILO.

Tribalat, M. (1995) *Faire France. Une Enquête sur les Immigrés et Leurs Enfants*, Paris: La Découverte.

— (1996) 'Chronique de l'immigration', *Population*, 1: 141–96.

Truong, T.D. (1996) 'Gender, international migration and social reproduction: implications for theory, policy, research and networking', *Asian and Pacific Migration Journal* 5(1): 27–52.

Truong, T.D. and Del Rosario, V. (1994) 'Captive outsiders: trafficked sex workers and mail-order brides in the European Union', in J. Wiersma (ed) *Insiders and Outsiders: On the Making of Europe II*, Kampen: Pharos.

Turner, B. (1990). Outline of a theory of citizenship. *Sociology*, 24: 189–217.

Uçarer, X. (1998) 'Trafficking in women and international organizations' Conference of the International Studies Association, Minneapolis.

Uçarer, X. and Puchala, D. (eds) (1997) *Immigration Into Western Societies. Problems and Policies*, London: Pinter.

UMA (1999) *The Newsletter of Young Women from Minorities*, 8, Spring.

Vogel, U. (1988) 'Is citizenship gender-specific?', in U. Vogel and M. Moran (eds) *Frontiers of Citizenship*, London: Macmillan, 58–85.

Wagner, A.C. (1998) *Les nouvelles élites de la mondialisation: une immigration dorée en France*, Paris: Presses Universitaires de France.

Walby, S. (1990) 'Is citizenship gendered?', *Sociology* 28(2): 379–95.

Walker, A. and Maltby, T. (1997) *Ageing Europe*, Buckingham: Open University Press.

Walter, B. (1997) 'Contemporary Irish Settlement in London: women's worlds, men's worlds', in J. MacLaughlin (ed) *Location and Dislocation in Contemporary Irish Society*, Cork University Press.

Waylen, P. (1998) 'Gender, feminism and the state: an overview', in V. Randall and G. Waylen (eds) *Gender Politics and the State*, London: Routledge, 1–18.

Weinert, P. (1991) *Foreign Female Domestic Workers: HELP WANTED!*, Geneva: International Labour Office.

Werbner, P. and Modood, T. (1997) *Debating Cultural Hybridity. Multi-cultural Identities and the Politics of Anti-racism*, London Zed.

Werner, H. (1994) *Integration of Foreign Workers into the Labour Market – France, Germany, the Netherlands and Sweden*, World Employment Working Papers. Geneva: International Labour Organization.

Wieviorka, M. (ed.) *Racisme et Xénophobie en Europe. Une Comparaison Internationale*, Paris: La Découverte.

Wihthol de Wenden, C. (1990) 'The absence of rights: the position of illegal immigrants', in Z. Layton-Henry (ed) *The Political Rights of Migrant Workers in Western Europe*, London: Sage, 27–46.

— (1994) Immigrants as political actors in France, *West European Politics* 17(2): 91–109.

Williams, F. (1989) *Social Policy: a Critical Introduction, Issues of Race, Gender and Class*, Cambridge: Polity.

— (1995) 'Race/ethnicity, gender and class in welfare states: a framework for comparative analysis', *Social Politics* 2(2): 127–59.

Wilson, M. (1993) *Mental Health and Britain's Black Community*, London: NHS Management Executive, King's Fund.

Wrench, J. and Solomos, J. (eds) (1993) *Racism and Migration in Western Europe*, Oxford: Berg.

Yuval-Davis, N. (1991) 'The citizenship debate: women, the state and ethnic processes', *Feminist Review* 39: 58–68.

— (1997a) 'Ethnicity, gender relations and multiculturalism', in P. Werbner and T. Modood (eds) *Debating Cultural Hybridity*, London Zed, 193–208.

— (1997b) *Gender and Nation*, London: Sage.

— (1998) 'Women, empowerment and coalition politics', in N. Charles and H. Hintjens (eds) *Gender, Ethnicity and Political Ideologies*, London: Routledge, 168–89.

Yuval-Davis, N. and Anthias, F. (eds) (1989) *Woman–Nation–State*, London: Macmillan.

Zehra, X. (1987) 'Different roots, different routes', *Trouble and Strife* 10: 11–15.

Zincone, G. (1998) 'Multiculturalism from above: Italian variations on a European theme; in R. Baubock and J. Rundell (eds) *Blurred Boundaries: Migration, ethnicity and citizenship*, Aldershot, Ashgate, 143–84.

Zlotnik, H. (1990) 'International migration policies and the status of female migrants', *International Migration Review* 24(1): 372–81.

— (1995) 'The South to North migration of women', *International Migration Review* 29(1): 229–54.

Index